SYMPTOMS

SYMPTOMS

A complete A–Z of thousands
of symptoms and signs

DR ROBERT YOUNGSON

BLOOMSBURY

First published in 1996 by Parragon Book Service Limited in arrangement with Bloomsbury Publishing plc
2 Soho Square
London, W1V 6HB

Copyright © 1995 by Dr R.M. Youngson

The moral right of the author has been asserted

A copy of the CIP entry for this book is available from the British Library

ISBN 0 7525 1663 9

10   9   8   7   6   5   4   3   2   1

Designed by AB3
Typeset by Hewer Text Composition Services, Edinburgh
Printed by Guernsey Press

INTRODUCTION – AND A WARNING

This book is not intended to be a do-it-yourself guide to medical diagnosis. It has quite a different, if no less important, purpose.

When anything goes wrong with your body, the fact is almost always signalled to you by *symptoms* and *signs*. These are not the same. Symptoms are what you experience internally; signs are indications that can be perceived by others. Symptoms are subjective; signs are objective. You are not likely to miss your symptoms – pains, aches, itches, visual disturbances, anxieties, depression, faintness, fatigue, weakness, and so on -- but you might not be aware of what they mean. It is also possible for you to miss important signs and, again, their significance might escape you. This is not something you should take chances on. Certain symptoms and signs can be of profound importance for your future health and possibly even your survival.

Although no book can replace a proper medical consultation with a doctor, you have to have some reason to consult your doctor in the first place. That is where this book comes in. Symptoms can have widely differing implications in different circumstances. A headache that has plagued you for years whenever you get tense is a very different matter from a headache that started two weeks ago, has never gone away, and is associated with sudden vomiting and weakness down one side of your body. The former is hardly a reason for an emergency appointment but the latter certainly is. If a mole you have had for years starts itching, should you worry? (You most certainly should – see **Itching mole**.)

Signs, too, may have differing significance, and if you notice that something has changed in your body, you may have great difficulty in deciding whether or not you should be perturbed. If you develop a prominent brown network pattern on your legs, should you worry? (Probably not, but you should know what it could mean – see **Network pattern on the legs**.) Most of the entries in this book are concerned with physical signs and what they mean. You will find much that you read in this book reassuring but, although this may be useful and comforting, it is not the primary purpose of the book. In a minority of cases this book will bring to your notice matters that require medical attention – sometimes urgent attention (such cases are highlighted by the symbol ⚠). It is tragic when life is lost or serious illness occurs through the lack of a little knowledge about what our bodies are telling us. The central purpose of this book is to provide that knowledge.

Doctors make the distinction between symptoms and signs mainly because they can reliably assess signs while they have to take their patients' word for symptoms and can only guess at their severity. But this argument does not apply in a book of this kind so we can safely ignore the distinction. From now on you can think of signs as symptoms.

HOW TO USE THIS BOOK

This is an A to Z book and I have put all the entry titles in plain, non-medical language. Because there are far more possible *causes* of symptoms than there are symptoms, and because most medical conditions have several symptoms, I have had to make decisions about these entry titles. In many cases I have selected for the heading the principal symptom of the condition being discussed – the symptom that will always be experienced by anyone with that condition. Sometimes it has been necessary to include more than one symptom in the title.

Some symptoms are common to many medical conditions. Pain, for instance, is a symptom of thousands of different diseases. For this reason, I have had to include fairly long sections under certain symptoms such as breathing difficulty, drug effects, itching, loss of appetite, mental problems, pain, skin changes and so on. These sections are arranged in alphabetical order and, within them, the headings are also in alphabetical order.

Once you have started to browse and become familiar with the book, you should find it easy to get to the section you want. However, because of the many permutations and combinations between the symptoms and the wide range of possible conditions I have also compiled an extensive index. So if you are having difficulty in finding the information you need, or if you think there should be more information than you have found about the symptom you are interested in, check the index.

Dr Robert Youngson

A

Absence of menstrual periods

Accident proneness

Ageing

Age spots

Agitation

Air swallowing

Allergies

Amnesia

Anal protrusions

Antisocial attitudes

'Ants' crawling under skin

Anxiety

Arthritis

Absence of menstrual periods

This is called *amenorrhoea* and it has many causes. Menstruation usually begins after the age of 11 and should be occurring by 16. If periods have not started by this age, see your doctor. When periods stop after they have been occurring regularly, it may be due to a number of factors, the commonest being pregnancy. Stopping the contraceptive pill after using it for a time usually results in absent periods for six to eight weeks but sometimes for much longer – even up to a year. Other causes include:

- severe emotional disturbance;
- anorexia nervosa;
- intense and prolonged athletic activity;
- cysts or tumours of the ovaries;
- the menopause.

The menopause may occur as early as 40 but more usually when a woman is between 45 and 50. Amenorrhoea is permanent, of course, if the womb is removed surgically (hysterectomy).

Accident proneness

Some people are certainly more prone to accidents than others, but this is not a symptom of any particular disease. People who are emotionally upset and preoccupied and, as a result, less watchful than

3

normal, have an increased tendency to mishaps. The same is true of aggressive men who often behave in such a way as to cause accidents to themselves and others. Some people are just plain careless.

Ageing

Ageing is not a disease but it is sometimes blamed for symptoms that are caused by disease. Although the tissues of the body do gradually deteriorate with age, many of the disorders that affect elderly people are due to other factors. These include:

- lack of exercise;
- the wrong kind of food;
- too much exposure to sunlight;
- smoking;
- excessive drinking;
- conforming to expected patterns of behaviour (in a way that elderly people think they should behave rather than how they feel).

Memory need not decline severely with age and is usually well preserved in people who are in the habit of using their minds. Elderly people are more conscious of normal lapses of memory than the young and are liable to worry unnecessarily about these, thinking that they might be developing dementia or Alzheimer's disease. The first real indication of either is when someone gets lost in formerly familiar areas. This is called disorientation. However, great philosophers and scientists have been known to get lost simply because their minds were on other things.

Sexual activity need not decline much with age. The reason some elderly people are less sexually active is often only because of a lack of opportunity.

Age spots

See **Skin spots in elderly people**.

Agitation

This shows itself by constant, aimless, physical restlessness, and it is usually caused by anxiety. If there is a real cause for the anxiety, agitation is normal and is known as *reactive anxiety*. But if there is no appropriate cause, agitation suggests an anxiety disorder, often with an underlying physical cause, possibly alcohol or drug withdrawal. Depression in the elderly often causes agitation. Some drugs, especially those used to treat psychiatric conditions, cause constant movements of the body. This is called *akathisia* and it is not the same as agitation.

Air swallowing

Everyone swallows some air from time to time, but greedy or anxious people, or those who regularly feel the need to belch, may swallow a great deal of air. This causes a feeling of fullness that is relieved only by bringing the air up again. People who belch frequently at times other than after eating are usually air swallowers. There is no great harm in this but it can be boring for others. Air swallowing is sometimes a symptom of stomach ulceration or indigestion from unsuitable diet and eating at irregular times.

Allergies

See **Contact reactions**.

Amnesia

See **Loss of memory**.

Anal protrusions

The commonest protrusions are internal piles (haemorrhoids) that have slipped down. These cause a lot of irritation (see **Itching anus**).

A more major and dramatic condition causing anal protrusion is prolapse of the rectum. This is a condition in which the mucous membrane lining of the anus (the lower part of the rectum) turns inside-out and passes out of the anus. In incomplete prolapse, only the lining of the anus appears, but in complete prolapse the whole thickness of the bowel protrudes as a thick cylindrical mass with the mucous membrane lining on the outside.

Incomplete prolapse is common in young children and usually requires no treatment. At the most, they will have their buttocks strapped together or be given a small injection to encourage internal adhesion of the lining. Complete prolapse occurs in adults, mostly in women, because of weakness of the muscle ring around the anus (anal sphincter), or of the supporting floor of the pelvis, following childbirth. Anal surgery or haemorrhoids may also predispose adults to the condition.

Prolapses are easily pushed back in but tend to recur. Complete prolapses usually require a surgical operation to tighten the anal sphincter or to fix the rectum internally.

Antisocial attitudes

People with persistent difficulty in getting on with others may have what is sometimes described as a borderline personality disorder. This is a rather vague name for a vaguely defined condition, lying somewhere between a social disorder and an actual mental illness. The unfortunate people in this category may be:

- moody;
- unreasonable;
- prone to outbursts of anger;
- incapable of forming or maintaining long-term relationships;
- addictive gamblers;
- petty criminals;
- prone to self-damaging or even suicidal behaviour.

Changes of mood are rapid and often inappropriate. Psychiatrists argue about this condition; some say that it is a psychiatric condition calling for treatment, others claim that it is not. It seems likely that the condition arises from unfortunate early life experience with lack of parental affection and the absence of consistent guidance on acceptable conduct.

People who consistently behave without regard to the rights or safety of others, and who refuse to conform to normally accepted standards of behaviour, are said to have an antisocial personality disorder. They used to be called psychopaths or sociopaths and many of them are actual criminals. Antisocial personality disorder almost certainly originates early in life as a result of defective training or conditioning and often a serious lack of parental affection and concern. Occasionally parents insist, however, that such people were 'born bad'. It is possible that there might be a hereditary element. Behaviour therapy or residence in therapeutic communities is sometimes successful in correcting the defect.

'Ants' crawling under skin

See Itching.

Anxiety

No one is wholly free from anxiety, which is a normal and necessary part of life. Anxiety – an unpleasant sense of uneasiness or fear – becomes medically significant only when these fear reactions occur without obvious external cause and interfere with normal living. There is a fair range of disorders in which anxiety is the main feature. These affect about one person in 25 and include generalized anxiety disorder (previously known as anxiety neurosis),

panic attacks, phobias, post-traumatic stress disorders and obsessive/compulsive disorders. If you have an anxiety disorder you will certainly be aware of the fact.

Anxiety, from whatever cause, is always associated with the release within the body of the hormone adrenaline, and with overaction of the part of the nervous system concerned with involuntary control of the internal organs (the autonomic nervous system). As a result, there are few parts of the body that are not affected by anxiety. These effects are purely physical. They include:

- fast pulse;
- awareness of the heartbeat;
- 'butterflies in the stomach';
- dryness of the mouth;
- trembling of the hands;
- tightness in the chest;
- sighing and overbreathing (hyperventilation);
- tense muscles.

Tightening the muscles persistently soon results in aching and tiredness. (Prolonged muscle tension is a common cause of backache and neck pain.) It also affects the urinary system, causing frequent desire to empty the bladder, and even affects the skin, causing blushing or pallor and sweating.

Anxiety is additionally known to disrupt the intestinal system causing:

- loss of appetite;
- a sense of fullness;
- difficulty in swallowing (sometimes);
- nausea;
- vomiting;
- belching;
- irritable bowel with frequent diarrhoea.

Abnormal anxiety features constant fears. These might be fear of death, serious illness, psychiatric breakdown, financial loss, social disasters or work inadequacy. With this anxiety comes an increased dependency on others, fatigue, insomnia and frightening dreams. A strong and persistent conviction that one is suffering from a serious disease is common. This is called *hypochondriasis* – sufferers are hypochondriacs.

Anxiety is the hallmark of most neurotic disorders and, although various theories have been put forward to explain it, no one really knows its cause. Anxious people deserve every sympathy and need help. There is little evidence that psychoanalysis can cure anxiety, but there *are* effective remedies. Wise psychotherapy by a mature and experienced counsellor, behaviour therapy, learning relaxation techniques or carefully selected drug treatment can help greatly. The tricyclic antidepressant drugs are often useful in panic conditions. Fluoxetine (Prozac) is really only appropriate if the condition is basically a depression. It is best to avoid the benzodiazepines – drugs like Valium – if possible, because it is all too easy to get addicted. Beta-blockers can help anxiety, and much can be done to relieve the problem, especially if you have a sympathetic doctor.

Arthritis
See **Pain in the joints, generally**.

B

Baby birth injury	Bent finger
Backache	Bent penis
Bad breath	Bent toe
Baldness	Black eye
Bandy legs	Black stools
Bat ears	Blackening and loss of the extremities
Bedsores	Blackheads
Bedwetting	Blackout
Belching	Blackwater fever

Bleeding during
pregnancy

Bleeding gums

Bleeding into the skin in
childhood

Blistered skin

Blocked nose

Blood poisoning

Blue baby

Blue hands

Blue-eyed baby with a
mousy smell

Blushing

BO

Body odour

Bones easily broken

Bow legs

Bowel problems

Brain death

Breast lump

Breast tenderness

Breath-holding

Breathing deliberately
suppressed

Breathing difficulty

Breathing exaggerated

Breathing stopped

Breathing through the
mouth

Breathlessness

Brittle bones

Broken veins

Bruising

Buck teeth

Bug-eyes

Bulging at the navel

Bunion

B

Baby birth injury

Most babies are born with a minor injury such as bruising, temporary deformation of the head or face, or a swelling on the scalp. These are normal side-effects of birth and may be fairly conspicuous if the labour was unduly prolonged or if forceps or a ventouse vacuum extractor were used. Forceps can cause temporary paralysis of the face as a result of pressure on the nerves that activate the facial muscles. The ventouse often produces a large blood swelling on the top of the scalp (called a cephalhaematoma) which is eventually absorbed. Premature babies often suffer birth injuries. Even limb fractures may occur during difficult deliveries, but healing is remarkably easy and rapid in babies and there are seldom any adverse long-term consequences. Bottom-first (breech) deliveries tend to cause injuries to the nerves of the arms, sometimes causing temporary paralysis.

Contrary to the widely held belief, cerebral palsy is not a common consequence of birth injury, nor are epilepsy and mental retardation. These are more likely to be due to other factors not related to the birth.

Backache

See **Pain in the back**.

Bad breath

The medical euphemism for bad breath – *halitosis* – is rarely used today but bad breath is still a problem for many. It is unusual because those most concerned that they might have bad breath usually don't, and those worst affected are usually oblivious to the fact.

All smells, pleasant or otherwise, are caused by tiny chemical molecules floating in the air. Bad-smelling breath may acquire these odorous molecules from the mouth, nose or lungs – rarely from the stomach. Food debris in the mouth, especially around the teeth, will inevitably ferment and produce odours, unless it is removed by regular brushing. Some foodstuffs, such as garlic, are highly efficient and persistent odour-producers when fresh, let alone when decaying. For these, the only remedy is to wait for the odour to dissipate. Oil of garlic, taken in capsules, does not have the same odour as cooked or raw fresh garlic and so causes much less offence to others.

Bad breath can also be caused by:

- infection of the gums (gingivitis);
- rotten teeth;
- some degenerative conditions of the nose lining;
- sinusitis;
- tonsillitis;
- throat infections;
- pharyngeal pouch (an abnormal sac which forms at the top of the oesophagus – see **Swallowing difficulty**).

Added to the above, nearly everyone has slight bad breath in the morning because the self-cleaning mechanisms of the mouth also 'go to sleep' during the night. Normal tooth brushing will deal with this.

A few ingested substances, including some of the ingredients of alcoholic drinks, are partially excreted in the breath, but beware any persistent and genuine odour in the breath which comes from deep in the lungs. This suggests a cause arising in the body. These possible causes and types of odour include:

- diabetes – an acetone-like smell;
- kidney failure with build-up of waste products in the blood (uraemia) – a urine-like smell;
- lung abscess, lung cancer, or abnormal widening of the air passages with stagnation of secretions (bronchiectasis) – a putrid odour;
- liver failure – a mousy smell.

Forget the common notion that the state of the breath somehow reflects the condition of the digestion or the function of the bowels. In general, this is nonsense. Only in rare instances, such as stomach cancer with outlet blockage and food retention, will foul-smelling belching occur.

Many people suffer from the unjustified conviction that they have bad breath. Mostly this is no more than a mild social anxiety, but sometimes it is an indication either of depression or of imagined illness – (hypochondriasis). Hypochondriacs usually exaggerate normal body activity in their own minds. Occasionally, a fixed conviction of bad breath may be a feature of a more serious obsessive or paranoid disorder. It may even result from the delusion that there is internal putrefaction. Rarely, there may be a genuine hallucination caused by temporal lobe epilepsy. The delusion is a false belief; the hallucination is a genuinely experienced but false sensation.

Most cases of bad breath are easily remedied. The real answer is to remove the cause rather than try to cover up the problem with peppermint or spearmint. Antiseptic mouthwashes and antibiotic lozenges are unsatisfactory because they interfere with the mouth's normal bacterial content and may encourage thrush. Unfortunately, most sufferers are often unaware that they have bad breath because they get used to it, and the majority of best friends lack the necessary moral courage to break the news.

Baldness

Common baldness is hereditary and affects males in early adult life. The medical term is *alopecia*. In toxic alopecia, which sometimes affects children, the hair loss occurs some weeks after a severe feverish illness such as scarlet fever. Baldness may also be caused by disease, anti-cancer chemotherapy or radiation and treatment with thallium compounds, vitamin A or the related group of chemical substances known as retinoids. Scarring alopecia may follow burns, skin atrophy, ulceration, fungus infection of the scalp (kerion) or skin tumours.

Alopecia areata is a form of patchy baldness, of unknown cause, often affecting only one or two small circular areas of the scalp, but sometimes affecting all the hair of the body. The drug minoxidil, sold under the trade names of Rogaine and Regaine, was first brought out as a treatment for high blood pressure. It can cause regrowth of fine fuzzy hair in many cases, but you have to keep using it and this gets expensive.

Bandy legs

See **Bow legs**.

Bat ears

This is a lay term for a minor childhood disfigurement in which the ears are larger and more protruding than usual. The problem may not, however, seem so minor for the child who may be subjected to abuse from his or her peers. Children's ears are always relatively large – the ear is three-quarters grown at the age of three and almost fully grown by eight – so any unusual prominence is more obvious than in an adult. Should there be a significant psychological disadvantage, the condition may easily be remedied by a simple plastic surgical procedure known as otoplasty.

The skeleton of the ear is a single piece of gristle (cartilage) of complicated shape, and this is covered with skin which is firmly stuck to the front surface but more loosely attached behind. This is convenient, because, to conceal the scars, the surgeon performs the operation on the back of the ear. If the prominence is due to a folding outwards of the cartilage, the aim is to thin, or weaken, it along an almost vertical line so that it can easily be bent backwards towards the head. If the ear prominence is due solely to a large angle between the ear and the head, a different operation is necessary. In this case, the skin removal behind the ear is more extensive. When this is done, the bared area includes the angle between the ear and the head. When the free edges of this area are sewn together vertically, the ear is brought close against the head and becomes less prominent. In very severe cases, where both angles are large, the two procedures may have to be combined.

Bedsores

These are often worse than most people realize. Bed- sores, technically known as *decubitus ulcers*, are especially likely in debilitated or unconscious patients or in people who have had a stroke or are paralysed. Unless such people are frequently moved, they suffer sustained compression of the skin against the bed or wheelchair in the areas that take the weight of the body. This leads to local loss of blood supply, local loss of feeling so that there is no pain and, eventually, local tissue death (gangrene) with ulceration. Skin can remain healthy and intact only if it has a constant supply of blood, carrying oxygen, sugars and other essential nutrients. Local pressure compresses the small skin blood vessels, so this supply is cut off. Bedsores may be very large and the ulceration may progress to complete local loss of skin with exposure of the underlying tendons or bone.

Bedsores are most likely to affect the buttocks, the heels, the elbows and the back of the head and are particularly common in people with defective sensation from neurological damage. They can be avoided by regular changes of position and by skilled nursing to detect and deal with early signs of trouble. Diabetics, and those with compromised blood supply to the limbs from arterial disease, such as atherosclerosis, are especially liable and require special attention. Modern technology has devised all kinds of ingenious beds, which, by differential air inflation of bed segments, or movement of fluid, constantly alter the sites taking the body weight. If economics allow, these can greatly help to reduce the risk of bedsores, but they do not eliminate the need for regular passive body movement and vigilance. The skin should also be inspected daily and kept clean, dry and in good condition.

Bedwetting

This is not usually a symptom of any organic disease, but it can be. Ordinary bedwetting usually occurs during sleep. The normal child develops adequate control early in life, but one in 10 still wets regularly at the age of five. With all children, accidents will occasionally happen, especially in times of stress, but persistent bedwetting after five is considered abnormal. Most children with this problem are merely slow in developing full nerve control and, unless there is some underlying disease, bedwetting nearly always stops before puberty.

Training to pass urine regularly during the day is helpful as is a simple, battery-operated electrical bed alarm which rings as soon as urine is passed. Avoid giving drinks last thing at night and insist on a visit to the toilet before bed. Persistent bedwetting should always be medically investigated. Possible organic causes include:

- urinary infection;
- kidney trouble;
- diabetes;
- sickle-cell anaemia.

The problem may also result from emotional disturbance. If no organic cause is found, counselling by a child psychologist is often helpful.

Belching

See **Air swallowing**.

Bent finger

See **Deformities of the hand**.

Bent penis

See **Penis problems: bending**.

Bent toe

See **Deformities of the foot**.

Black eye

See **Eyelids bruised after injury**.

Black stools

If your stools turn tarry black report the matter to your doctor at once. ⚠️ Black faeces (melaena) result from chemical change in blood released by bleeding into the stomach or upper part of the intestine. This is an important indication of disease such as gastric or duodenal ulcer. Blackening may also be caused by iron tablets taken for anaemia. Red

blood in the faeces usually comes from piles (haemorrhoids) but may be a sign of colitis or cancer of the rectum or colon, especially in older people. ⚠️ None of these signs should be ignored. Prudent people always take a quick look at what they have produced before flushing the toilet.

Blackening and loss of the extremities

This is a rather extreme symptom, but it can start in a small way and the earlier it is recognized the better. Death of body tissues is called *gangrene*. This usually occurs in an arm or leg because of an inadequate blood supply. Gangrene is commonly caused by severe arterial disease, such as atherosclerosis, in which the amount of blood able to get through the narrowed and easily obstructed arteries is not enough to keep the remoter parts alive. Diabetes also increases the possibility of gangrene, mainly because of its effect on the blood vessels, but also by encouraging infection. Other important causes include:

- embolism;
- thrombosis;
- severe arterial injury;
- Buerger's disease, an obstructive arterial condition (see below).

The rye fungus ergot can cause gangrene by inducing prolonged tight spasm that shuts off the arteries. Mechanical obstruction to the arterial blood supply can also cause gangrene, as occurs in the bowel with a strangulated hernia or a gangrenous appendix.

Limb gangrene usually starts in the toes or fingers. If the dead part does not become infected, it becomes dry and turns brown or black. At the junction between the dead and living tissue there is a zone of inflammation and sometimes this is where the dead part will drop off. This form of *dry gangrene* is commonest in the fingers and toes.

Wet gangrene occurs when flesh becomes infected and putrefies. Infection with anaerobic organisms, such as the common, gas-producing *Clostridium welchii*, which is present in most cultivated soils, causes the very dangerous *gas gangrene*. In this type, gas makes body tissue, especially muscles, swell greatly or balloon, and the gangrene spreads rapidly to healthy tissue. There is discoloration, a smell of putrefaction, and the affected person is gravely ill from poisoning. Gas gangrene was a major cause of death in World War I when so many deep wounds were contaminated by cultivated soil. The condition has nothing to do with poison gas.

Buerger's disease (also known as thromboangiitis obliterans) is a fortunately rare disorder affecting young adult males who are heavy smokers. It is a severe inflammation of the medium arteries and veins of the legs, and less commonly of the arms. The inflammation causes the blood vessels to block resulting in death of the tissues (gangrene) so that the affected limbs, or part of them, may have to be amputated. Initially, there is pain in the hands and feet with colour changes – white, blue then red (Raynaud's phenomenon) in cold weather. If the sufferer stops smoking, the disease will usually progress no further. The extraordinary thing is that, even after being told about this, many sufferers continue to smoke – some have done so until they have lost all four limbs.

Blackheads

See **Skin spots in adolescence**.

Blackout

This is not a medical term and is loosely applied to any condition in which there is loss of consciousness for a short time. Such conditions include:

- fainting;
- epilepsy;
- minor stroke;
- concussion;
- hysterical attacks.

The important thing is to try to identify possible causes. Consider these and also whether there are other symptoms (if so, look them up).

Blackwater fever

See **Fever and black urine**.

Bleeding during pregnancy

You must always take seriously any vaginal bleeding occurring early in pregnancy. This is an unmistakable sign that there is a risk that you might lose the baby, and is called *a threatened abortion*. Often there is a slight pain, like a period pain, in the lower abdomen. Although the embryo or fetus remains alive and still attached to the wall of the womb, the bleeding indicates that there is a threat of separation. There is a 25 per cent chance of spontaneous abortion, but more usually things settle down. If the bleeding stops, the pregnancy will continue to full term with delivery of a healthy, normal baby. In such cases, threatened abortion does not imply that there is anything wrong with the baby.

If the bleeding gets worse and the pain becomes more severe and cramping, there comes a point when you have to accept that abortion is inevitable. *Inevitable abortion* means that the cervix has opened and the contents of the womb are being expelled by contractions. Blood clots and membranes, enclosing the fetus, will have passed into the vagina. Sometimes bleeding from an inevitable abortion is very severe, and may even call for a blood transfusion. Often the expulsion is incomplete and a minor operation, under general anaesthesia, may be needed. This is called *evacuation of retained products of conception* (ERPC). The womb is emptied by suction, and the lining is carefully scraped with a sharp-edged spoon called a curette. A drug is then given to make the womb contract, and antibiotics may also be necessary.

When bleeding occurs from the vagina after the 28th week of pregnancy it is known as *antepartum haemorrhage*. Most cases are caused by partial separation of the afterbirth (placenta) from the inside of the womb or because the placenta is not in the normal position. Usually the bleeding itself is painless but there may be pain in the abdomen. Antepartum haemorrhage is a threat to the baby and sometimes to the mother as well. So this requires immediate investigation in hos-

pital. There the condition of the baby can be monitored and the mother can be treated, if necessary, for blood loss. Transfusion is sometimes required and, if the baby is at risk, delivery by caesarean section. ⚠

Bleeding gums

These usually occur when the gums are inflamed (gingivitis). This arises when normal tooth care has been neglected to the extent that plaque and tartar (dental calculus) accumulate around the necks of the teeth. Occasionally bleeding gums are due to severe vitamin C deficiency (scurvy). Inflamed gums are red, thickened, bulgy and will bleed even on minor tooth brushing. You can't get rid of tartar by brushing or flossing, but need to have your teeth scaled by your dentist or dental hygienist. Afterwards, resolve to prevent plaque from forming by regular flossing.

Bleeding into the skin in childhood

Spontaneous bruising, gum bleeding and tiredness in a

child should always arouse the suspicion of possible leukaemia. This is a kind of blood cancer in which certain groups of white blood cells reproduce in a disorganized and uncontrolled way so that they progressively replace, and interfere with, the normal constituents of the blood. Unless effectively treated, leukaemia usually ends fatally either from a shortage of red blood cells (anaemia), or from severe bleeding or infection. The cause is unknown but there are definite associations with radiation, with some drugs used in the treatment of other cancers, with certain industrial chemicals (such as benzene) and with certain viruses. The various types of leukaemia arise from different white cell types and have varying outlooks. Leukaemia often features:

- influenza-like symptoms;
- a feeling of great tiredness;
- sore throat;
- bleeding from the gums and into the skin;
- loss of appetite and weight.

There may be enlargement of the lymph nodes in the neck, armpits and groins. A blood check in a sufferer will show a severe anaemia and usually large numbers of primitive white cells.

The slower forms of leukaemia – chronic leukaemia – can almost always be cured by chemotherapy. Unfortunately the treatment is unpleasant and behavioural problems are common. Parents may need counselling and support.

Another cause of bleeding into the skin is purpura (see **Skin bruising without injury**). In children, purpura may follow a childhood infection. Fortunately, it usually clears up within a year.

Blistered skin

See **Skin blisters**.

Blocked nose

See **Nasal obstruction**.

Blood poisoning

This entry is included mainly to reassure worried people. If you have genuine blood poisoning you are extremely ill, fevered and probably collapsed. Blood poisoning or *septicaemia* means the presence of bacteria and their poisons (toxins) in the blood. This is a dangerous condition which may arise from a major infection anywhere in the body. The bacterial toxins released in septicaemia can cause widespread relaxation of arteries so that the volume of blood is insufficient to fill them. The heart rate is very fast and the pulse weak and thready. This is called *toxic shock* and is often rapidly fatal unless fluids are transfused and antibiotic treatment given to eliminate the bacteria. ⚠ You are unlikely to get blood poisoning until a fairly severe infection has built up elsewhere in the body.

Blue baby

This is the common term given to a baby whose blood does not contain enough oxygen to convert it to the normal bright red. Blood with insufficient oxygen is a dark purplish colour and this conveys a bluish tinge to the skin, especially obvious in the lips and tongue. The blue colouring is called *cyanosis*. It is usually due to a heart defect or to an abnormality in the large arteries running out of the heart. Such a congenital defect may cause the blood to bypass the lungs so that it is not able to take up oxygen. In some cases, narrowing of the arteries leading from the heart to the lungs seriously reduced the rate of flow of blood through the lungs and has the same effect.

Every baby showing cyanosis should have a thorough medical examination so that the cause can be established. Effective treatment is available for most of the likely causes.

Blue hands

Medically known as *acrocyanosis*, this condition features blueness, coldness and excessive sweating of the hands and feet. These effects result from partial closure of the small arteries supplying the hands with blood, usually as a result of exposure to cold.

The commonest cause of this is Raynaud's disease. See your doctor, and keep your hands warm in cold weather.

Blue-eyed baby with a mousy smell

Phenylketonuria is a genetic disease in which a normal constituent of dietary protein, phenylalanine, cannot be broken down normally but is converted to substances which are very poisonous and damaging to the brain, causing mental retardation. Phenylalanine is present in milk. The trouble is hereditary and happens because of a defect in the gene that produces a body enzyme that normally converts phenylalanine to a simpler and safe compound. As a result of this genetic mutation, the enzyme is missing.

About one baby in 16,000 has phenylketonuria and because some of the phenylalanine and its breakdown products are excreted in the urine, a simple urine test with a special paper test strip on a wet nappy will detect the problem. This test becomes posi-

tive at the age of four to six weeks, but a more sensitive test is available for babies at birth. This is called the Guthrie test.

Newborn babies with phenylketonuria are often strikingly blond with blue eyes and have an odd 'mousy' smell. Any affected baby taking milk will receive enough phenylalanine to cause damage to the brain. It is thus essential to ensure that the baby has a special diet, free from phenylalanine. Such a diet must be substituted for milk in the first few days of life. ⚠

Blushing

This is caused by a temporary widening of large numbers of small blood vessels near the surface of the skin of the face and the neck, usually as an involuntary and uncontrollable reaction to embarrassment, nervousness or a feeling of social insecurity. Blushing is also a feature of the temporary upset of blood vessel control that commonly occurs at the time of the menopause. In this case the blushing occurs without any of the usual causes.

Not much can be done to prevent embarrassment blushing except to analyse and try to learn to cope with the circumstances that cause it. Frequent blushing is a feature of adolescence and nearly always settles as the young person acquires social skills, poise and confidence. Menopausal blushing can usually be controlled with oestrogen hormones. Doctors are still arguing as to whether or not the problem is due to oestrogen deficiency.

BO

See **Body odour**.

Body odour

Fresh sweat is odourless unless you have been eating strong-smelling volatile substances such as garlic. Sweat from sweat-glands in the groins and the armpits contains fatty and protein material that is easily acted on by bacteria to produce very smelly compounds and these may contaminate clothing as well as the skin. This occurs within a few hours of sweating. Sweat from other parts of the body, including the feet, does not contain these materials but may still become smelly if it is allowed to accumulate and to soak into the clothing.

You are very unlikely to have a body odour problem, even in the hottest weather, if you wash all over every day, use an antiperspirant and change your clothes frequently. Put on clean underwear, socks, stockings or tights daily and, if possible, do not wear the same pair of shoes for long periods of time.

Bones easily broken

See **Brittle bones**.

Bow legs

Many mothers worry about the appearance of bow legs in toddlers, but such concern is usually unnecessary. Some degree of bowing is normal in infants and will usually correct itself as the child grows, so long as it is moderate and symmetrical and the child is healthy. Bulky nappies do not cause bow legs.

If the bowing is severe or affects one leg only, or if it is still present after the age of about six, you should seek medical advice. Children deficient in vitamin D will consequently be deficient in calcium, and may develop softening of the bones (rickets) and a bowing deformity. This is very rare in children on a reasonable diet and who are exposed to moderate amounts of sunlight. Sunlight causes the synthesis of vitamin D in the skin.

Bowel problems

See **Constipation** and **Diarrhoea**.

Brain death

This is the state in which all the functions of the brain, even the maintenance of breathing, have ceased and, by reason of physical damage to the nerve structure, cannot be restored. The heart can, however, continue to beat and the body organs can be kept alive by artificial ventilation with an air pump and by artificial feeding. A person with brain death is dead in every meaningful sense of the word.

Breast lump

This is a most important sign. Although most breast lumps do not mean cancer, every new lump felt should be considered as potentially serious until you have had a medical opinion. ▲

There are many causes of breast lumps, most of them innocent. Lumps may be caused by:

- the normal glandular tissue of the breast;
- fibrocystic disease (mastitis);
- harmless fluid-filled cysts that are usually most prominent during the week before the period starts;
- a benign tumour known as a fibroadenoma;
- a fatty tumour (a lipoma);
- breast cancer.

Don't make any assumptions and don't take any chances. Just see your doctor to check up on anything suspicious.

Breast cancer is the commonest cancer in women, affecting around one woman in 20, so it is extremely important for all women to know as much about the subject as possible. Early action is vital as in most of the women who die from breast cancer the disease has already spread beyond the breast when the diagnosis is first made. In cases in which the cancer is still confined to the breast, the outlook is excellent, so regular self-examination and mammography screening are essential.

Most cancers occur in the upper, outer part of the breast and can be felt as a firm lump which is seldom painful or tender. Breast cancer will sometimes cause the nipple to turn inwards (but note that retracted nipples from innocent causes are quite common) or may produce a darkish discharge from the nipple. Cancers may also cause local puckering of the skin of the breast, producing a kind of rough orange-peel effect.

Your best chance of detecting cancer early is to do a routine self-examination every month after your period. Look at your breasts in a mirror, compare the two sides; check for changes in appearance when you raise your arms; lie down and feel each breast all over with the flat of your hand. If you notice anything new or feel a firm lump, report it immediately to your doctor. *Never* delay for fear of possible consequences. Surgery in the early stages is often minor and the appearance of the breast afterwards can often be maintained by an implant, if necessary. **A**

Special X-ray mammography, every 3 to 5 years, is recommended for women over 40, especially if there is a family history of breast cancer.

Breast tenderness

Tenderness of the breasts is very common, especially just before a period, and is often associated with a feeling of fullness. This is normal. During breast feeding tenderness is especially common, mainly from the tension of milk engorgement, but sometimes from actual inflammation (mastitis) or from a breast abscess. Tenderness is not a principal symptom of breast cancer. See also **Pain in the breast**.

Breath-holding

See **Breathing deliberately suppressed**.

Breathing deliberately suppressed

Deliberate breath-holding is a highly effective form of parental control exercised by determined babies. One or two babies per 100 discover by experience that they can get their parents to do almost anything by holding their breath. They do this until they turn first red, then blue, then start to twitch as if they are about to have an epileptic fit. The more anxiously the parents respond, the more convinced the babies become of the value of the ploy. Soon every little pain, frustration or annoyance is signal for an attack on the parents' morale by breath-holding.

These episodes are not in the least dangerous and nature can be relied upon to force the child to start breathing again, even if the child faints. The secret is to ignore the performance – if you can. Breath-holding is rare after the age of about four.

Breathing difficulty

This is the result of any blockage or narrowing of the tubes carrying air down into the lungs. It may be due to asthma in which the circular muscles in the walls of the air tubes tighten abnormally (see below), or to inhaled food or another foreign body, or to swelling or disease of the lining of the tubes.

The most severe and dangerous form of allergic reaction – *anaphylactic shock* – may feature tight spasm of the breathing tubes so that the air supply is partly obstructed. This is an emergency and medical help should be summoned immediately. ⚠ People prone to this reaction may carry an adrenaline syringe and this should be given at once. It also helps if the victim lies down with the legs raised.

Mouth-to-mouth respiration or even heart massage may be needed. See also **Contact reactions (allergies)**.

Asthma is a disease in which the circular smooth muscles of the branching air tubes of the lungs, the bronchi, are liable to go into spasm so that the bronchi are narrowed and the passage of air impeded. It is often easier to breathe in than out and the lungs become inflated and cannot easily be emptied. A wheeze on breathing out is a regular feature of an asthma attack. The commonest kind is allergic asthma, but asthma can also be induced by infection, emotion and exertion. Asthma is not trivial and kills at least 2,000 people a year in Britain. Parents must know the signs of the condition worsening and what steps to take to overcome them. The best way to take drugs for asthma is by inhalation.

Narrowing of the tubes carrying air into the lungs, as a result of tightening of the muscles in their walls, is called *bronchospasm*. While bronchospasm is the main feature of asthma, it also occurs in other allergic conditions and in various lung diseases, such as emphysema and chronic bronchitis. The result of bronchospasm is a restriction in the flow of air. This is often worse on breathing out than on breathing in and there may be severe wheezing and a persistently inflated chest. It also causes coughing. Sometimes bronchospasm is so severe as to endanger life. Commonly it leads to an inadequate supply of oxygen to the tissues and the skin may appear bluish (cyanosis).

Severe breathing difficulty in small babies may be due to what is known as the *respiratory distress syndrome*. This is a condition where there is an increased amount of fluid in the lungs. This impedes the normal passage of oxygen into the blood, and the lungs become stiffer. The fluid in the lungs comes from the blood and may clot, causing the air sacs to collapse and further reducing the passage of oxygen to the blood.

The respiratory distress syndrome may occur in premature babies whose lungs are immature and do not inflate fully after birth. This is the result of the deficiency of a substance known as a *surfactant* which acts as a kind of detergent, or wetting agent, to lower the surface tension of the fluid in the lungs. Reduced oxygen in the blood prompts faster breathing, but the increased stiffness of the lungs makes this much more difficult. The result is increasing distress. Fatigue of the breathing muscles leads to a worsening of the situation. Breathing becomes heavy and laboured, and as the condition progresses, the skin becomes blue-tinged.

In the early stages, administration of oxygen by mask can raise the blood oxygen levels and this may be all that is required. If the condition worsens, a tube must be passed into the windpipe (trachea) and mechanical ventilation used to force oxygen into the lungs and inflate the air sacs, so that the volume of the lungs actually increases. The outcome depends on the severity of the condition and the effectiveness of treatment. In newborn babies, complications are common and the respiratory distress syndrome is still a common cause of death in premature babies. ⚠

Children with cystic fibrosis often have lung complications due to blockage of the air tubes with excessive mucus secretions and plugs of thick muco-pus. There is troublesome cough, wheezing and difficulty in breathing and the chest becomes barrel-shaped from the effort of breathing.

Breathing exaggerated

Hyperventilation is unusually deep or rapid breathing. It is normal when it occurs during the course of taking strenuous exercise. The term hyperventilation is more often applied to a degree of deep breathing which is inappropriate to the oxygen needs of the body and which, as a result, causes excessive loss of carbon dioxide from the blood. This leads to a reduction in blood acidity. This, in turn, affects the amount of calcium in the blood and brings about various changes in the conductance of nerves so that certain muscle groups, such as those of the forearms and calves, may go into intense spasm. The wrists may bend and the ankles extend.

Hyperventilation is a common manifestation of neurotic illness, either as a panic reaction associated with a feeling of 'not getting enough air', or as a resource in people who feel that they are not getting enough attention. In this instance, the activity is usually highly successful, but is not without danger. If the affected person can be persuaded to rebreathe for a few minutes into a small paper bag, the blood changes will soon be reversed and the more dramatic elements – the muscle spasms – abolished.

Rarely, hyperventilation can occur as an effect of organic disease and may be a feature of brain damage from infection or injury, poisoning, fever or thyroid gland overactivity.

Breathing stopped

Absence of breathing, usually for periods of seconds or a minute or two, is known as *apnoea*. It can be caused by damage to the part of the brainstem containing the breathing nerve centres. This is often an effect of a stroke, but may result from the effects of drugs or direct injury. It can also be caused by obstruction of the airway, for instance if the tongue falls back during sleep or when there is a foreign body in the voice box. Seriously ill people often have a form of apnoea that features spells of deep breathing alternating with periods of very shallow breathing or stoppage. This is called *Cheyne-Stokes respiration*. New cases of apnoea require urgent attention – call an ambulance. Apnoea should always be taken seriously. ⚠

Breathing through the mouth

Adenoids are probably the commonest cause of mouth-breathing. These are swellings on the wall of the back of the nose above the tonsils, and they contain masses of white cells (lymphocytes) that help to combat infections. In doing so, they enlarge and this may cause complications. Most children's adenoids shrivel away after the age of about five, and it is uncommon for them still to be present at puberty.

Trouble starts if adenoids get so big that they obstruct the movement of air from the nose to the throat. This causes mouth-breathing, a nasal quality to the voice and snoring. Enlarged adenoids can block the openings of the Eustachian tubes which connect the nose to the middle ear. This can cause deafness and, by preventing drainage of secretions from the middle ear, encourage middle ear infection (otitis media). Children may require antibiotics or even a minor surgical operation to drain pus from the middle ear.

If your child is a mouth-breather, sleeps with his or her mouth open, snores a lot, is much troubled by ear-ache or seems to be deaf, the problem might well be adenoids. See your doctor to check whether anything need be done. The operation to remove adenoids is called *adenoidectomy*.

Breathlessness

This is normal in response to exertion or sometimes extreme emotion, but breathlessness at other times, or from minor exertion, is always a sign that something is wrong. The number of possible causes of breathlessness is considerable. Here are some of the more important:

- an over-full stomach;
- aneurysm of the aorta in the chest;
- anxiety (causing hyperventilation);
- asthma;
- bronchiectasis;
- bronchitis;
- collapse of the lung;
- croup;
- emphysema;
- heart failure;
- heart muscle disorders;
- heart valve disorders;
- high altitudes;

- kidney failure;
- lung scarring from pneumoconiosis;
- lung cancer;
- obesity;
- partial blockage of the windpipe or larynx;
- pleurisy;
- pneumonia;
- 'popped lung' (spontaneous pneumothorax);
- pregnancy;
- severe anaemia;
- smoking;
- tuberculosis of the lung;
- unduly thick blood (polycythemia);
- unfitness or debility;
- whooping cough.

The length of this list is an indication of the vital importance of oxygen. Anything that tends to prejudice the supply of oxygen to the body immediately leads to an increase in respiration – breathlessness.

The commonest cause is simple unfitness and the obvious remedy is to take more exercise and become fit. Obesity (carrying too much weight) is another common cause. Being at a high altitude will also cause breathlessness because the oxygen pressure of the atmosphere is less than normal. Another cause is anaemia, in which the oxygen-carrying power of the blood is reduced.

More serious causes of breathlessness include heart disease, in which the blood cannot be circulated fast enough to maintain the oxygen supply to the tissues, and lung diseases in which there is obstruction to the access of air to the parts of the lungs in which oxygen passes into the blood. Heart conditions that cause breathlessness include aortic incompetence, aortic stenosis and heart failure.

Aortic incompetence does not mean incompetence of the aorta but of the heart valve at the start of this major artery. If the valve becomes leaky, it allows blood to flow back into the main pumping chamber, the left ventricle. The result is that the muscular wall of the chamber has to work harder than normal to pump out the extra blood and may become enlarged. There is a noise from the abnormal blood flow, which can be heard with a stethoscope as a murmur. Mild aortic incompetence may cause little trouble but sometimes the extra load is too much for the heart, which becomes unable to keep the blood flowing fast enough to prevent stagnation in the lungs. This is called heart failure and it causes accumulation of fluid in the tissues and breathlessness. Always report breathlessness that seems to be unrelated to effort or occurs for no obvious reason. ▲ Heart valve replacement may be necessary.

Aortic stenosis is an abnormal narrowing, or failure of proper opening, of the heart valve at the outlet of the main pumping chamber on the left side. The effect of this is to force the muscular wall of the heart to work much harder than normal to maintain the circulation of the blood throughout the body. As a result, the heart wall becomes thicker. Depending on the degree of narrowing, there may be few symptoms or there may be serious lack of energy, or even fainting, from a poor blood supply to the body and the brain. The coronary arteries, which branch off the aorta just above the valve, may not get enough blood and this may cause angina. The damming back of blood in the lungs may cause breathlessness. The condition can be relieved by timely heart valve replacement.

Heart failure does not mean that the heart has stopped or that it is in imminent danger of doing so. Heart failure is the condition in which, as a result of various forms of heart disease, the heart is no longer capable of producing an adequate output of blood so as to meet the needs of the body for oxygen and nutrition. In heart failure the blood flow to the tissues and to the lungs is diminished and slowed. Congestion results, with engorgement of the veins and other small blood vessels, leading to obvious signs and symptoms. Heart failure is commonly caused by coronary artery disease, high blood pressure and rheumatic heart disease, but may result from one of many different heart disorders. The features may vary considerably but breathlessness is a principal sign.

If blood returning from the body to the right side of the heart cannot be pushed on to the lungs quickly enough, this is called right heart failure. The result is blueness (cyanosis) and the accumulation of fluid in the tissues (oedema), ankle swelling, enlargement of the liver and, in severe cases, a considerable accumulation of fluid within the abdomen (ascites). When the left side of the heart is unable to clear the blood from the lungs quickly enough, and fluid accumulates in the lungs, this is called left heart failure. The main symptom of left heart failure is breathlessness, which may occur on mild exertion or even when the affected person is at rest. There may be attacks of sudden breathlessness during the night. As the condition worsens, the tendency to breathlessness increases. Eventually, the degree of disability becomes extreme and the state pitiful. In both right and left heart failure there is severely restricted activity.

Heart failure can usually be treated effectively, especially if the underlying cause of the heart damage is remediable. The drug digitalis is valuable in increasing the strength and effectiveness of the heartbeat (contraction) and its use often greatly improves the condition of the affected person. Fluid in the lungs and the tissues can be removed by the use of diuretic drugs, which greatly increase the urinary output. After effective treatment for heart failure, the greatly relieved patient may spend long periods in the toilet disposing of excess water. Abdominal fluid may sometimes be removed by suction through a wide-bore needle.

Smoking can cause breathlessness in several ways. It turns a proportion of the haemoglobin in the blood into a form that cannot carry oxygen; it causes chronic bronchitis which is often associated with airway obstruction; and it affects the heart's ability to benefit from exercise. Again, the remedy is obvious – give up smoking or at the very least cut down dramatically on the number of cigarettes you smoke.

Breathlessness is sometimes the result of a panic conviction that one cannot breathe. This is called *hyperventilation* – a form of hysterical overbreathing. The effects on the nervous system tend to make matters worse (see **Breathing exaggerated**). Another psychogenic breathing pattern takes the form of deep sighing respirations regularly repeated.

Breathlessness should be distinguished from breathing difficulty although it may be caused by it. Conditions causing breathing difficulty include asthma in which the air tubes are severely narrowed by spasm of the muscles in their walls; pleurisy, which interferes with breathing because of pain on expanding the lungs (see **Pain in the chest**); disorders of the chest wall causing pain on movement of the ribs; and airway obstruction from an inhaled foreign body.

Brittle bones

People who suffer bone fractures on minor injury have bones that are much weaker than normal. There are several possible causes for this, the most important being:

- osteoporosis;
- osteomalacia;
- secondary cancer;
- osteogenesis imperfecta.

Osteoporosis is a reduction in the density of the protein (collagen) scaffolding of the bones and of the calcium salts deposited on the protein. Like other tissues of the body, the bones are in a state of constant physical and chemical change, losing and gaining calcium and protein, to and from the bloodstream. These changes are controlled by various growth and sex hormones, and alteration in the amounts of these in the body affects the strength of the bones. As a result, diseases of the hormone-producing glands may cause osteoporosis. This is a feature of:

- overactivity of the thyroid and parathyroid glands;
- disorders of the adrenal glands;
- reduced output of sex hormones;
- disorders of the pituitary gland;
- oestrogen deficiency after the menopause;
- underactivity.

Osteoporosis also occurs in Cushing's syndrome, acromegaly, prolonged thyrotoxicosis and diabetes.

The bones are thickest and strongest in early adult life. Thereafter, they become gradually thinner with age, as a result of progressive loss of the protein structure and of calcium. Bones stay strong by being used. Under-use, such as occurs in the bedridden or in astronauts living in zero gravity, leads to osteoporosis. Even a change from an active to a sedentary life can cause osteoporosis, as do the ordinary processes of ageing, with associated loss of

activity and reduced hormone levels. Women are worse off than men in this respect because while men continue to secrete sex hormones into old age, women have an oestrogen shutdown at the menopause and begin to lose calcium in the urine, with progressive weakening of the bones. Adequate dietary calcium in youth and plenty of exercise are important in minimizing the risk, especially in women.

In most cases of osteoporosis there are no symptoms until some effect of the weakening in the bones occurs. This may be:

- loss of height from shrinkage of the bones of the spinal column;
- severe curvature of the spine;
- sudden collapse of a bone in the spine with severe pain and disfigurement;
- a wrist or forearm fracture;
- an unexpected fracture of the neck of the hip bone following a quite

minor stumble or fall. (About one woman in four over the age of 75 suffers this misfortune and the consequences may be very serious, often shortening life.)

There is still some controversy about the effectiveness of oestrogen hormone replacement therapy (HRT) in reducing the risk of osteoporosis in women after the menopause. Oestrogens certainly retard the process of bone loss, but do not increase bone bulk. They also have some disadvantages, especially in causing a slight increase in the risk of thrombosis and cancer of the womb. Most doctors, however, are strongly in favour of oestrogens and often prescribe them in combination with progesterone. Such combined therapy minimizes the risk of uterine cancer but restores periodic bleeding and may slightly increase the risk of breast cancer.

Male sex hormone treatment, in men, is useful only in those relatively rare cases in which osteoporosis is due to inadequate natural sex hormone production. In both sexes, calcium supplements are valuable and help to strengthen bones.

The bone-softening disorder, osteomalacia, results from a severe shortage of vitamin D. This leads to inadequate mineralization of bone, with softening and an increased tendency to fracture. The condition occurs in adults and is similar to rickets, the childhood disease.

When cancer from a primary site, such as the breast, lung, womb, large intestine or prostate gland, spreads remotely, it often settles in the bones. Some cancers are very destructive and can so weaken bones that they will break spontaneously or under quite minor force. When a bone breaks because it is diseased the condition is called a *pathological fracture*. These are sometimes quite unexpected and may be the first indication of widespread cancer.

In young people, brittle bones and frequent fractures suggest the inherited brittle-bone disease, *osteogenesis imperfecta*. People with this condition usually have an unusual blue tinge to the whites of their eyes, because of undue thinning of the tissue.

Broken veins

The medical term for this minor but annoying condition is more impressive than the condition might be thought to warrant. It is *telangiectasia*. The veins are not, in fact, broken. The condition is a localized increase in the size and number of small blood vessels in the skin, and most commonly affects the skin of the nose and the cheeks, causing permanent redness. In many cases a tendency to broken veins is present from birth but it also results from loss of support to the blood vessels from collagen damage due to undue exposure to sunlight and adverse environmental conditions (wind, rain, cold temperatures and so on). Persistent flushing from the effects of alcohol is also said to be a cause.

Broken veins are the main feature of the blushing disorder *rosacea*, but occurs in a number of other disorders, including psoriasis, lupus erythematosus and dermatomyositis. When the condition is restricted to a number of very small patches it produces characteristic spots known as *spider naevi*. Large numbers of these suggest liver disease. In the rare condition of *hereditary haemorrhagic telangiectasia*, frequent bleeding occurs from small rounded patches of dilated vessels around the mouth and nose.

Bruising

See **Eyelids bruised after injury** and **Skin bruising without injury**.

Buck teeth

This popular term is given to protruding or splayed upper front teeth. This is not just a cosmetic problem; buck teeth are not moistened properly by saliva and are more prone than normal teeth to decay. They are also more liable to physical injury. You don't have to put up with buck teeth. Sustained pressure on one side of a tooth will cause the bone of the socket to absorb on the other side and new bone to grow on the same side. The result is that the tooth can be gradually moved into a new position which it will maintain permanently. Pressure needs to be applied by an orthodontic appliance, such as a brace which may be removable or fixed. Sometimes it is necessary to take out side teeth to make room.

Bug-eyes

See **Eyes protruding**.

Bulging at the navel

Umbilical hernia, as this condition is known medically, is common in Afro-Caribbean babies, who may have a protrusion at the navel resembling a small elephant's trunk. The cause is a weakness in the tummy wall, at the navel, caused by a slight separation of the two central longitudinal muscles, allowing a knuckle of small intestine to protrude under the skin and push it forward. The conventional treatment is to push the hernia back and keep it in place with a coin wrapped in a cloth. This is likely to push the muscles further apart but, fortunately, most umbilical hernias correct themselves without treatment. In rare cases a surgical repair may be necessary.

Bunion

See **Pain in the foot**.

Car sickness

Cellulite

Chills

Choking

Colic

Colour blindness

Compulsions

Concussion

Constipation

Contact reactions
(allergies)

Convulsions

Corns and callosities

Coughing

Crying baby

Crying baby (high
pitched)

Car sickness

See **Travel sickness**.

Cellulite

Hypodermic fibrosis sounds like a genuine medical condition, but it is really a cosmeticians' buzz term – the same goes for the alternative description *cellulite*. You will not find 'cellulite' in dermatology textbooks. Cellulite is simply a lay term for what happens when too much fat gets laid down under the skin and the normal strands of fibrous connective tissue, that keep the skin in place, act like mattress strings and cause dimpling. Regrettably, there is no magic cure. Try to lose some weight and take more exercise.

Chills

Feverish colds are caused by viruses. These are spread, not by coughs and sneezes, but by hand to hand contact. The route of transfer of viruses is from the nose of the sufferer to his or her hands; from there, directly or indirectly, to the hands of a susceptible person; and from there to the new victim's eyes or nose. The mouth is not an effective means of entry.

People do not acquire useful resistance to cold viruses because there are over 200 of them and they are constantly changing. But you can reduce the number of your colds, and those of your children, if you know how they are passed between people. Watch how a person with a cold contaminates his or her environment by face-to-hand-to-surroundings contact. Don't touch anything touched by the sniffler. If you can't avoid this touching or being touched, simply keep your hands away from your own face until you have washed them thoroughly. There is no practical treatment for a cold.

Choking

This is what happens when any solid or liquid material obstructs the air passages, particularly at the opening to the voice box (the larynx). This is especially likely if solid material is inhaled, which may happen if a sudden, unexpected breath is taken during eating. For this reason, laughing with a full mouth is not a good idea.

If you inhale a small quantity of solid or liquid, you will cough and the cough's repeated blasts of air will usually drive out the unwanted material. Total blockage is rare, but a large foreign body, and the resulting swelling of the surrounding tissues may cause this – in which case, death from suffocation is inevitable unless the obstruction can be overcome. ⚠

Attempts to dislodge the obstruction should be made by suddenly and forcibly squeezing the abdomen below the ribs in a bear hug from behind or rapid upper abdominal thrusts from the front (called the Heimlich manoeuvre). If babies are choking, hold them face down and slap them on the back. Failing this, give them a chest thrust – placing your hand below the nipples. If this fails, the only hope of saving life lies in boldly cutting an opening into the windpipe, in the midline, on the front of the neck just above the notch on the top of the breast bone (tracheostomy). Use the barrel of a fairly wide pen to keep the hole open.

Colic

This is pain caused by stretching of any tubular structure in the body. The intestine is very sensitive to stretching, and when the contents passing along it are impeded, segments become ballooned and stretched. The result is colicky pain which rises to a peak, as the bowel is stretched, and the pain then subsides, as the bowel relaxes. The same effect can occur if the intestine contracts strongly around a hard object, such as a lump of undigested food.

Bowel colic is usually caused by inadequately chewed food, but may occur when there is genuine intestinal obstruction. In biliary and renal colic the pain is caused by contraction of the bile duct or ureter around a stone.

The term *infantile colic* is used to describe a distressing baby problem that, in fact, has nothing to do with colic. The affected infant is healthy, feeds well and gains weight, but seems exceptionally hungry and will suck vigorously on anything offered. The feature which drives parents crazy is the apparently endless frantic crying, often at around the same times of the day or night. This crying often causes the baby to swallow air and this may lead to distention of his or her abdomen and the passage of wind from either end.

There is no reason to believe that the original reason for the crying is colic, or anything else connected with the bowels. If crying is due to insufficient feeding, the baby will not gain weight; if due to bowel upset there will be other signs, such as diarrhoea, fever and dehydration. In bottle-fed babies, milk intolerance may sometimes be the cause, and it may be worth trying a change of brand.

Some babies are naturally hyperactive and these can often be calmed down by wrapping them up firmly in a small sheet. Powerful crying is never harmful to the baby, however severely it may affect the unfortunate parents. Infantile colic nearly always ceases by the age of three or four months. See also **Pain in the abdomen**.

Colour blindness

This is better described as colour perception defect because full colour blindness, with no perception of any colours, is almost unknown. Colour perception defect is common, especially in males, and involves varying degrees of difficulty in seeing either red, green or blue, or some combination of these. It is almost always inherited, the defective gene being recessive and on the X chromosome. Men only have one X chromosome; women have two. X-linked recessive conditions always occur in males if the gene is present. For women to show the trait, both of their X chromosomes have to carry the defective gene. So, although almost 10 per cent of males have some degree of colour perception defect, the condition is rare in women – less than 0.5 per cent are affected.

Colour perception defect can also arise later in life, and is a fairly common consequence of optic nerve fibre damage from any cause, such as multiple sclerosis, diabetes or drug or chemical toxicity. In cases of one-sided damage, comparing the colour intensity of an object, as viewed by each eye, will show an obvious difference.

Colour perception can be tested in various ways. The Ishihara, multi-dot test is a quick and useful screening test. People with normal colour vision see one sequence of numbers, those with colour problems see another. Colour matching is also a sensitive test of perception, as is placing in sequence a large series of discs of gradually changing colour value.

For certain occupations, normal colour perception is needed and young men with ambitions to join the Armed Forces should be tested well in advance. Colour perception defect is not an absolute bar to recruitment, but denies entry to certain occupations and trades. Commercial flying calls for good colour perception, and seafaring people are also often required to have a high standard of colour vision. Most coloured signals on the ground, such as traffic lights, can easily be interpreted by colour-defective people.

Compulsions

A compulsion is a kind of inner drive that makes you do things that you don't really want to do, such as washing your hands or repeatedly checking that you have locked the front door. Compulsions are always linked to obsessions so the problem is known as an *obsessive-compulsive disorder*. An obsession is an intrusive thought or feeling that constantly recurs with little or no relevance to current events. You might, for instance, be obsessed with the idea that you are constantly being observed. Many of us have obsessions; most of us have compulsions, and these are normal and often valuable aids to efficiency and success. A little bit of compulsive tidiness can be very useful.

In the obsessive-compulsive disorder, these feelings recur with sufficient frequency and irrelevance to cause distress or disability. The victim, who is usually of above-average intelligence and educational level, may have an obsession, a compulsion, or both, and is perfectly aware that the situation is irrational but is unable to control it. Complying with the compulsion does not relieve the associated anxiety.

People with the obsessive-compulsive disorder are often deeply preoccupied with cleanliness and fear of contamination, especially with faeces. Some wash so much that they develop a severe dermatitis of their hands. The checking compulsion is also common and can severely interfere with the normal conduct of life. The obsession that actions must be performed meticulously, slowly and in a certain order can also be very disabling. Affected people are also often preoccupied with aggression and go in for 'magical thinking' – the feeling that events can be brought about by thinking about them. This can result in much concern over aggressive thoughts.

The obsessive-compulsive disorder usually starts in early adult life often after a stressful event such as a bereavement or a sexual problem of some kind. Usually the sufferer keeps quiet about the matter and often does not seek help for as long as 10 years. One third of these unfortunate people develop clinical depression and suicide is not uncommon.

The condition has long been classified as a neurosis, but today the tendency is to avoid this term and simply refer to it as a behaviour disorder. There is some evidence that this condition is associated with subtle brain damage, possibly, in some cases, from prenatal effects or birth injury. Freudians have their own explanation, claiming that the problem results from a defensive regression to the pre-oedipal anal-sadistic phase, however that might be interpreted.

Treatment with tricyclic antidepressant drugs, especially clomipramine, can be valuable, but the best results have been achieved by behaviour therapy and family therapy. There is no evidence that psychoanalysis can cure the condition.

Concussion

As the term implies, this is a shaking-up of the brain. Concussion occurs when a force is applied violently to the head causing an immediate brief period of unconsciousness, lasting for seconds to hours. Concussion is caused by head injury, usually without skull fracture, from sudden forcible acceleration or deceleration forces. The living brain is soft and jelly-like and these forces cause it to swing forwards or backwards so that it is squashed against the inside of the skull. Alternatively, it may twist on its stem and suffer compression against protrusions on the skull. The injury is probably always associated with some bleeding inside the brain and it is known that in many cases nerve tissues are destroyed.

Happily, the supply of nerve tissue is liberal and a single episode of concussion is unlikely to have observable permanent effects. Repeated episodes of concussion, however, such as those sustained by boxers, will inevitably cause major, widespread and irremediable brain damage (the 'punch-drunk' syndrome).

Anyone who has suffered concussion and who has lost consciousness, after a head injury, even for a few seconds, should be seen by a doctor. In many cases it is safest to admit the victim to hospital for 24 hours' observation. So the next time you watch a film in which the hero is constantly being knocked out only to get up and proceed with the action, remember that this is not what should or probably would happen in real life.

Constipation

This is a disorder of civilized societies and is unknown among peoples whose diet is largely vegetable with a high fibre content. Such people are free from many of the colonic problems suffered by those of us who enjoy more expensive diets.

Many people believe that if they fail to empty their bowels at least once a day they will come to harm. This is nonsense. Constipation causes symptoms but they are not the result of the absorption of toxins from the bowel. These symptoms – a sense of fullness, headache, furred tongue, loss of appetite and depression – can be produced by packing the rectum with sterile cotton wool.

Anxious, fastidious people often feel that it is essential to get rid of 'unclean' excreta every day, and dose themselves, and their children, with laxatives. This can turn an imaginary disorder into a real one. The way to cure constipation is to ensure adequate bulk in the stools. This can be done by replacing refined sugary carbohydrate in your diet with foods containing a high proportion of vegetable fibre. Eat plenty of fruit, leafy and other vegetables and bran-containing cereals. These will produce bulky, soft stools and regular motions. As a bonus, you might even lose a bit of weight.

Contact reactions (allergies)

The body's immune system protects us against *any* foreign substance, not just bacteria and viruses. It does so by producing antibodies which will attack the invader. Allergy is an abnormal reaction of the immune system to contact between any such substance and the skin, the lining of the nose, throat or lungs, or the lining of the digestive system.

In people with allergies the antibodies produced become fixed to special cells called mast cells. These are full of histamine and other powerful irritants. Any substance causing allergy in a sensitive person is called an allergen. Contact between the allergen and the antibody on the mast cells triggers off the release of the irritating substances from these cells. The result may be skin weals (urticaria), dermatitis, asthma or hay fever (allergic rhinitis), depending on the type of allergen and on where the mast cells and their antibodies are situated.

The most dangerous form of allergic reaction is called *anaphylactic shock*. This only affects people with a special sensitivity and usually follows injection of a drug, such as penicillin or serum, or an insect sting. The reaction causes widespread relaxation of arteries, leading to a critical drop in the blood pressure. There may also be a widespread skin rash and often tight spasm of the breathing tubes so that the air supply is partly obstructed. This is an emergency and medical help should be summoned immediately. ⚠ Remember that people who have had this reaction before often carry an emergency adrenaline syringe. If available, adrenaline should be given immediately to anyone known to be prone to this reaction who is having breathing problems. It also helps if the victim lies down with the legs raised. You may need to give the kiss of life or even heart compression if there is no breathing or heartbeat.

Severe airway obstruction is a critical emergency. If the obstruction is complete, the victim has only minutes to live. Foreign bodies can often be expelled by gripping the victim around the upper abdomen from behind and forcibly thrusting the clenched fist up into the angle between the ribs. This must be done rapidly and repeatedly. Sometimes food blocking the entrance to the airway can be moved if the tongue and jaw are pulled forward with one hand and the forefinger of the other swept round far down at the base of the tongue. If a person who has choked on food is unconscious and there is no inward movement of air, life can sometimes be saved by stretching back the head and cutting into the windpipe just below the Adam's apple with any available sharp instrument. Bleeding should be ignored. Keep the hole open with a tube, such as a pen barrel.

Convulsions

These are fits or seizures. A fit may involve the whole or part of the body and may or may not be followed by loss of consciousness. In the major fit of epilepsy (grand mal), there is a sudden violent contraction of most of the volun-tary muscles of the body (tonic contractions) followed by relaxation and then a succession of smaller jerky contractions (clonic contractions), persisting for a minute or so.

Convulsions occur in many brain conditions, of which epilepsy is only one. In children, the commonest type are fever fits (febrile convulsions) and these do not imply epilepsy. They are caused by raised temperature, especially prolonged fever. They should be prevented, if possible, by bringing down the temperature (sponge the body with tepid water) and by treating the cause of the fever. There is reason to believe, however, that repeated fever fits might predispose to epilepsy later in life.

Corns and callosities

These are the way your body protects itself against undue friction or pressure on the skin overlying a bony bump. Such trauma can do a lot of damage but, fortunately, the body has an answer to the problem. This is to thicken up the threatened skin by forming a corn or a callosity – they are really the same thing. A common form is the corn on a toe caused by a tight or pointed shoe or by an abnormally positioned toe. The tern 'corn' comes from the process – cornification – which is a thickening, flattening and compaction of the outer layer of skin (the epidermis). The greater the trauma, the thicker the cornification.

Callosities form whenever stong skin pressure occurs over bone. Students get them on their elbow, guitarists on their fingertips. saints on their knees, and marathon runners on their heels. In the days of manual labour, callosities on the palms of the hands were natural to most working men. So long as the cause persists, it is illogical and foolish to remove callosities. But if the cause is removed the callosity no longer has any function and will soon disappear.

Coughing

Coughing is an automatic reflex by which the lungs are able to get rid of potentially dangerous semi-solid material in the bronchial tubes. These tubes are normally guarded against the entry of unwanted solid material by the cough reflex, but such material may accumulate within them by secretion from the glands in the tube linings. In coughing, a deep breath is taken and the vocal cords are pressed tightly together. The diaphragm is then forced upwards to compress the air in the lungs. The vocal cords are then sharply released so that a blast of air passes upwards from all parts of both lungs. This carries out any material, such as excess mucus, sputum or small foreign bodies. Many persistent (chronic) chest disorders feature regular coughing because of the production of excessive bronchial secretions.

Never neglect a persistent cough. early treatment may prevent it from becoming chronic. There are many causes of coughing but they all involve irritation of the linings of the air tubes. They include:

- upper respiratory tract infections;
- lower respiratory tract infections;
- smoker's cough;
- bronchitis;
- bronchiectasis;
- bronchopneumonia;
- whooping cough.

'*Upper respiratory tract infections*' is rather a mouthful, so doctors refer to them as 'URTIs'. URTIs are usually caused by viruses and are seldom dangerous. They include common colds, tonsillitis, sore throat (pharyngitis), sinusitis, laryngitis and croup.

Most URTIs lead to nasal congestion and this causes distress, mouth-breathing and, in babies, difficulty in both breast- and bottle-feeding. Nasal catarrh, with mucus accumulation, will cause similar problems. Coughing, which is a constant feature of URTIs, should not automatically be treated, as the cough is part of the defensive mechanism of the respiratory system. But tiring and distressing coughing may helpfully be relieved in children over one year, who are not otherwise unwell, by a mild antihistamine and soothing expectorant mixture. Medical experts deplore the widespread practice of treating URTIs with antibiotics, because they are justifiably worried that this will lead to a rapid increase in antibiotic resistance. On the other hand, streptococcal infections of the throat can lead to serious conditions such as rheumatic fever and kidney disorders, and, in such cases, antibiotics are important.

Lower respiratory tract infections are, in general, more serious. They affect the breathing tubes (trachea and bronchi) and the lungs, and include acute bronchitis, acute bronchiolitis and various kinds of pneumonia.

Smoker's cough is no joke. It is an indication that persistent damage is being done to the linings of the air tubes in the lungs. This leads to loss of the normal character in the lining cells, which often progresses to lung cancer. Sufferers should give up smoking for good.

Bronchitis indicates that something is causing inflammation of the lining of the air tubes. The resulting irritation causes excess mucus to be produced and this may become infected causing a cough, phlegm (sputum), pain in the chest and fever. Bronchitis tends to get worse and to come on each winter. The principal cause of bronchitis is smoking cigarettes. Long-term bronchitis may lead to narrowing and obstruction of the air tubes and may progress to emphysema, in which the lung air sacs become widened and inefficient. This may cause breathlessness.

Bronchiectasis is an unpleasant lung disorder featuring local widening of some of the smaller air tubes with stagnation of secretions and infection. This results in a persistent cough with the production of much green or yellow, blood-streaked phlegm containing pus. The stagnant secretions in the bronchi may cause bad breath and the par-

tial obstruction to the air tubes may cause breathlessness. Much can often be done, both by antibiotic treatment and by surgery, to improve the situation of people with bronchiectasis.

Bronchopneumonia is now the commonest kind of pneumonia. It involves widespread, patchy inflammation of the lung tissue and the smaller air tubes, some of which are filled with pus. Bronchopneumonia usually follows some other illness, such as whooping cough, measles or flu, or is related to some other misfortune, such as inhaling vomit. There is a cough, high fever, rapid breathing, breathlessness, sputum, and pain in the chest. Bronchopneumonia is often the final event in people seriously ill from other causes. The death-rate is highest in the very young and the elderly.

In children, the most worrying form of persistent cough is whooping cough. This is an acute, highly infectious disease occurring almost exclusively in children under five years of age and spread by droplet infection. It is also known as *pertussis* and is caused by the organism *Bordetella pertussis*. The early, infectious stage cannot be distinguished from a cold, so epidemics commonly occur in susceptible children. The incubation period is seven to ten days.

The disease, which can be very distressing, lasts for about six weeks. After the first week or two of cold symptoms, the characteristic cough begins and the number of paroxysms of coughing varies from two or three to as many as 50. These bouts are more common at night. The child is seized by an uncontrollable succession of short, sharp coughs, so insistent and rapid in sequence that there is no time to draw breath between them. The lungs thus become almost emptied of air and the cough sequence is followed by a long, deep inspiration which often features a whooping sound. The final paroxysm in a series is often followed by vomiting. The process is exhausting to child and parent alike.

Whooping cough may be complicated by pneumonia, collapse of a segment or lobe of a lung, epileptic seizures from lack of oxygen in the brain, ulceration of the central membrane under the tongue and pushing out (prolapse) of the rectum. Antibiotics are of no value once the paroxysmal stage has been reached, unless secondary infection occurs, but effective cough suppressants, such as methadone, are available. Vomiting may interfere with nutrition, but feeds are usually retained if given immediately after vomiting.

In very rare cases, whooping cough vaccine has caused epileptic-like seizures or brain damage and public knowledge of this has led to a decline in acceptance of vaccination in Britain. It is important to state that the risks of vaccination are much less than the risks of the disease. Prior to the introduction of the vaccine in 1957 over 100,000 cases of whooping cough were officially notified each year, and many more occurred which were not notified. The death rate was about one per 1,000, overall, but the rate was much higher in children under one year of age. By 1973, vaccination of 80 per cent of children had led to a reduction in annual notifications to about 2,400 cases. But public anxiety thereafter caused a drop to 30 per cent acceptance and major epidemics occurred in 1977-79 and 1981-83.

Since then, acceptance has again risen and acceptance in 1986 was 67 per cent. Major epidemics have not occurred since. Most doctors advise that this disease should be prevented by active immun*i*zation of all infants, from three months of age, unless the child is suffering from any other acute illness or shows an adverse reaction to the first injection of the vaccine. Decisions may be difficult in the case of children with a history of brain damage or seizures, or a family history of epilepsy. In these the risk of vaccination may be higher, but so may be the risks of whooping cough.

Babies under three months should be protected, as far as is possible, from contact with children who may be infected with whooping cough. They do, however, have considerable protection from antibodies acquired from the mother before birth.

Crying baby

See **Colic**.

Crying baby (high pitched)

See **Fever and neck stiffness**.

55

D

Deafness	Déjà vu
Deformities of the bones	Delay in development
Deformities of the chest	Dementia
Deformities of the face	Diarrhoea
Deformities of the foot	Dizziness
Deformities of the hand	Double vision
Deformities of the limbs	Drooping eyelid
Deformities of the skull	Drug abuse effects
Deformities of the spine	Dry mouth and eyes

Deafness

See **Hearing problems**.

Deformities of the bones

Rickets is a childhood disorder affecting body calcium and phosphorus, mainly involving the bones, and caused by vitamin D deficiency. This vitamin is necessary for the absorption of calcium from the intestine. Vitamin D is found in dairy products and fish oils. Vitamin precursors in the diet are also converted to vitamin D by the action of sunlight on the skin, and poorly nourished children, such as vegans, who are deprived of sunlight are more likely to be affected. Rickets involves a diminished amount of calcium being deposited in the bones, so that they are consequently weakened and softened. The result may be:

- bowing of the legs;
- a pigeon breast deformity;
- curvature of the spine;
- an increased tendency to bone fracture and softening;
- squaring off and flattening of the skull;
- delay in teething;
- softening of tooth enamel after the tooth has grown.

Rickets is treated by adequate, but not excessive,

doses of vitamin D and plenty of calcium-containing nourishment, such as milk.

Osteomalacia is a bone softening condition similar to rickets except that it affects adults who are deficient in vitamin D. The bones can become deformed under the weight of the body and there is considerable discomfort or pain. The muscles are weak and the gait often waddling. Spontaneous fractures of bone can occur. The condition responds dramatically to vitamin D therapy.

Dyschondroplasia is a rare progressive disease of the growing parts of bone, affecting children and causing growth retardation. Bones are abnormally, and often unequally, shortened and show nodular swellings. The arms, legs and fingers are commonly affected, but the skull, spine, ribs and pelvis are usually spared. The process continues until early adult life but, by then, severe deformity may have resulted, with limbs of unequal length. Disability from finger deformity may also be a problem.

Deformities of the chest

There are several of these. In *pigeon chest* the breastbone (sternum) projects rather sharply, like that of a bird. This may be a natural shape, present from birth, or it may be the result of nutritional deficiencies, especially a shortage of vitamin D that has led to childhood rickets. This is now almost unknown in Western societies and, if present, will arouse the suspicion of neglect.

In *funnel chest* the breastbone is depressed, producing a distinct hollow which may be quite deep. This, too, can be either natural or the result of rickets. As a rule, neither pigeon chest nor funnel chest causes any real harm, apart from looking unnatural.

Asymmetry of the chest is usually due to a twisted spine of the type known as *kyphoscoliosis* (see **Deformities of the spine**). It may, however, be the result of serious lung problems such as collapse of the lung, tuberculosis or pleurisy. Chest asymmetry should always be investigated and the cause corrected, if possible. If the child is entirely well, the condition need not in itself be harmful.

A *barrel-shaped chest* – one that looks as if the person is breathing in all the time – is the hallmark of emphysema. This is a lung disease featuring destructive changes in the small air sacs (alveoli) where oxygen passes from the air into the blood and carbon dioxide passes out. As a result of disease, the walls of the alveoli break down so that larger air spaces are formed. The effect is that the surface area available for gas exchange is greatly reduced and there is diminished oxygen supply to the vital organs and a rise in the amount of carbon dioxide in the blood.

Bronchitis is commonly associated with emphysema and because bronchitis narrows the bronchial tubes, it becomes even more difficult for air to pass through and the situation becomes worse. When air is trapped in the enlarged alveolar spaces, the lungs become overinflated.

This is why the chest becomes barrel shaped. The sufferer wheezes and is short of breath. The deficient oxygen supply also leads to a reduction in the amount of exertion possible and, eventually, the affected person may be able to do no more than sit up in bed. Even then, there may be breathlessness and blueness of the skin (cyanosis) requiring oxygen by mask for survival. Smoking and recurrent respiratory infections make matters worse.

The primary cause of emphysema is still unclear, but smoking is the most important known factor. Inhalation of industrial pollutants can also contribute to the development of the condition. In some cases there is a strong family history of the disease, but this does not necessarily imply a genetic factor.

Deformities of the face

Facial deformities are particularly distressing as they commonly affect the attitudes of other people, especially strangers. These deformities include:

- enlargement from pituitary hormone;
- gargoylism;
- lupus vulgaris;
- cleft palate;
- the elephant man disorder;
- lion-like appearance;
- Bell's palsy.

Acromegaly is a rare disorder resulting from overproduction of pituitary gland growth hormone. It features gradual enlargement of the jaw, tongue and nose, as well as other parts of the body.

Hurler's syndrome, or *gargoylism*, is one of the group of inherited disorders called the *mucopolysaccharidoses*. It is due to the absence of the enzyme alpha-iduronidase and features dwarfism, widespread skeletal deformity, mental retardation, heart abnormalities, clouding of the cornea and early death.

Now that milk is reliably free from the tubercle bacillus, lupus vulgaris is a rare disease. It is a form of skin tuberculosis that was formerly the cause of much facial deformity, especially around the nose and the inside of the mouth. It causes painless ulceration and, unless treated, loss of tissue. In extreme cases, the nose may be lost. Lupus – the name comes from the Latin word for 'wolf' – was once commonly confused with leprosy and syphilis.

A cleft palate, one of the commonest birth defects, is a gap in the roof of the mouth, which may partially or completely divide the palate. A cleft palate may occur on its own, or with a cleft lip. A cleft lip may be no more than a small notch, or it may extend right up to join one nostril. Sometimes there are two gaps in the upper lip, extending up to both nostrils and these may be associated with partial or complete cleft palate.

The surgical management of these conditions has improved immeasurably in recent years and it is now rare to see obvious deformity from a cleft lip (hare lip). Babies with a cleft palate cannot breast-feed and must be fed from a bottle. Although good surgical repair is possible, usually around one year of age, there may be a long-term problem with speech, with therapy often necessary and helpful.

Neurofibromatosis, also known as *von Recklinghausen's disease*, affects about one in 3,000 people. It is a genetic disorder with dominant inheritance but about half the cases occurring result from a new mutation. The disease varies in severity from a few minor skin features to severely disfiguring and dangerous involvement of other parts of the body, including the nervous system.

Diagnosis is usually made by observing six or more *café au lait* patches, more than 15 mm in diameter, on the skin, and freckles in areas not normally exposed to the sun, such as the armpits. In the fully established condition, the fibrous sheaths of numerous nerves in the skin and elsewhere develop soft tumours called *neurofibromas*. In most cases these are confined to the skin and have cosmetic significance only.

But in about 20 per cent of cases serious complications arise when massive amounts of skin or the central nervous system become affected. The celebrated Elephant Man, made famous by the English surgeon Sir Frederick Treves (1853–1923), probably had neurofibromatosis.

The tumours can involve the brain and spinal cord; the eye sockets, leading to increasing protrusion of the eyes; the bones, leading to spontaneous fractures; and the spine, causing severe deformity and sometimes paralysis. Mental retardation, usually mild, occurs in a proportion of cases. People with neurofibromatosis need support and help and, in Britain, this is supplied by such organizations as LINK (Let's Increase Neurofibromatosis Knowledge). Similar organizations exist in other countries.

Paget's disease (see **Deformities of the skull**) affects bone formation and can produce a face that looks rather like that of a lion's. Another cause of facial deformity is

Bell's palsy (see **Facial weakness or paralysis**). See also **Nasal deformity**.

Deformities of the foot

Clubfoot or *talipes* is a congenital deformity affecting the shape or position of one or both feet. The commonest type is called *talipes equinovarus* and in this the entire foot, including the heel, is twisted inwards, so that the sole lies almost in a vertical plane. The arch of the foot is greatly exaggerated. 'Talipes' is the Latin word for 'clubfoot' and 'equinovarus' combines the word for a horse with the word for an inward deviation.

Talipes is thought to be caused by a lack of balance in the muscles which stabilize the foot, and the condition has a definite familial tendency. Treatment must begin at, or as soon as possible after, birth, and consists of repetitive deliberate manipulations in which the inturn and the high arching are gently but positively corrected, followed sometimes by the application of a splint. If started during the first week of life, splints may not be necessary and the parents, after careful instruction, may be able to continue the manipulation themselves. If the start of treatment is delayed for three weeks, splints will probably be required. The longer the delay, the more difficult the problem will be to correct. If full correction has not been achieved by six months of age, surgical correction will be needed.

Hammer toe is a condition in which a toe is permanently bent at the joint and fixed in this position so that the outer bone points downward like the head of a hammer. The condition may affect one or more toes and arises because the tendons which bend the toe are unduly tight.

The foot deformity underlying a bunion is a distortion of the bones in the big toe called *hallux valgus*. See **Pain in the foot**.

Deformities of the hand

Hand deformities, present at birth, are commoner than

might be expected. In fact, one person in 2,500 is born with some degree of hand deformity. These may be:

- failure of parts or all of the fingers to develop;
- overgrowth of one finger (producing a giant finger);
- fewer fingers than normal;
- additional fingers;
- fusion of two or more fingers into one;
- webbed skin between fingers;
- spider fingers (see **Spider-like fingers**).

Additional fingers, fusion of two or more fingers into one and webbed skin are all easily corrected.

Dupuytren's contracture is a condition of inflammation, scarring, thickening and shortening of a fibrous layer under the skin of the palm of the hand so that one or more fingers are pulled into a permanently bent position. The ring (third) finger is usually the first to be affected, then the little finger, the middle finger and the index finger.

The right hand is affected more often than the left and the condition affects men far more frequently than women. It starts with a painless, nodular thickening on the palm. This gradually extends to form a thick, longitudinal irregular firm cord, to which the skin becomes stuck so that it can no longer move freely. Slow, progressive contraction then occurs, with disabling bending of the finger or fingers. The rate of progress is variable and in some is very slow.

In the days of widespread manual labour, Dupuytren's contracture was assumed to be due to constant trauma to the palm from hand tools. This view is no longer held and its cause remains uncertain. The condition occurs with increasing frequency after middle age and is found most often in diabetics, in people with AIDS, in those with cirrhosis of the liver and in those with tuberculosis of the lungs. The only effective treatment is careful surgical removal of the thickened, contracted tissue.

Trigger finger is an effect caused by localized swelling of the tendon by which the finger is bent (flexor tendon), and of the tendon sheath. The swelling in the tendon occurs near the base of the finger. When the finger is bent, the swollen tendon is able to slip normally out of the end of its sheath but cannot easily slip back in again. The finger thus remains bent unless straightened passively, which may cause an audible click. Permanent correction is possible by surgery – the tendon sheath is opened (decompressed) so that the tendon is no longer obstructed. See also **Finger clubbing**.

Deformities of the limbs

The drug Distaval – the trade name for thalidomide – was widely advertised as the safest sedative yet produced, and was prescribed to millions, including many women in early pregnancy. In 1961 it was found to be linked with a syndrome of severe congenital malformation featuring especially gross stunting of the limbs, which were often replaced by short flippers. This condition is called *phocomelia*. Research then showed that the drug was interfering with the normal development of the fetus early in pregnancy. About 10,000 babies with such deformities were born, half of them in Germany, where the drug was most widely used, and these unfortunate people are now coping as well as they can with severe disabilities.

This tragedy prompted much stricter governmental control on the testing and safety of new drugs, all of which are now checked for any tendency to interfere with fetal development, as well as for other hazards. Thalidomide has been found useful in the treatment of certain forms of leprosy and Behçet's syndrome.

Deformities of the skull

Babies and small children sometimes suffer a skull deformity resulting from an increased pressure in the fluid which bathes the brain. 'Water on the brain' – the medical term is *hydrocephalus* – is an abnormal accumulation of the cerebrospinal fluid within, and around, the brain. Hydrocephalus results when the fluid cannot be properly reabsorbed, usually because its flow is blocked, either by a congenital abnormality or later acquired disease.

In babies or young children the pressure from accumulated fluid expands the skull, sometimes greatly, and if the cause cannot be removed it is necessary to shunt, or bypass, the normal channels by passing a tube into one of the spaces in the brain (ventricle), carrying it down under the skin of the neck and inserting it into the heart through a jugular vein. Alternatively, the shunt tube can be carried right down to open into the abdominal cavity. In both cases, the tube contains a one-way valve so that fluid can pass out of the brain but not back in. Unfortunately, blockage of the tube is common

and replacements may be required.

Unrelieved hydrocephalus causes compression of the brain, especially after the skull bones have fused together, and this leads to headache, vomiting, and damage to the way the body functions, including visual disturbance.

Paget's disease is a bone disease, sometimes called *osteitis deformans* because of its tendency to cause softening and distortion of any of the body's bones. It affects men more frequently than women and often runs in families. It is rare before the age of 40, but increasingly common thereafter, affecting up to three per cent of the elderly population. Recent evidence suggests that the disease may be due to a virus infection of one of the two types of bone cells (osteoclasts).

The bones most often involved are the skull, the collar bones (clavicles), the spine (vertebral column), the pelvis and the leg bones. Sometimes the bones of the face become distorted to produce the lion-like appearance known as *leontiasis ossea.* There is an increased blood flow though the affected bones and the area involved may feel unusually warm. Affected bones are enlarged and distort under pressure. The legs may become bowed; spinal distortion may affect the spinal cord, causing paralysis; spontaneous fractures may occur; and skull enlargement and thickening may cause headache and deafness from compression of the acoustic nerves.

Paget's disease is treated with pain-relieving drugs and with the hormone calcitonin, which decreases the rate of bone turnover and allows more calcium and phosphorus to be lost in the urine. People with Paget's disease who are confined to bed often develop very high levels of calcium in the blood and are at risk from kidney stones and other complications. A high fluid intake, and measures to reduce blood calcium, are important.

Another cause of skull deformity is the blood disorder *thalassaemia.* This is a condition of abnormal haemoglobin in the red blood cells, leading to unduly rapid breakdown of the cells and severe anaemia. Haemoglobin is the pigment in red blood cells which transports oxygen. The haemoglobin abnormality can take various forms, but all are due to the inheritance of an abnormal gene or an abnormal gene pair. One gene causes a minor disturbance, but inheritance of both genes causes a much more serious type, with breathlessness, easy tiredness, jaundice and enlargement of the spleen. These symptoms are caused by the anaemia and the reduced oxygen-carrying capacity of the blood. The body responds by attempting to produce more red cells in the bone marrow and this may cause characteristic enlargement of bones, such as 'bossing' of the temples and the cheekbones in children.

Thalassaemia may require transfusion of normal blood cells so as to allow normal development. Accumulation of iron in the body, from red cell breakdown, must also be treated, or this will cause complications including cirrhosis of the liver.

Deformities of the spine

These may take various forms and have a range of causes. Postural curvature is the commonest problem. Abnormal bowing in the back region is called *kyphosis* and sideways curvature is called *scoliosis*. These are usually the result of poor habits when standing and can be checked if children are constantly encouraged to 'walk tall'. Kyphoscoliosis is a spinal deformity in which an abnormal degree of kyphosis is combined with scoliosis. Wry neck (torticollis) can cause severe distortion of the upper part of the spine.

Bone disease, such as tuberculosis, is now uncommon but can cause severe spinal deformity by collapse of one or more bones of the spine (vertebrae). This condition is known as *Pott's disease* and was once very common. Pott's disease features acute angulation of the back. This was once a frequent cause of

the disfigurement known popularly as 'hunchback' but, happily, is now rare. The infection was usually acquired from bovine tuberculosis in milk, now largely eliminated by pasteurization.

Spina bifida is a developmental defect in which the rear part of one or more vertebrae remain incomplete. As a result, the spinal cord, which runs down through a series of holes in the vertebrae, is relatively unprotected in the affected area. In spina bifida occulta, the condition is hidden and unsuspected and usually discoverable only on X-ray. In more serious cases, the coverings of the cord (the meninges) pass back through the opening to form a cyst-like swelling called a *meningocele*. In the worst cases, the spinal cord, itself, is exposed. This is called a *myelocele* and there is usually paralysis of the legs and loss of sensation. There is often an associated hydrocephalus and subsequent brain damage.

Spina bifida, especially if severe, is easily diagnosed before birth, by amniocentesis, alphafetoprotein estimation and ultrasound examination. In severe cases, detected early in pregnancy, the option of termination of the pregnancy may be considered. Surgery to correct the defect may be performed as soon as possible after birth.

Déjà vu

Nearly everyone has experienced this odd phenomenon and, if it happens occasionally, there is no cause for concern. Frequent episodes, however, could be significant. Déjà vu means 'already seen' in French, and the term is applied to the sudden mistaken conviction that a current new experience has happened before. There is a compelling sense of familiarity, usually lasting for only a few seconds, and a persuasion, almost always immediately disappointed, that one knows what is around the next corner.

By definition, déjà vu does not relate to actual repeat experiences or memories, so the interest lies in why the conviction occurs. One possible explanation is that the phenomenon results from a brief neurological short circuit, with data from the current observation reaching the memory store before they reach consciousness. The conscious experience of such a memory would be very strong, as it is so recent.

Some experts suggest that memory is not a matter of recalling a fixed, established event, but is a process of reconstruction, from stored components, which involves elaborations, distortions and omissions. Each successive recall of the event is merely the recall of the last reconstruction. The sense of recognition involves achieving a good 'match' between the present experience and the stored data, but this may now differ so much from the original event that you 'know' you have never experienced it before.

Psychologists are still arguing about déjà vu and will continue to do so until much more is known about the mechanisms of the brain.

Déjà vu, occurring often, is a possible symptom of disorders resulting from brain damage, such as temporal lobe epilepsy. So if this is something that happens to you a lot, it would be a good idea to see your doctor and suggest a neurological examination.

Delay in development

This refers to mental, rather than physical, development. There are many reasons why a child should not achieve abilities and behaviour patterns appropriate to his or her age. These include:

- serious and prolonged general diseases especially of the heart and lungs;
- poor nutrition;
- brain damage before, during or after birth;
- severe deafness;
- very poor vision;
- lack of parental affection or attention;
- lack of adequate guidance in acceptable conduct;
- lack of mental or physical stimulation.

Some of these causes may be unapparent and, in some cases, they can be corrected so that development can return to normal. For this reason, if you have any suspicion that there may be developmental delay you should insist on immediate medical investigation.

For newborn babies, attention will be paid to:

- weight;
- length;
- head circumference;
- presence of any congenital abnormalities;
- reaction to noise;
- reaction to light;
- clarity of lenses of the eyes;
- state of the fontanelles;
- possible hip dislocation;
- possible jaundice;
- pulses;
- whether testes are present in the scrotum;
- possible floppiness.

At six months, the doctor will be interested in:

- interaction with environment;
- interaction with parents;

- physical development;
- vision;
- hearing;
- sounds produced;
- possible squint;
- ability to roll over;
- ability to sit up without support;
- laughter.

At two years, all the above points will be reviewed and the doctor will additionally check:

- walking;
- ability to climb stairs;
- speech;
- vocabulary;
- response to commands;
- tightness of sphincters.

When a normal baby is supported, face down, with a hand under the chest, the head is held back, the back is held straight, or almost so, and the arms and legs are partly bent. A floppy infant droops over the hand like an inverted 'U'. This state is called *hypotonia* and it is not, in itself, a disease, but is an indication of one of a wide variety of conditions. Investigation is needed to determine whether any of

these conditions are present. The possibilities include:

- any major debilitating disease;
- malnutrition;
- a hormonal disorder such as hypothyroidism;
- a chromosomal abnormality such as Down's syndrome or Turner's syndrome;
- a connective tissue disorder such as Marfan's syndrome, osteogenesis imperfecta or the Ehlers-Danlos syndrome;
- a birth brain injury;
- progressive spinal muscular atrophy;
- a muscular dystrophy or other muscle disorder (myopathy);
- myasthenia gravis (a rare autoimmune disorder);
- infection with the botulinum organism (infant botulism).

Many floppy infants do not have any of these disorders, but this should not discourage investigation, in case urgent treatment is needed.

Developmental delay is a very large subject and it is inappropriate to go into more detail in a book of this kind. The essential point is that children are sometimes unnecessarily held back and may be permanently disadvantaged by conditions that can be corrected at an early stage, if they are detected.

Dementia

See **Loss of memory**.

Diarrhoea

In adults, this is nearly always trivial and self-correcting. Because the bowels can usually be relied on to get rid of the irritant that is causing the diarrhoea, it is not a good idea routinely to use medicine to cure the problem like codeine or Lomotil.

In babies, however, because of the ever-present risk of dehydration, diarrhoea should never be taken lightly. Breast-fed babies are much less likely to suffer intestinal infection – a common cause of diarrhoea – than those on the bottle, but normally pass very soft stools. If the faeces are very watery and runny and if there is any sign of general upset, such as fever, vomiting or failure to feed, then medical attention is urgently required. ⚠ Babies with gastroenteritis can go downhill very rapidly.

Diarrhoea can be caused by lactose intolerance due to deficiency of lactase, the enzyme which splits milk sugar. Unsplit milk sugar attracts fluid into the intestine, causing diarrhoea, tummy distention, bowel noises and failure to thrive. The same problem may occur if excessive sugar is added to the feed or if fruit juices are given too concentrated (they should be diluted as instructed). Even sugary-based medicines can cause diarrhoea. The move to solid food (weaning) can also cause diarrhoea because of the unaccustomed bowel irritation. In such a situation, formulas of low lactose, easy-to-digest carbohydrate, with adequate vitamin content may be useful for a short period.

Irritable bowel syndrome (IBS) is a very common, persistent and distressing disorder associated with recurrent pain in the abdomen, and intermittent diarrhoea, often alternating with constipation, for which no organic cause can be found. The condition is also known as *spastic colon, nervous diarrhoea* or *idiopathic diarrhoea*. It is responsible for about half the medical attendances for bowel upset.

IBS most commonly affects women between 20 and 40, and women suffer three times as often as men. It features:

- rapid transit of food with frequent bowel motions;
- a sense of fullness;
- an awareness of the bowel action;
- abdominal pain;
- frequent diarrhoea;
- extreme and embarrassing urgency to empty the bowels, often soon after a meal;
- loud abdominal rumblings and squeaking (borborygmi);
- excessive gas production (flatus);
- headache;
- tiredness;
- a sense of incomplete emptying after defaecation;
- anxiety.

The processes of peristalsis (the rhythmical way muscles move food and waste through the digestive system) are stronger and more frequent than normal and there is often intolerance to known kinds of food. Pain – usually felt in one of the four corners of the abdomen – is sometimes brought on by eating and is often relieved by going to the toilet. The stools are usually ribbon-like or pellet-like and may contain mucus.

IBS often begins during a period of emotional stress, as after marital discord, divorce, bereavement or business worry. It tends to affect anxious, tense, intelligent, conscientious women, especially those who worry unduly about personal, family and financial matters. There may be an underlying fear of cancer. Full investigation, including barium meal X-ray, shows no objective abnormality but, on examination, the colon is seen to be in a state of unusual activity, contracting and relaxing in an abnormally rapid manner.

A diet high in roughage is helpful in regulating the bowel action, and there are several drugs effective in quieting down the excessive bowel activity and relieving the pain. Drugs can be taken in anticipation of events which might provoke an acute attack. Useful drugs include Diarrest, Lomotil or Imodium (prescription only) and Kaodine or Kaopectate (which can be bought over the counter). After careful investigation to exclude organic causes, strong reassurance is often, in itself, therapeutic.

Dizziness

See **Vertigo**.

Double vision

See **Vision doubled**.

Drooping eyelid

See **Eyelid drooping**.

Drug abuse effects

This subject is included because it is always worth reminding people that there is a good deal to be said for avoiding recreational drugs altogether. No substance that has these effects on the body can be considered harmless.

Amphetamine overdose causes:

- shakiness;
- trembling of the hands;
- fast pulse;
- a rise in the blood pressure;
- headaches;
- palpitations;
- anxiety;
- sweating;
- difficulty in sleeping.

In some cases there may be psychiatric symptoms such as false beliefs (delusions) and false perceptions (hallucinations). Occasionally fits (seizures) occur. Long-term amphetamine use may lead to drug dependence.

Cocaine overdose can be extremely dangerous to health. The commonest serious physical effects are:

- epileptic-type fits;
- loss of consciousness – 'tripping out';
- unsteadiness;
- sore throat;
- running and bleeding nose;
- sinusitis;
- pain in the chest;
- coughing blood;
- pneumonia;
- severe itching ('the cocaine bug');
- irregularity of the heart;
- loss of appetite;
- stomach upset.

Some of the chest and throat problems are probably caused by the high temperature of the inhaled cocaine fumes. The nose and sinus disorders are due to the constricting effect of cocaine on the blood vessels in the nose linings. This is followed by rebound swelling, but is sometimes severe enough to destroy part of the partition between the two halves of the nose, leaving a perforation.

Crack, like amphetamine, can lead to a short-lived, acute form of mental illness. This is called a cocaine psy-chosis. The symptoms in-clude:

- severe depression;
- agitation;
- delusions;
- ideas of persecution;
- hallucinations;
- violent behaviour;
- suicidal intent.

People with a cocaine psychosis often have 'lucid intervals' in which they seem normal and will often deny using the drug. Cocaine psychosis usually follows long binges or high doses.

Solvent abuse is the deliberate inhalation of the vapour from various solvents for their narcotic effect. Substances used include:

- any of the solvent-based commercial adhesives;
- volatile cleaning fluids;
- lighter fuel;
- petrol;
- paint thinner solvents;
- marking ink;
- anti-freeze;
- nail varnish remover (acetone);
- butane gas;
- toluene.

Usually, a small quantity of the solvent is poured into a polythene bag which is held tightly against the nose and mouth. The effects are generally intoxicant, with loss of full awareness of the surroundings, loss of coordination and muscle control and, sometimes, hallucinations. Unconsciousness may occur and death may result from asphyxiation, inhalation of vomit, or accident. Solvent abuse is responsible for many cases of brain, liver and kidney damage, especially in children who have become addicted. The practice is often performed in groups and many youngsters take to it as a result of peer pressure. For many, however, glue-sniffing episodes are merely experimental and of little importance.

Dry mouth and eyes

These are common symptoms and usually mean no more than thirst and a mild irritative conjunctivitis. In most cases of 'dry eyes' a quick look in a mirror will show that there is a perfectly adequate tear film along the lid margin, indicating that the dry feeling is an illusion. But if your mouth and eyes are really dry all the time, you have a problem.

Sjögren's syndrome is a condition featuring dryness of all parts of the body which are normally kept moist by fluid secretion. It thus affects the eyes, mouth, nose, respiratory system and vagina. The disorder is often found in conjunction with immune system upsets, such as rheumatoid arthritis, systemic lupus erythematosus, myasthenia gravis, dermatitis herpetiformis or autoimmune liver or thyroid disease. Twenty-five to 50 per cent of people with rheumatoid arthritis have Sjögren's syndrome and 90 per cent of those affected are women, usually middle-aged and often post-menopausal. The peak incidence is between 40 and 60 and the cause is unknown. About two per cent of the population is affected, but the condition is often missed.

The most obvious feature of Sjögren's syndrome is the dry

eye condition known as *keratoconjunctivitis sicca*. There is a sense of grittiness in the eyes, a burning and itching sensation, redness, dimness of vision and sensitivity to light. A lack of saliva makes the mouth feel dry; it becomes difficult to chew food, the tongue is sore and the salivary glands swell. There is commonly a loss of taste and smell. Dryness of the nose can be painful and is often associated with a hoarse voice and persistent chest infection. Dryness of the vagina causes difficulty and discomfort in sexual intercourse.

In Sjögren's syndrome the dryness results from reduced secretion of various kinds of glands following invasion and damage by immune system white cells (lymphocytes). There is no specific treatment to restore the glands to normal function, but much can be done by the use of artificial tears, frequent sips of fluid or polyvinyl alcohol sprays in the mouth, careful dental hygiene, and the use of K-Y jelly for vaginal lubrication.

Earache

Ears, noises in

Eating dirt

Elation

Enlarged 'glands'

Erection difficulties

Excessive sweating

Excessive thirst

Excessive urinary output

Eye inflammation

Eye irritation from lashes

Eye watering

Eye with white ring
around cornea

Eyelids bruised after
injury

Eyelid drooping

Eyelid retraction

Eyelid with hard, pea-
shaped swelling

Eyelid with yellow head on margin

Eyelids inturned

Eyelids out-turned

Eyelids reddened

Eyelids squeezed tight uncontrollably

Eyes crossed (squinting)

Eyes protruding

Eyes sunken

Eyes wobbling

Eyesight problems

E

Earache

See **Pain in the ear**.

Ears, noises in

See **Noises in the Ears**.

Eating dirt

The medical term for this is *pica*. This is a persistent tendency to eat non-nutritional substances such as earth, ice, match-heads, coal, chalk or wood. Pica is common in children under eighteen months and, in these, is not considered abnormal. Pica in pregnancy has been known throughout the ages and the bizarre catalogue of substances eaten include mothballs, soap, insects, clay, baking soda and excrement. Pica is also a feature of nutritional deficiency and iron-deficiency anaemia and sometimes succeeds in providing a needed supply of minerals. It will often stop if anaemia is effectively treated. As well as in pregnant women, pica commonly occurs in mentally retarded people and in people with severe psychiatric disorders.

In most cases, pica does little harm, but there have been many medical reports of obstruction or perforation of the bowel, lead poisoning, parasite infestation and other misfortunes from this cause. No satisfactory explanation of many types of pica has been produced.

Elation

This is a very good thing which, unfortunately, occurs all too seldom. But to qualify as a blessing, elation must have an appropriate cause. Elation without a cause can be a real problem. It is called *mania* and is one of the phases of a distressing condition known as *manic depressive illness* – a serious disturbance of the emotions. In some cases the affected person may show only mania or only depression. Such people are said to have *unipolar* disorders. If both phases occur, the disorder is said to be a *bipolar* disorder. The cause is unknown, but studies of identical twins suggest that hereditary factors may be involved.

This illness features an association of diametrically opposite kinds of mood disorder – on the one hand an abnormal elation (mania), and on the other, one of pathological depression. The depressive phase usually comes first and about 10 per cent of people thought to be suffering from unipolar depression have a manic episode six to 10 years later, usually in the early 30s. No real distinction is now drawn between the depressive phase of manic-depressive illness and psychotic depression generally.

During the manic phase the features are:

- speeding up of thought and speech;
- severely disordered judgement and mental reliability;
- ever-changing flights of ideas;
- constant elation or euphoria;
- inappropriate optimism;
- grandiose notions;
- a gross overestimation of personal ability.

The latter may be reflected in unrealistic plans and expressed intentions or even in socially and financially ruinous behaviour. The affected person sleeps poorly and may engage in an unusually high level of sexual activity. About three quarters of those with this disorder engage in personal assault or threatening behaviour, often against people in prominent positions. They are notoriously unreliable and characteristically engage in deceit and lying.

In the depressive phase there is mental and physical slowing, loss of interest and energy, loss of concentration, sadness, pessimism, self-doubt, self-blame and thoughts of suicide. Depressive episodes, if untreated, last for about six months to one year. The average patient suffers five or six episodes over a twenty-year period. Most treated episodes clear in about three months, but if treatment is stopped before about three months, relapse is very likely. The manic phase, if it occurs, usually comes after two to four depressive episodes.

Both phases may feature the characteristic psychotic elements of hallucinations and delusions. The spontaneous recovery rate in manic-depressive illness is very high – about 90 per cent recover. The relapse rate, however, is also high.

Depression is treated with antidepressant drugs and careful and sympathetic counselling. The doctor is aware of the ever-present threat of suicide, and advises accordingly. The mainstay of the treatment of mania is lithium.

Enlarged 'glands'

What are popularly known as 'glands' are, in fact, not glands at all but lymph nodes. They have no glandular properties or function, but with this understood it is easier to discuss them using the better-known term. The commonest cause of enlarged glands is inflammation of the lymph nodes. This is known as *adenitis*. You can't feel healthy lymph nodes but inflamed glands become enlarged and more firm, so that they can be made out as small, rubbery bean-like objects. They are sometimes tender to the touch. The main collections of lymph glands are in the neck, the armpits and the groins. Neck glands become inflamed in the course of throat infections such as tonsillitis. Armpit nodes become inflamed following infection in the arm and breast, and groin glands following infection of the leg. All these lymph nodes may be inflamed in glandular fever.

There are also large numbers of lymph nodes inside the abdomen. If these become infected they cause the condition of *mesenteric adenitis* which has symptoms very similar to those of appendicitis. Adenitis suggests a fairly severe infection with spread of germs beyond the original site. See your doctor. ⚠

Another important cause of lymph node enlargement is *glandular fever*. In childhood, this disease is usually mild and unapparent, and most children acquire the infection without knowing it. One attack confers permanent immunity. During the acute phase and convalescence the virus is present in large numbers in the saliva. This is why the condition is sometimes called the 'kissing disease'.

In an obvious case, there is misery, fever, headache, sore throat and a general enlargement of lymph nodes which may be felt, as rubbery swellings, in the neck, armpits, elbows, groins and behind the knees. In about 10 per cent of cases there is a rash of small, slightly raised, red spots. If this does not occur spontaneously, mistaken treatment with ampicillin will bring it on. The lungs may be involved, with chest pain, difficulty in breathing and a cough. Usually there is complete recovery in less than a month, but one person in ten complains for months, or even years, of fatigue with occasional recurrences of fever and lymph node enlargement. There is no specific treatment, but bed rest is desirable during the acute stage and strenuous exercise should be avoided while the spleen is enlarged.

A much less common cause of lymph node enlargement is the group of leukaemias. These are blood cancers in which certain groups of white blood cells reproduce in an entirely disorganized and uncontrolled way so that they progressively replace, and interfere with, the normal constituents of the blood. The leukaemias are progressive conditions which, unless effectively treated, will usually end fatally either from a shortage of red blood cells (anaemia), or from severe bleeding or infection. There are two main groups – the acute leukaemias, with a very short life expectancy and the chronic leukaemias in which the affected person may live for years. Certain types of chronic leukaemia can be cured.

Acute leukaemias often start with influenza-like symptoms: a feeling of great tiredness, sore throat, bleeding from the gums and into the skin, and loss of appetite and weight. There may be enlargement of the lymph nodes in the neck, armpits and groins. A blood check shows a severe anaemia and usually large numbers of primitive white cells. It is important for a precise diagnosis to be made of the type of cell involved, as the treatment will differ accordingly.

Chronic leukaemias have a slow, insidious onset, gradually followed by lassitude and fatigue, and a slow increase in the size of the spleen until it becomes massive, causing a dragging weight and pain in the upper left side of the abdomen. There is slow loss of weight, aching in the bones, nose bleeds and sometimes unwanted and prolonged erections (priapism) in men. There may be intolerance to heat and undue sweating.

Another serious group of conditions causing general lymph node enlargement are the lymphomas. These are cancers affecting lymphoid tissue, mainly in the lymph nodes and the spleen. There are two main kinds – *Hodgkin's lymphoma* and *non-Hodgkin's lymphoma*. Hodgkin's lymphoma usually begins in adolescence and early adult life, but can occur at any age. It affects the sexes equally. There is painless lymph node enlargement all over the body, the nodes being rubbery, easily felt, and occasionally slightly tender to pressure. Later, the spleen and the liver enlarge, and this is part of the general involvement of lymph tissue throughout the body. Persistent but variable degrees of fever are common, as is anaemia. The pressure of the enlarging nodes on adjacent structures (sometimes the disease even spreads to these) causes many secondary effects, including neurological damage, obstruction to veins, difficulty in swallowing or breathing, and jaundice. Occasionally the bone marrow becomes involved, usually late in the disease. This is a serious complication.

Non-Hodgkin's lymphomas usually consist of clonal masses of white blood cells called B lymphocytes. They vary considerably in their degree of malignancy and have many features in common with certain leukaemias. Some progress very slowly, and even the more malignant will often respond well to treatment. Again, the commonest tangible sign is widespread, painless, firm lymph node enlargement. There is tiredness, loss of weight, and sometimes fever. When the disease process reaches a certain stage, there may be pressure on various structures of the body. In many cases, no treatment is needed and often patients are watched for years without intervention. But when treatment is required, radiotherapy is often best and may be a cure.

Almost all cancers can spread to the nearest group of lymph glands. The most obvious spread of this kind occurs when a breast cancer progresses to the point where the lymph nodes in the armpit become involved and are enlarged and easily felt. Unfortunately, this is rather a bad sign and the outlook is likely to be worse than if the cancer has not spread to the nodes.

Erection difficulties

See **Penis problems: unresponsiveness**.

Excessive sweating

The medical term for this is *hyperhidrosis* and the condition is due to overactive sweat glands. These may occur all over the skin, or may be confined to certain areas, such as the palms of the hands, the armpits, the groins and the feet. In severe cases, the skin may be affected by the constant moisture, becoming soggy, soft and crumbly (macerated). Hyperhidrosis is often associated with strong body odour, caused by the bacterial breakdown of the sweat and the surface cells of the skin. This is called *bromhidrosis*.

Excessive sweating is usually just a variant of the normal, but may be caused by thyroid gland overactivity, fever or, rarely, by a disease of the nervous system. In some cases, hyperhidrosis is due to stress reactions or other psychological causes. It can be treated by local applications to reduce the activity of the sweat glands, or even, in extreme cases, by the surgical removal of the most active groups of glands. Many people just naturally sweat a lot, and these should set themselves a higher-than-average standard of personal hygiene and wash their clothes and bodies regularly. Emotional sweating usually calms down with time and maturity.

Excessive thirst

Thirst is a normal response to lack of water in the body. There is no need to be concerned about thirst so long as there is an obvious cause of water lack, such as sweating or inadequate intake.

Excessive thirst without obvious cause should always arouse the suspicion of diabetes, especially if there is also an unusually large output of urine. Diabetes is a wasting disease in which sugar, the normal fuel of the body, cannot be properly used and is passed in large quantities in the urine. There is a great increase in the volume of urine produced and corresponding severe thirst. Fat and muscle protein are converted to sugar, so there is severe loss of weight. The disease is due to a shortage of insulin, the hormone produced by the pancreas.

Damage to the pancreas is probably related to a virus infection which alters pancreas tissue so as to render it unrecognizable as 'self' to the immune system.

Diabetes affects one per cent of the population and causes untold distress. It requires life-long treatment with insulin by injection, constant checking of the sugar level in the blood and in the urine, and a regular watch for complications.

Another disease also causes excessive thirst. This is diabetes insipidus, a rare disease that has nothing to do with ordinary diabetes mellitus. Its main feature is the production of excessive quantities of dilute urine and a consequent great thirst. One of the pituitary hormones is the anti-diuretic hormone (ADH) or *vasopressin*. This substance acts on the kidneys to allow a massive return to the blood of water which has passed into the tubules (tiny tubes in the kidneys) after being filtered. In the absence of ADH this water passes out into the urine. Diabetes insipidus is caused by a reduction in ADH. This may result from a variety of pituitary disorders including tumours, infections, blood supply deprivation, pressure from local swelling on arteries (aneurysms) and injuries in the course of skull fracture.

The affected person has to spend much of the time emptying the bladder and may pass as much as 30 litres of water a day. This leads to continual thirst and an equal quantity must be drunk if dehydration is to be avoided. The condition is treated with injections of ADH, or the use of an ADH-containing nasal spray, about four times a day. Diabetes insipidus can also occur from a kidney disorder in which the kidneys are abnormally insensitive to the anti-diuretic hormone.

Excessive urinary output

Production of excessive quantities of urine, or *polyuria*, may simply be due to the excessive intake of fluid, as in the common case of the over-enthusiastic beer drinker, but it can also be a sign of diseases such as diabetes mellitus, diabetes insipidus (see above) or certain diseases of the kidney, known as 'salt-losing' states. Excessive urine output also occurs when oedema from any cause is treated with diuretic drugs to get rid of the excess fluid accumulated in the tissues of the body.

Excessive urination is not necessarily the same as abnormally frequent urination. In the latter, it is common for the affected person to be able to pass only small quantities of urine on each occasion. Frequency of this kind may be stimulated by the infection of an irritated bladder (cystitis – see **Pain on urination**). In elderly men, the commonest cause is enlargement of the prostate gland which so obstructs urine outflow that only a small quantity can be passed each time. As a result, the desire to urinate soon recurs.

Eye inflammation

The medical term for the common 'pink eye' is *conjunctivitis* and this is usually caused by infection. In babies it may be

associated with failure of the tear drainage duct to open up. In this case there will be an overflow of tears and a tendency to produce pus and mucus. In any infective conjunctivitis, pus tends to accumulate on the lashes causing them to stick together. Most infections clear up on their own but simple remedies, like Brolene, can be helpful.

A special case of infective conjunctivitis is that which occurs in new-born babies. The concern here is that the infection might be caused by gonorrhoea and acquired during birth from an infected mother. The gonococcus can cause havoc in the eye – even blindness, by perforation of the cornea – so it is important that any new-born baby with sticky or inflamed eyes should be urgently treated. ▲

It is important to note that eye inflammation is not necessarily caused simply by conjunctivitis. A red eye can be a sign of a much more serious condition such as acute glaucoma, corneal ulcer, a foreign body or the internal eye inflammation known as *uveitis*.

In all these cases there will be other symptoms, in particular pain and/or loss of vision. When eye inflammation is associated with pain or visual disturbance, you are in an emergency situation and need specialist attention urgently. ⚠

Eye irritation from lashes

This may be due to *trichiasis*, in which the lashes grow in an abnormal direction and cause discomfort and pain by rubbing on the eye. Inturning of the lid margin (entropion) causes similar effects. Pulling out the offending lashes is only a temporary solution to trichiasis and short, growing lashes may be more troublesome than full-grown lashes. Trichiasis and entropion can be cured by lid surgery.

Eye watering

Eyes water for one of two reasons: either there is overproduction of tears (lacrimation) or the tears are unable to drain away into the nose as they should and run over (epiphora). Lacrimation is caused by an irritant such as a foreign body or an infection. When this is detected and treated, the lacrimation will cease. Tear drainage blockage is often more difficult to fix.

Babies commonly suffer a constantly watering eye because the duct carrying tears into the nose has not opened up properly. Regular finger pressure over the inner corner of the eye may clear this, but sometimes the duct has to be cleared by passing a fine metal probe down the tear duct. This is done under a general anaesthetic.

In adults, persistent watering is usually due to the condition called *dacryocystitis*. This is an inflammation of the lacrimal sac, the tiny bag situated in the eye socket, just inward from the inner corner of the eye. The lacrimal sac acts as a kind of suction pump to draw tears away from the eye and pass them down the naso-lacrimal duct into the nose. Inflammation always causes problems with tear drainage and usually results in permanent blockage of the naso-lacrimal duct. Sometimes an abscess forms and this may burst externally below the inner corner of the eye. Whether or not this happens the problem invariably causes overflowing of tears in the affected eye.

Tear drainage can be restored by an operation, known as *dacryocystorhinostomy*, in which the lacrimal sac is connected to the inside of the nose by way of an artificial opening through the bone. Occasionally, watering is due to blockage of the tiny tubes – the canaliculi – that carry tears from the eye to the lacrimal sac. This can be a more difficult problem but there are surgical procedures in which a tiny glass tube is used to drain the tears directly into the nose.

Eye with white ring around cornea

This is called *arcus senilis*. The appearance is actually caused by a narrow, grey-white band near the edge of the outer lens of the eye (the cornea) in elderly people. Arcus senilis does not affect vision and is not considered to be of medical importance. A similar condition in young people (arcus juvenilis) should, however, be investigated as this is sometimes associated with excess cholesterol in the blood (hyperlipidaemia).

Eyelids bruised after injury

The medical term for black eye – *periorbital haematoma* – is impressive but simply means that some blood has been released into the loose tissues around the eye. Black eye almost always results from injury to the network of veins, lying under the skin, from direct violence. Incidentally, it is widening of these veins, in conjunction with the thinness of the skin in this region, that cause the appearance of dark circles under the eyes. A cold compress applied immediately after the injury will help to reduce the amount of bleeding and minimize the bruised appearance (raw steak has no effect whatsoever, unless it is straight out of the fridge – it is the coldness that is important).

Free blood in the tissues is gradually absorbed by phagocytes and the process leads to an interesting succession of colour changes, ending up with a nice lemon yellow stage before your appearance returns to normal. If you sustain a black eye you should always check that the vision in the appropriate eye is normal, that the eye can move fully and that there is no double vision. Don't take aspirin for the pain as this can encourage further bleeding. Take paracetamol (Panadol) if you need a painkiller.

Eyelid drooping

The medical term for a persistent droop of an upper eyelid is *blepharoptosis*, usually shortened to *ptosis*. This may be present from birth (congenital) or it may occur later in life. In the latter case, the droop may occur either for no obvious reason or may be the result of injury or disease, such as myasthenia

gravis. Ptosis is usually due to a weakness of the thin muscle that pulls up the upper lid or to interference with the nerve supply to the muscle. Severe congenital ptosis, in which the drooping lid covers the pupil, must be corrected as a matter of urgency so as to allow normal vision to develop. An uncorrected ptosis that covers half the pupil or more will result in life-long partial blindness of the eye concerned. This failure of visual development is called *amblyopia*.

Acquired ptosis without obvious cause may be a sign of a neurological disease, such as a brain tumour or a cerebral aneurysm, and should be immediately investigated by a doctor. ▲

Eyelid retraction

This refers to the upper eyelids. These may sometimes be pulled upwards and backwards in such a way as to produce a strikingly staring effect. The lids may even remain pulled upwards for a short time after the affected person looks down. Normally, lids drop as the person looks down. Eyelid retraction is almost always a feature of a thyroid gland upset and it is usually associated with the protrusion of the eyes known as *exophthalmos*. See also **Eyes protruding**.

Eyelid with hard, pea-shaped swelling

If you have a round, painless, hard, pea-like swelling in your upper or lower eyelid, you almost certainly have a *meibomian cyst* (also known as a chalazion). The swelling arises because the outlet of one of the meibomian glands that lubricate the edge of the eyelids is obstructed. If the swelling is allowed to grow large enough, pressure on the lens at the front of the eye (the cornea) may cause blurred vision.

Meibomian cysts can occur at any age and are especially common in people suffering from the skin conditions acne, acne rosacea, or seborrhoeic dermatitis. If the cyst becomes infected, the eyelid becomes more swollen, red and painful. About one third of chalazions disappear without any treatment, but large cysts usually need to be removed surgically (from the inside of the eyelid) under a local anaesthetic.

There is another meibomian problem called *meibomitis*. This is an inflammation of the glands on the eyelid, which causes the normal, oily secretion to thicken. Meibomitis usually affects middle-aged people, often those with inflammation of the eyelid (blepharitis), and frequently leads to recurrent meibomian cysts.

Eyelid with yellow head on margin

This common condition, known as a *stye*, is an infection around the root of an eyelash. A stye is a small abscess, usually caused by staphylococcal germs, the follicle being stretched painfully by the collection of pus which usually causes the small 'yellow head' at the base of the eyelash. In these cases relief may sometimes be obtained, if somewhat painfully, by pulling out the lash and so allowing the pus to get out. This takes courage but is usually effective.

Styes tend to recur because the infection spreads to adjacent lash follicles. Antibiotic eye ointment, applied to the lid margins two or three times a day for two or three weeks will help to prevent this. If styes prove very persistent, you may need a check on your general health and you should have a urine test for sugar to eliminate diabetes.

Eyelids inturned

This is a common problem in older people and commonly affects the lower lid. It is called *entropion*. There is great discomfort if the lashes touch the eyeball, especially the cornea, and there is sometimes danger of corneal damage and ulcer formation. Try to get the lid to turn out by gentle pressure below the margin with the finger. Do not delay unduly – consult your doctor as soon as is convenient. The condition can usually be cured by a simple operation.

There is also an eyelid-inturning condition that affects fat babies. This is called *puppy-fat entropion* and, although it looks very uncomfortable, the remarkable thing about it is that the affected babies don't seem to be worried. The fact is that, at that age, the eyelashes are so soft that they are very unlikely to do any harm even if they lie on the cornea. Eye specialists never operate on puppy-fat entropion as the condition can be relied on to clear up on its own.

Eyelids out-turned

This condition mostly affects older people and usually results from laxity of the lid margin and weakness of the flat muscle surrounding the eye. It may also be caused by scarring and contracture of the skin on the outside of the lid. The condition is called *ectropion*. Ectropion of the lower lid causes severe watering because the tear duct opening (in the inner corner of the lid) no longer rests in the tear film. See your doctor. Ectropion is easily treated in the early stages by a simple operation. But, if it is left too long, contraction of the lid occurs and the treatment becomes much more difficult.

Eyelids reddened

This is called *blepharitis* and the redness is due to inflammation. The main features of blepharitis are redness of the lid margins, a collection of greasy scales around the roots of the lashes and considerable itchy discomfort. Sometimes the whites of the eyes are also inflamed and reddened. In severe cases the lid margins may even become ulcerated and lashes may change to grow in a different direction or there may be local loss of lashes. Blepharitis is often associated with dandruff (which should be kept under control by means of a selenium shampoo) or eczema and is a very persistent condition with a

strong tendency to recur after treatment.

You should try to prevent too much accumulation of scales by cleaning with cotton buds dipped in water or a mild detergent prescribed by your doctor. Severe blepharitis needs to be looked at by a dermatologist or an eye specialist.

Eyelids squeezed tight uncontrollably

This unpleasant condition is called *blepharospasm*. It is a kind of tic in which one or both eyes are tightly closed by an involuntary and prolonged contraction of the flat muscles just under the skin surrounding the eyes. This occurs for no immediately obvious reason, either occasionally or so frequently as to be severely disabling. It may be brought on by anxiety or as a hysterical reaction to various stimuli such as bright lights. Tics of this kind are difficult to treat as they are essentially symptoms of an underlying neurotic problem. Some cases of blepharospasm are not of psychological origin but are caused by a disorder of the nerve supply to the muscle around the eye. Such disabling blepharospasm can be treated by injecting a powerful paralysing poison called *botulinum toxin* derived from bacteria.

Blepharospasm is also commonly caused by a foreign body in the eye, a corneal abrasion or ulcer, or any other painful eye condition. In this case the remedy is to treat the cause – when this is done the blepharospasm will disappear.

Eyes crossed (squinting)

In a squint, medically known as *strabismus*, only one eye looks at the object of interest. The other eye may turn in, out, up or down. A squint most commonly starts in early childhood, usually when the brain mechanisms that keep the eyes aligned, so as to fuse the two images into one, have not yet developed fully. The most important cause of a squint, at this stage, is 'long-sight' (hypermetropia). This forces the child to focus strongly to see clearly and this makes the eyes turn inwards. Such a squint causes double vision and, to overcome this, the brain immediately rejects the signals from the deviating eye. From that moment on, visual development stops in the squinting eye, and the result, unless effective treatment is given, is a severe and permanent defect of vision in that eye, known as *amblyopia*. Amblyopia cannot be corrected after the age of eight, and the earlier it is treated the easier it is to correct.

Treatment involves the child wearing spectacles to stop him or her from making the excessive focusing effort, and covering up the good eye with a patch (occlusion) for varying periods, until vision is restored to its former level in the squinting eye. At this stage, the squint will often alternate from one eye to the other. This is an encouraging sign and a muscle balancing operation at this stage will often complete the cure.

Crossed eyes occurring for the first time later in life also require urgent attention. This may result from the breakdown of an earlier and well-treated childhood squint but many cases are due to organic disease (see **Vision doubled**) Never neglect this. ⚠

Eyes protruding

'Bugging-out' of an eyeball is called *exophthalmos*. As the eye comes forward it forces the eyelids apart and causes a staring appearance. Exophthalmos is caused by an increase in the bulk of the contents of the bony eye cavern (orbit) behind the eye. This occurs most commonly as a result of an immune system disorder associated with the thyroid gland. In this case, the protrusion is caused by enlargement of the small eye-moving muscles behind the globe as a result of the presence of antibodies (immunoglobulins) and an accumulation of white cells (lymphocytes) and fluid. *Dysthyroid exophthalmos* does not necessarily occur at the same time as the active thyroid

gland malfunction. The protrusion may occur months or years after a thyroid upset, or may, on occasion, even precede it.

Persistent and disfiguring exophthalmos may be treated by removing the bony floors of the eye sockets or by reinforcing the lids with mersilene mesh implants (mersilene is a tough plastic that the body tolerates well).

Although thyroid problems are by far the most common cause of exophthalmos, even if only one eye appears to be affected, protrusion of an eyeball may be caused by the presence of other material in the orbit, such as a cancer or a mucus-filled cyst (mucocele). It should always be regarded as a potentially grave sign and should never be ignored. ⚠ See also **Eyelid retraction**.

Eyes sunken

Backwards displacement of the eyeball into its bony socket is the opposite of exophthalmos and is called *enophthalmos*. When this happens, the lids tend to come together, producing an obvious narrowing of the aperture between them. Enophthalmos is common in old age as a result of the loss of the normal amount of fat within the eye socket.

Sudden enophthalmos occurs when the floor of the socket is fractured by direct violence and the fat is lost downwards into the sinus (maxillary antrum). This is called a *blowout fracture* and is usually caused by a direct blow to the front of the eye from a fast-moving ball or a fist, or it may occur if a person falls onto a blunt object. In blowout fracture, one or more of the small muscles that move the eye may become trapped so that the eye cannot move fully. This requires urgent specialist attention. ▲

Eyes wobbling

Persistent jerky or wobbling movement of the eyes, usually together, is called *nystagmus*. The movement is most commonly horizontal, but may be vertical, or even circular. The commonest type of nystagmus, 'sawtooth' nystagmus, involves a repetitive slow movement in one direction followed by a sudden recovery jerk in the other. This kind can be observed daily, as a normal phenomenon, in underground railway passengers trying to read the station name from a moving train. Permanent sawtooth nystagmus is almost always present from birth (congenital) and seldom implies anything serious. Although the eyes are normal, it is, however, usually associated with a slight reduction in visual acuity.

A searching type of nystagmus, as if the affected person is constantly looking for something, is a feature of very severe visual defect, such as might occur from dense congenital cataract or other serious eye defects present from birth. Nystagmus appearing for the first time later in life indicates a probably serious disorder of the nervous system and should prompt immediate medical attention. ▲

Eyesight problems

See entries under **Vision**.

F

Face puffy

Face swollen

Facial disfigurement

Facial pain

Facial pallor

Facial puffiness

Facial weakness or
paralysis

Failure of recognition

Failure to urinate

Fainting

Fatigue

Fatness

Fear

Fear of disease

Fear of dying

Fear of public places

Feeling full

Fever

Fever after exposure to heat

Fever and a fine, scarlet spotty rash

Fever and black urine

Fever and facial swelling in new babies

Fever and 'hamster face'

Fever and mottled rash

Fever and neck stiffness

Fever and progressive muscle weakness

Fever, vomiting and delirium

Finger clubbing

Fingers turning black

Fishy smell when washing

Fits

Floaters

Flushing

Food poisoning

Forgetfulness

Fright

Face puffy

See **Facial puffiness**.

Face swollen

See **Fever with 'hamster face'** and **Tooth abscess**.

Facial disfigurement

See **Deformities of the face**.

Facial pain

See **Pain in the face**.

Facial pallor

A pale face is often thought to be an important sign of illness but, apart from cases of severe anaemia or surgical shock – both of which have obvious additional features – this is seldom the case. Many perfectly healthy people have naturally pale faces and this is usually due to a slightly thicker skin than average and minor changes in the blood vessels. If you remember that pinkness of the skin is simply a matter of how readily well-oxygenated blood in the small arteries can be seen through it, you will understand how these changes in the appearance occur.

Sudden changes are common and these are due to sudden alterations in the degree to which the small blood vessels are open. A severe fright, for instance, may cause your face to become deathly pale simply because the blood vessels temporarily close down tightly under the influence of adrenaline.

Facial puffiness

There are several possible causes for this. One of the most striking, but fortunately one of the least common, is thyroid gland underactivity. *Myxoedema*, as it is called, affects women five times as often as men. The skin is dry, scaly, cold, thickened, coarse and puffy. The hair is scanty, coarse and brittle. Often the eyebrows are greatly thinned or even partly absent. The lips are thickened, mauve and there is bad breath. The affected person does not complain, but is lethargic, readily fatigued, and slowed in body and mind. She also suffers muscle aches, loss of menstruation, deafness, angina pectoris, heart failure, anaemia and constipation. All these effects can be reversed by the administration of thyroid hormones.

Facial puffiness from fluid in the tissues (oedema) is a common feature of the kidney inflammation condition known as *glomerulonephritis*. This is an immunological disorder in which the kidney is no longer able to retain the important soluble proteins in the blood. These proteins have many functions, one of which is to draw water from the tissues into the blood. So nephritis is liable to cause an accumulation of water in the tissues. This oedema is so generalized that it even affects the face. The loose skin around the eyes may be especially puffy.

Glomerulonephritis commonly affects children causing, in addition to generalized swelling of the body tissues, fever, loss of appetite, vomiting and headache. The blood pressure is usually raised and examination of the urine shows that this is scanty and contains blood and protein – both highly abnormal constituents. In severe cases the urine may stop altogether, for a time. After two or three days the signs and symptoms lessen, the output of urine increases and apparently full recovery occurs. There may, however, be abnormalities in the urine for weeks or months afterwards and, in some cases, the episode of glomerulonephritis is later seen to have been an episode in a prolonged course of progressive disease which may end in complete kidney failure.

There are several varieties of glomerulonephritis, some with a more serious outlook than others, and these are best distinguished by removing a small sample of kidney tissue (renal biopsy) for microscopic examination.

Facial puffiness may also be caused by burns and general oedema (when other parts of the body are swollen). Major facial trauma – such as going through a windscreen or suffering a vicious assault – always produces severe swelling (oedema).

Facial weakness or paralysis

Bell's palsy is a common and distressing complaint, first described in the early 19th century by the Scottish surgeon and anatomist Sir Charles Bell (1774–1842).

Bell's description holds good to this day. Within a matter of hours of onset, some or all of the muscles on one side of the face become paralysed so that the corner of the mouth droops, the lower eyelid falls away, and the affected side of the face becomes flattened and expressionless. Sometimes the paralysis is preceded by a pain in the bone behind the ear on the affected side. The facial muscles, on which all facial expression depends, are forced to contract by electrical impulses passing along the two facial nerves, one on each side, which come directly from the brain, emerging from the skull by way of narrow channels through the temporal bone. Although not proved, it is believed that inflammation of one of the nerves, from virus infection or other agency, causes it to swell and become compressed within this channel so that it is no longer able to conduct nerve impulses to the muscles.

The result of the above is a one-sided paralysis. This may

be total or partial, depending on the severity. In partial paralysis, recovery always occurs, although this may take weeks or months. At least one fifth of those with total paralysis recover fully, but the outcome is always uncertain. Sometimes, in these severe cases, the regenerating nerve fibres in the facial nerve trunk become redirected to the wrong muscles with surprising results, such as a wink when you really mean to smile.

Permanent facial paralysis is a grave disfigurement and affliction. However, much can be done by plastic surgery to improve the lopsided appearance and to prevent secondary effects, such as eye watering. If there has been no recovery in six months, surgery should be considered. Delay leads to the skin and muscle contracting.

Failure of recognition

Known medically as *agnosia*, this is the inability to recognize things for what they are, or to remember what they are

used for. Agnosia is the result of brain damage usually from stroke, brain tumour or head injury. It usually affects only one form of sensation – either vision, hearing or touch. People with visual agnosia have normal vision but cannot identify what they see, although they may be able to describe them in detail. Those with tactile agnosia can recognize something seen but may not be able to identify something that is felt with the hands without looking at it. People with auditory agnosia may have normal hearing but cannot recognize sounds. There is often partial or complete recovery from agnosia caused by a stroke.

Failure to urinate

See **Stoppage of urine output**.

Fainting

Fainting is a temporary loss of consciousness. It happens when there is a drop in the blood pressure so that the brain doesn't get enough oxygen and glucose fuel. Blood pressure may drop because the heart isn't pumping blood fast enough or because many of the arteries of the body have temporarily widened. Common faints usually occur after a person has been standing for a long time, especially in hot conditions, or when a severe fright or shock causes the heart to beat abnormally slowly. Fainting is also more likely when the volume of the blood is reduced as may occur if there has been fluid loss from persistent diarrhoea or excessive sweating. People who faint on taking exercise may have heart disease.

A fainting person falls and lies flat and this is exactly what is required to restore the flow of blood to the brain. Raising the legs is a great help. On no account force a fainting person to sit up or stand. Convulsions or even brain damage can result if a fainting person is foolishly kept upright.

It is quite normal and common to feel faint during pregnancy, so this is no major cause for alarm.

Fatigue

See **Tiredness and weakness**.

Fatness

See **Obesity**.

Fear

See **Unreasonable fears**.

Fear of disease

Everyone fears serious disease, but it is abnormal to have the reaction known as *hypochondriasis*. This is a defect of the personality leading to a constant, but unjustified, conviction of illness and unjustified fear of impending death. The hypochondriac is convinced that he or she is suffering from one or other of any number of serious organic disorders, and there is a tendency, as time passes, for the nature of the disorder to change. The derivation of the term is rather complicated and comes from the Greek for 'under' (hypo) and 'cartilage' (chondros). The hypochondrium is the area of the front of the abdomen under the lower rib cartilages on each side. The Greeks believed that the spleen, which lies in this area on the left, was the seat of melancholy and pessimism – hence hypochondriasis.

Professor William Cullen of Edinburgh published a classic description of hypochondriasis in 1816: 'In certain persons there is a state of mind distinguished by a concurrence of the following circumstances: a languor, listlessness or want of resolution and activity with respect to all undertakings; a disposition to seriousness, sadness and timidity; as to all future events, an apprehension of the worst or most unhappy state of them; and therefore, often upon slight grounds, an apprehension of great evil. Such persons are particularly attentive to the state of their own health, to every smallest change of feeling in their bodies; and from any unusual feeling, perhaps of the slightest kind, they apprehend great danger and even death itself. In respect to all these feelings and apprehensions, there is commonly the most obstinate belief and persuasion.' In spite of the language, this account can hardly be bettered.

There is a salutary reminder to doctors, too ready to ascribe symptoms to hypochondriasis, in the history of the French playwright and comic actor Jean Baptiste Molière (1622–73). While acting in his own play *Le Malade Imaginaire* (*The Hypochondriac*), Molière, who was, himself, a noted hypochondriac, suffered chest pains, was hurried off the stage and died two hours later from a heart attack.

The cardiac neurosis is a common form of hypochondriasis. This may take two forms. The first is an excessively high level of anxiety suffered by someone who has had a heart attack and has recovered. The anxiety is apt to manifest itself by a frequently recurrent acute fear of dying. Symptoms such as chest pain and tightness, breathlessness and palpitations are experienced, although these are not due to recurrence of the disease, and the affected person finds great difficulty in returning to a normal life. The second is an unjustified conviction that one is suffering from heart disease. This is notoriously persistent and difficult to treat. Often, there is a family background of heart trouble and a belief that heart disease is hereditary – which it is not. The conviction is usually fortified by various symptoms, especially harmless palpitation, and chest pain, usually arising from heartburn.

Strong medical reassurance, even after comprehensive examination and investigation, seldom succeeds in dispelling the belief and the unfortunate mental sufferer goes from doctor to doctor almost as if hoping for confirmation of the fears. There is little to be done to help people with this unfortunate problem. Logical arguments, and demonstration that they are capable of physical exertion impossible for people with heart disease, do not impress. In most cases, the cardiac neurotic lives a long and medically uneventful life. In some cases, as in Molière's, he does not.

Herein lies the doctor's dilemma. In the great majority of cases the complaints are entirely imaginary and to carry out repeated examinations and tests is not only a waste of medical time and resources, but will also strengthen the patient's fears and make the hypochondriasis worse. The wise doctor will spend a good deal of time in careful history-taking before deciding that the patient is a hypochondriac, and will then offer a full scheme of examination and tests, with the explicit understanding that, if these are negative, that will be the end of investigation of the current complaint.

Unfortunately, the true nature of hypochondriasis remains obscure, so no logical approach to treatment is possible. It has been thought to be a form of pathological depression, but it doesn't respond to anti-depressive treatment. The patient has full insight and cannot, by definition, be considered psychotic. The nearest reasonable classification is to view it as an inherent personality defect characterized by a low threshold to fear, to sensation and to the awareness of the normal functions of the body. The hypochondriac is, essentially, a person who is constantly looking inwards instead of out.

Fear of dying

See **Fear of disease**, **Pain in the chest** (heart attack).

Fear of public places

This panic syndrome is known as *agoraphobia*. It is an abnormal fear of entering public places where other people are present. Agoraphobia causes panic attacks and sufferers spend most, if not all, of their time at home. There are effective treatments for agoraphobia and panic. Behaviour therapy is often the best approach. See also **Anxiety**.

Feeling full

See IBS under **Diarrhoea**.

Fever

This describes a rise of body temperature above the normal range of 37°–37.5° Celsius (98.6°–99.6° Fahrenheit), taken in the mouth. Rectal temperatures are a little higher.

In childhood, fever is nearly always caused by infections such as tonsillitis, otitis media, measles, mumps and chickenpox. Infecting organisms grow best at normal body temperature and are discouraged by fever. So it is not always a good idea to bring down the temperature. But high temperatures in children commonly cause fever fits (febrile convulsions) and should always be brought down. Tepid sponging all over the body is best. Temperatures above about 44.5°C (112°F) usually cause fatal brain damage and, in such cases, urgent cooling, by any available means, is vital. ▲

Fever after exposure to heat

Heat stroke is what happens when the body's temperature regulating mechanism is unable to cope with excessive heat, or when, as a result of disease or other causes, it fails altogether. The temperature rises rapidly and the situation is highly dangerous. Initially, there may be warning indications in the form of faintness, dizziness, headache, dry skin, absence of sweating, thirst and nausea. Later there may be lethargy and confusion or agitation progressing to epileptic-like fits, coma and death. This is a medical emergency. The rising temperature causes brain damage which worsens the longer the high temperature continues. ⚠

The treatment is to get the temperature down by any available means. The whole body should be immersed in cool water and ice packs and fans used to supplement the cooling. The temperature must be monitored continuously and not allowed to drop below 38°C (101°F) as excess cooling may convert hyperthermia to hypothermia.

Fever and a fine, scarlet spotty rash

Scarlet fever is caused by a streptococcus which infects the throat and is passed on by coughs and sneezes or contaminated hands or food. Two to four days after contact there is fever. The tongue is at first white coated and it then develops a 'strawberry' look. The rash quickly spreads all over the body. It consists of thousands of tiny scarlet spots which blanch briefly when pressed. The area round the mouth remains pale (circumoral pallor). After about a week the rash fades and the skin peels. The complications can be more serious. They include:

- middle ear infection (otitis media);
- sinusitis;
- inflammation behind the ears (mastoiditis);
- pneumonia;
- rheumatic fever;

- inflammation in the kidneys (glomerulonephritis).

Fortunately, the streptococcus is very sensitive to penicillin and this is usually given for 10 days to prevent complications.

Fever and black urine

Blackwater fever is a dangerous complication of malaria caused by the most dangerous of the several malarial parasites – the *falciparum* type. Like other malarial blood parasites this one breaks down the red blood cells, releasing the contained haemoglobin. It is only in *falciparum* malaria that this can occur to such a degree that the haemoglobin appears in the urine, turning it a dark brown, almost black, colour. This is an indication of a heavy and dangerous infection calling for urgent treatment, but the affected person will already be so obviously ill, with fever, shivering, vomiting and even loss of consciousness, that medical attention is likely already to be at hand. Blackwater fever occurs only in the tropics. ⚠

Fever and facial swelling in new babies

Mumps is rare in babies under one year so this combination of signs raises the possibility of *listeriosis*. Although this is a rare disease, it is becoming commoner. Listeriosis is caused by an organism which can resist low temperatures and has been recovered from lamb kept at 0°C (32°F) for 24 days. The organism is present in most domestic and farm animals and many birds and fishes. It has been found in soft cheeses and various precooked foods. Over half the chickens in Britain carry the organism, either internally or externally, but proper cooking will kill it. It is common in sewage and in the stools of up to 30 per cent of healthy people.

Babies can be infected before birth but this is rare – only about one baby in 18,000 is affected. Those who are, however, may suffer widespread damage to most of the systems of the body, and about a quarter of the babies severely infected in this way are born dead.

Human listeriosis is commonest in babies and old people, affecting the throat, the eyes, the skin and the nervous system. The great majority of cases are mild and pass unnoticed. Some have an upset similar to glandular fever. There is fever, conjunctivitis, mumps-like swelling of the salivary glands, and sometimes pustules on the skin. Listeriosis responds well to antibiotics, which greatly reduces infant mortality from listeriosis. The outlook for the disease in adults is good.

Fever and 'hamster face'

In children over one year of age, this is almost certainly mumps. Mumps is a virus infection, most commonly affecting children. There is fever and the salivary glands in front of the ears (the parotid glands) swell up until the affected person looks a bit like a hamster. One attack of mumps confers permanent immunity.

The disease is spread by aerosol droplet transfer during coughing and sneezing and the first symptoms appear about three weeks after infection. The fever only lasts for two or three days and the illness is often very mild, frequently amounting to no more than a slight discomfort in front of the ears and on chewing. In more severe cases there may be headache. The swelling of the parotid glands settles in about 10 days. Occasionally a mild form of meningitis may occur, but this is seldom serious.

The complication that most commonly causes concern is inflammation of the testicle. This is no fun and is called *orchitis* (see **Pain in the testicle**).

Fever and mottled rash

Measles is a highly infectious, often epidemic, childhood disease, caused by a virus usually acquired by inhaling infected droplet material. Every two or three years a sufficient number of susceptible children accumulate and an epidemic occurs. About 14 days after infection, and shortly before the rash appears, tiny 'salt-grain' spots (Koplik's spots) may be seen inside the cheeks. There is fever, cough, sneezing, general misery, conjunctivitis, and an irregular, red, mottled, slightly raised rash which lasts for about a week and then fades.

Complications include otitis media, bronchitis and pneumonia, all of which will usually respond to antibiotic treatment. Much less commonly, there may be encephalitis. Measles cannot cause squint but may precipitate it in children with severe 'long sight'.

Most people have measles during childhood and a second attack is rare. The disease can be prevented by a vaccine which should be given to all children, aged one to two years, for whom there is no valid medical objection.

German measles or *rubella* is caused by a virus which infects the respiratory tract and, during a long incubation period of up to three weeks, multiplies and spreads to local lymph nodes, especially those in the back of the neck. There is a mild illness, swollen nodes and a scattered rash of slightly raised red patches where the virus has settled in the skin. The disease is so mild that it often passes unnoticed. In adults, the virus sometimes attacks the joints causing an arthritis which may occasionally become persistent (chronic). The natural infection produces lifelong immunity.

The chief importance of rubella is that, in pregnant women, viruses circulating in the blood can localize in the placenta and infect the fetus. Until this fact was known, rubella was a major cause of congenital heart disease and other malformations, blindness, deafness and mental retardation. The fetus is especially susceptible to the toxic effects of the virus during the first three months of pregnancy and if the virus is circulating at the time that the brain, the eyes, the ears and the heart are undergoing their early development, serious effects are likely.

In the combined results of five separate studies, the incidence of congenital defects, when rubella occurred during the first month of pregnancy, was 50 per cent; during the second month, 25 per cent; during the third, 17 per cent; during the fourth, six per cent; and after the fourth month, less than two per cent.

Immunization against rubella could eliminate this disease. All young girls and women of childbearing age who are found to be free of antibodies (seronegative) should be vaccinated, but vaccination should never be done during pregnancy as it is thought possible that the vaccine can affect the fetus. If there is a risk of pregnancy, effective contraception should be used for three months after vaccination.

Fever and neck stiffness

This combination of signs, especially in an obviously ill child, should immediately raise the suspicion of menin-

gitis – inflammation of the membranes covering the brain and spinal cord (the meninges). The commonest cause of meningitis today is infection with viruses such as the herpes simplex virus, the chicken pox virus, the polio virus, echo viruses, coxsackie viruses and mumps virus.

Viral meningitis is often a minor disorder but may be acute, with headache, fever and drowsiness which may progress rapidly to deep coma. In severe cases there may be weakness of the muscles, paralysis, speech disturbances, double vision or partial loss of the field of vision, and epileptic fits. Most children make a complete recovery, but some may have residual effects. There is no specific treatment for most virus infections, but in the case of herpes meningitis, the drug acyclovir can be valuable.

Meningococcal meningitis is an epidemic form which may occur in institutions and overcrowded dwellings such as orphanages or boarding schools. There is a sore throat, a rising temperature, severe headache, marked stiffness of the neck and vomiting. A rash of red spots appears on the trunk and because of this typical rash, the condition is sometimes called 'spotted fever'. The affected child may become gravely ill within a day of onset and may pass quickly into a state of confusion, drowsiness and coma. Babies and infants show fever, vomiting, convulsions and have a characteristic high-pitched cry. In babies, the soft areas on the head between the skull bones (the fontanelles) often bulge outwards and feel much tenser than normal. Without treatment, death may occur within days or even hours. So treatment is urgent and should never be delayed. Fortunately, bacterial meningitis nearly always responds well to antibiotics and full recovery is usual. ⚠

Fever and progressive muscle weakness

Poliomyelitis is an infectious disease caused by viruses which inhabit the intestine and are passed in the stools in large numbers for up to six weeks after the start of the illness. At one time, poliomyelitis was by far the commonest cause of paralysis in young people and, for this reason, was known as 'infantile paralysis'. Polio was also once a common cause of death, but the widespread use of oral vaccine has greatly reduced this outcome. Just as the dangerous viruses were once spread by direct faecal contamination of food by fingers and by coughing, so the modified but live viruses in the oral vaccine are also spread. In this way, many more people acquire protection than those who have the oral vaccine.

Even in unprotected people, most cases of polio are mild, causing a brief, unidentified illness with headache, fever and sometimes vomiting. But in some cases, this stage is followed by a more major illness, with severe headache, neck stiffness, high fever and progressive muscle weakness and paralysis. This reaches a peak at the end of the first week of the severe symptoms and, thereafter, recovery is gradual.

Muscles which show no sign of movement by the end of a month are permanently paralysed. If the upper part of the spinal cord or the brain stem are involved, death may occur from paralysis of respiration during the acute stage, unless some form of artificial respiration is used. Using an 'iron lung' was once the only way of saving the lives of those in this situation, but it has now been replaced by better methods.

Oral polio vaccine is completely successful in preventing this catastrophic disease and should be given to everyone.

Fever, vomiting and delirium

Reye's syndrome is a childhood disease in which brain swelling and severe liver inflammation (hepatitis) occur following infection with one of several viruses including chickenpox, influenza, rubella, herpes simplex and echovirus. Brain swelling causes uncontrollable vomiting, delirium, disorientation, fits, and rapid onset of stupor and coma. ⚠ The liver disorder is also severe and there is reason to believe that the effect on the brain may be secondary to the liver damage. In fatal cases, the average time between admission to hospital and death is four days.

Treatment is aimed at controlling brain swelling by steroids and drugs to withdraw fluid. Artificial ventilation may be needed. With increasing understanding of the condition and its management, the death rate from Reye's syndrome has dropped from about 50 per cent to about 10 per cent. Some children, unfortunately, suffer permanent brain damage.

It is generally accepted that Reye's syndrome is connected with taking aspirin and the evidence for this is so strong that the medical authorities in Britain and the United States have advised that children suspected of having chickenpox or influenza should not be given aspirin. Some have gone further and have recommended that aspirin should *never* be given to children. The British pharmaceutical industry appears to have accepted this advice, and paracetamol has replaced aspirin in paediatric painkillers.

Finger clubbing

This surprising condition features enlargement of the soft tissues of the end segment of the fingers or toes, with loss of the angle at the root of the nail. Finger clubbing occurs in:

- heart disease that causes lack of oxygen in the blood and consequent blueness (cyanosis) of the skin;
- infection of the heart inner lining (endocarditis);
- cancer of the lung;
- widening of the lung air tubes (bronchiectasis);
- ulcerative colitis.

It also occurs in several other conditions. Finger clubbing is more of a medical curiosity than a valuable diagnostic aid, but the development of clubbing usually indicates that something serious is happening. You are not going to develop finger clubbing if you seem perfectly well, but if it does happen you should certainly see your doctor.

Fingers turning black

See **Blackening and loss of the extremities**.

Fishy smell when washing

Gardnerella vaginalis is a germ commonly found in the genitalia of both sexes. In women, it infects the vagina, producing a thin, greyish-white vaginal discharge with small bubbles in it. The most striking – and perhaps the only significant – characteristic of this germ is an obvious fishy-smelling odour produced when it comes into contact with a mild alkali, such as that found in toilet soap. Indeed, this effect is so specific to this organism that it is used as a laboratory test for it. There are no other symptoms, but both the organism and the odour can be sexually transmitted to a partner. The infection tends to be stubborn, but responds well to treatment with the drug metronidazole (Flagyl).

Fits

See **Convulsions**.

Floaters

See **Vision affected by floating specks**.

Flushing

See **Blushing** and **Hot flushes**.

Food poisoning

See **Pain in the abdomen**.

Forgetfulness

See **Loss of memory**.

Fright

See **Unreasonable fears**.

G

Gasping for breath	Greasy stools
Genital blisters	Growth problems
Goose pimples	

G

Gasping for breath

See **Breathing difficulty**.

Genital blisters

See **Skin blisters around mouth or nose**.

Goose pimples

These occur simply because the skin around hair-follicle openings retracts slightly when the tiny muscles that cause the hairs to stand up tighten. These muscles, the arrector pili muscles, tighten under the influence of adrenaline or the sympathetic nervous system. The same thing happens in very cold conditions or when people try to kick the heroin habit. With the latter, however, the goose pimples are associated with sweating. This is known in the trade as 'cold turkey'.

Greasy stools

After certain kinds of surgery on the intestines it sometimes happens that a loop of bowel is not cleared constantly in the normal way. The contents stagnate and bacteria are able to multiply to an abnormal extent. These interfere with the function of the rest of the intestine causing failure of normal fat and vitamin absorption. The result is that the stools are very greasy, bulky and pale and difficult to flush away. Because of the failure to absorb fat and other nutrients, there is loss of weight and debility. Often the condition can be treated effectively with antibiotics but it is sometimes necessary to remove the blind loop surgically.

Greasy stools are also a feature of conditions in which bile from the liver is not getting to the intestine, or various other conditions in which dietary fats are not properly absorbed. Fats must be broken down by the enzyme lipase before they can be absorbed – this enzyme comes from the pancreas. Lack of lipase will also result in greasy stools. See also **Pale stools**.

Growth problems

Body growth is influenced by many factors. Heredity is one of the most important: tall parents tend to have tall children, for instance. Certain genetic disorders, such as achondroplasia, feature very short stature. Hormones, especially the growth hormone from the pituitary gland, can have a major effect. Deficiency of growth hormone in childhood causes dwarfism and this can be treated by giving the hormone. Too much of the hormone causes gigantism. Deficiency of thyroid hormones in childhood and sex hormones at puberty also lead to impaired growth.

Nutrition and general health early in life are also important. Severe, long-term illnesses can limit growth, as can the use of steroid drugs in childhood. General social and parental deprivation often leads to short stature.

H

Hair loss

Hallucinations

Hands, feet and jaw enlargement

Hangover

Hare lip

Headache

Head permanently on one side

Hearing problems

Hearing voices and seeing things

Heart attack

Heartburn

Heat stroke

Herpes

Hiccups

Hot flushes

Hyperventilation

H

Hair loss

See **Baldness**.

Hallucinations

See **Hearing voices and seeing things**.

Hands, feet and jaw enlargement

During adult life, abnormal enlargement of the hands and feet can only be due to acromegaly. This is a rare disease caused by excessive production of growth hormone by the pituitary gland after the growing ends of the long bones have fused. The hormone acts only on the skull, the jawbone and the hands and feet, which be- come abnormally enlarged. The excess growth hormone comes from a tumour in the pituitary gland. In addition to the enlargement of the extremities, the face becomes elongated and the features become coarsened. Victims notice that they need increasing shoe sizes and that their voice becomes deeper. There may be headache and loss of vision to the sides.

Any suspicion of acromegaly should be reported at once. There are effective treatments.

Hangover

This is the state of physical and mental distress you experience on waking after an evening of overindulgence in alcohol. Ethyl alcohol (ethanol) is toxic to the brain, probably because it interferes with what are called GABA neurotransmitter receptors, altering the passage of nerve impulses from cell to cell in a manner which degrades the higher functions of the brain. Drinkers acquire a degree of tolerance to the effect on the GABA receptors so that when it is withdrawn the brain 'protests'. The immediate cure for these withdrawal symptoms is a 'hair of the dog'. Alcohol also irritates the stomach lining and often causes an erosive gastritis.

The alcohol and aldehyde congeners – the secondary products of alcoholic fermentation which give character to alcoholic drinks – are believed by many to be even more toxic than pure alcohol. Congeners are present in highest concentration in drinks such as port and brandy and are lowest in purer spirits such as gin and vodka. It is thought to be the congeners, primarily, which give rise to the depression, nausea, headache, remorse,

shakiness, 'toothbrush heaves' and vertigo which characterize the unhappy state of the too-indulgent reveller, after the anaesthetic effects of the ethanol have passed.

Alcohol is a diuretic – that is, it causes the kidneys to pass out more fluid than the volume drunk. This is the basis of, and often the justification for, the beer-drinker's 'thirst', but it is also one of the factors contributing to the discomfort of the hangover. Alcohol promotes diuresis by causing the pituitary gland to produce less of the antidiuretic hormone, vasopressin.

The headache in hangover is due to widening and stretching of blood vessels in the scalp and around the brain and is of the same sort as occurs in migraine. Alcohol is a potent dilator of vessels – hence the flushed face of the drinker, but it also has analgesic effects and generally reduces sensitivity. Dilatation persisting after much of the alcohol has left the body is thought also to be due to breakdown products such as acetalde-hyde or to other factors such as smoking, excessive eating, undue excitement and loss of sleep.

Recovery from hangover is normally merely a matter of time, but in true alcoholics, the hangover may include withdrawal symptoms and be more severe and persis-tent. Many suggestions have been made on how to avoid a hangover (drinking plenty of water before retiring helps some people), but only those measures which reduce the total intake and rate of ab-sorption of alcohol are likely to be of any value.

Hare lip

The appearance caused by a badly repaired cleft lip. With advances in understanding of the principles of plastic sur-gery and a recognition that these principles, and the ap-propriate skills, should al-ways be available when congenital cleft lip is to be repaired, the condition has become quite rare. See **Defor-mities of the face**.

Headache

See **Pain in the head**.

Head permanently on one side

Medically known as *torticollis* or *wry neck*, this condition features persistent or perma-nent twisting of the neck and an abnormal head position. Common causes of torticollis include:

- damage at birth to one of the main longitudinal neck muscles so that it is shortened and the head tilted to one side;
- whiplash injury to the neck with painful muscle spasm;
- lack of balance in the eye muscles so that a tilt is needed to avoid double vision;
- severe scarring and shortening of the skin of the neck.

The treatment of torticollis depends on the cause. Conge-nital muscle shortening from injury should be corrected by early stretching and perhaps surgery otherwise the skull and face will probably be permanently asymmetrical. Skin contractures call for plastic procedures and eye balance problems for surgery on the eye-moving muscles. Muscle spasm from injury will usually settle with rest and time.

Hearing problems

There are two principal kinds of deafness, conductive deafness and nerve deafness (sensori-neural), and the distinction is important. Conductive deafness results from any defect of the mechanical part of the hearing system. This part is situated outside the inner ear. Nerve deafness results from defect of the innermost part of the ear in which the sound vibrations are converted into nerve impulses which are then carried to the brain.

Conductive deafness may occur from:

- wax blocking the external auditory tube, through which air vibrations pass to the eardrum;
- damage, such as

perforation, to the drum itself;
- gumming up of the auditory ossicles (see below);
- a condition known as otosclerosis.

Otosclerosis is a hereditary ear disease leading to progressive deafness of the 'mechanical' or conductive type. The vibration of the eardrum, under the influence of sound waves, is conveyed to the inner ear by a chain of three small bones, known as the *auditory ossicles*. The innermost of these, the stapes, is shaped like a stirrup and the 'footplate' of this bone fits into an oval window, in the outer wall of the inner ear, in such a way that it is free to vibrate in the window. In otosclerosis, the fibrous seal surrounding the footplate becomes replaced by bone so that the stapes becomes progressively immobilized. People with otosclerosis can hear best in noisy surroundings, but eventually become severely deafened.

The condition can be treated only by microsurgery. In

one procedure, the loop of the stapes is detached and a small hole is drilled in the footplate to take an artificial metal or plastic piston. This is then linked to the middle ossicle so that when the eardrum vibrates, the piston moves in its hole. The results of this delicate operation can be excellent.

Nerve deafness is due to damage or destruction of the delicate inner ear mechanisms in the cochlea. This contains thousands of sensitive hair cells which are stimulated by vibration to produce nerve impulses which inform the brain of the pitch and loudness of the sounds. Such damage results from:

- prolonged exposure to loud noise;
- sudden shattering sounds, as from explosions;
- a slap on the ear, which can literally shake the hair cell apparatus to pieces;
- certain toxic chemicals and drugs;
- the effects of ageing.

The main drugs that damage hearing are:

- the aminoglycoside antibiotics (streptomycin, gentamicin, neomycin, etc);
- some diuretic drugs (frusemide and ethacrynic acid);
- salicylates, including aspirin;
- quinine.

All the above drugs have to be taken in larger than usual dosage to cause ear damage. They may, however, have this effect if the kidneys are unable to excrete them normally, as may occur in certain kidney diseases.

Nerve deafness is commonly associated with singing in the ears (tinnitus) and it is seldom possible to cure this. It is thus important for people to avoid those things that cause it, especially loud noise, so as to minimize the long-term damage. Don't be embarrassed about putting your fingers in your ears in conditions of loud noise. Keep away from pop concerts, where the noise level is commonly dangerously high.

A rare but important cause of nerve deafness is acoustic neuroma. This is a tumour of the nerve that connects the ears with the brain. It is not a cancer, but because the nerve passes through a confined area close to many important structures, the enlarging tumour can do a lot of damage. It causes pain in the ear, deafness, noises in the ear (tinnitus) and loss of balance. Later, the expanding tumour can cause pain in the face and paralysis of an eye-moving muscle leading to double vision. Any such symptoms should be reported without delay and require the attention of an Ear, Nose and Throat (ENT) specialist. ⚠ Treatment is by surgery.

Conductive deafness is much more easily treated than nerve deafness. Ear wax can be removed, drum perforations can be repaired, middle ear infections can be controlled and the bones sometimes freed, and otosclerosis can be treated by surgery. The only thing to do about inner ear deafness is to have a cochlear implant fitted. At best, this is a poor substitute for normal hearing.

Hearing voices and seeing things

Hallucinations are sense perceptions not caused by an external stimulus. It is thus a hallucination to hear voices which do not come from any present source of sound or to see something that is not there. Hallucinations should be distinguished from delusions, which are mistaken ideas.

Hallucinations are very common, both in health and disease, and are a feature of many psychiatric disorders. They may be:

- visual;
- auditory – sometimes musical;
- tactile;
- of taste or smell (gustatory or olfactory);
- of the size of things (Lilliputian).

Hallucinations commonly occur in normal people as they

125

are falling asleep (hypnagogic hallucinations), or while waking (hypnopompic hallucinations). They occur in alcoholic delirium (delirium tremens), from cocaine abuse and from the use of hallucinogenic drugs. They are a common feature of schizophrenia, temporal lobe epilepsy, depression and organic brain disease.

Heart attack

See **Pain in the chest**.

Heartburn

This is the symptom caused by what doctors call acid reflux – the upward passage of some of the strongly acid and irritating contents of the stomach into the lower end of the gullet. The gullet lining is not protected like stomach lining and the acid causes it to become inflamed. This is the cause of heartburn. Acid reflux is common during pregnancy and in overweight people. It is also a feature of the condition hiatus hernia, in which part of the upper stomach passes up, through the gullet opening in the diaphragm, into the chest.

Occasional heartburn is likely to be due to greedy over eating, but if it occurs frequently you should see your doctor.

Heat stroke

See **Fever after exposure to heat**.

Herpes

See **Skin blisters around mouth or nose**.

Hiccups

Hiccups are a succession of involuntary spasms of the diaphragm, each followed by the vocal cords suddenly closing, which checks the inrush of air and causes the characteristic sound. Hiccups can be caused by irritation of the nerves to the diaphragm (phrenic nerves) or by abnormal stimulation of the input nerves which supply the respiratory centres in the brain. In most cases the cause is unknown and harmless. However, hiccups are a feature of many serious conditions, including:

- pleurisy;
- pneumonia;
- uraemia;
- disorders of almost any of the abdominal organs.

Sometimes hiccups are so persistent that they are seriously exhausting.

The tendency to hiccup is reduced if the level of carbon dioxide in the blood is raised. This is most easily achieved by holding the breath for as long as possible or by re-breathing air in a small plastic bag. Other tricks include drinking water out of the 'wrong' side of a glass, pulling on the tongue or pressing – not too firmly – on the eyeballs. Various sedative drugs are helpful, but if all else fails, the phrenic nerve can be temporarily prevented from transmitting impulses by injecting a small dose of local anaesthetic around it.

Hot flushes

Most women pass easily, and relatively unaffected, through the menopause, relieved of the risk of pregnancy and anxious to get on with their lives. Perhaps a quarter suffer in some way, mainly from hot flushes affecting the face and neck. These vary greatly in frequency and duration. For some women they are very brief and infrequent; others may have many episodes in a day that last for as long as 15 minutes. Flushes do not indicate a rise in blood pressure, but merely a rise in the blood flow through the affected parts as a result of the blood vessels temporarily widening. The cause of the autonomic nervous system instability that underlies flushes remains uncertain, but many doctors are convinced that they have something to do with oestrogen deficiency.

Other menopausal symptoms include night sweats, insomnia, headaches and general irritability. Like hot flushes, these can be attributed to a general instability of the nerve or hormonal control of the small blood vessels. Often they are severe

127

enough, in themselves, to justify treatment. It is by no means certain and has never been proved that these symptoms are due to oestrogen deficiency. But the placebo effect of oestrogen treatment is so strong that most people believe it is responsible for the resulting improvement.

Hyperventilation

See **Breathing exaggerated**.

I

Inability to make sense of words

Inability to perform purposeful movements

Inability to sit still

Inability to speak

Inability to speak

Inability to write

Insomnia

Irregular pulse

Itching

Itching after heavy sweating

Itching anus

Itching between toes

Itching elbows and knees

Itching genitals

Itching groin

Itching inflamed areas with white patches

Itching mole

Itching wrists

Itching scalp

I

Inability to make sense of words

This distressing condition is called *alexia* or sometimes 'word blindness' and, of course, makes it impossible to read. People with alexia are also usually unable to name colours, but can often identify numbers accurately. In some cases of alexia, the victim is able to write fluently and correctly but is then unable to read what has been written. Alexia is caused by localized brain damage and is usually an effect of a stroke. Alexia should not be confused with dyslexia (see **Word blindness**), which is normally present from birth and which causes much less severe reading difficulties.

Inability to perform purposeful movements

The medical term for this misfortune is *apraxia*. Although the muscles, their nerves and coordination are normal, purposeful voluntary movements cannot be made. Apraxia is due to damage in the small hind brain (the cerebellum) that carries out the computations necessary to perform purposeful movement. The affected person is perfectly aware of what he or she wants to do but is unable to do it. Apraxia is not a form of paralysis and the movements can often be performed unconsciously. The cerebellar damage is usually the result of stroke, head injury or brain tumour. A person with apraxia needs the attention of a neurologist. ⚠

Inability to sit still

Known medically as *akathisia*, this is usually a side-effect of antipsychotic drugs or a complication of Parkinson's disease.

Inability to speak

Loss of the ability to speak or write or to understand language, or of all of these abilities, is known as *aphasia*. This is due to brain damage, usually on the left side, and usually as a result of interference with the blood supply or from bleeding within or around the brain. It is a common feature of stroke and may also follow head injury. The areas of the brain affected are well known.

Aphasia takes various forms. Comprehension may be normal but the expression of ideas may be impossible. On the other hand, the expres-sion of thoughts may be normal but comprehension affected. The nerves and muscles which enable speech are not affected, but speech is slow and difficult with severe loss of fluency. Writing may or may not be affected. If comprehension is damaged, although speech may be fluent many words are poorly or wrongly selected and grammar and logic are defective. In nominal aphasia there is difficulty in naming objects. In global aphasia, all language functions are lost.

Aphasia often improves with time.

Inability to write

A person who cannot write in spite of normal hand and arm movement is said to be suffering from *agraphia*. This is caused by brain damage that interferes with the mental processes involved in writing. It is usually the result of loss of local blood supply causing a stroke, or head injury or brain tumour. There is usually also inability to read. As in agnosia and aphasia, gradual recovery of some or all of the function is common.

Insomnia

Difficulty in sleeping, or disturbances of the normal sleep pattern, are very common. Many people, however, are unaware of the wide individual variation in sleep requirements and that elderly people often have greatly reduced sleep needs. There is no reason to believe that shorter sleep periods are in any way harmful.

Difficulty in falling asleep is often caused by worry or tension, while early waking, with difficulty in going back to sleep again, tends to be a feature of depression or advancing age. A tendency to lie awake for what seems like hours, unable to relax or allow oneself to drift off to sleep, is often due to tension caused by business, personal, marital or other worries. These concerns are likely to seem insoluble, especially in the middle of the night, but the proper approach is to try to resolve them during waking hours and to make a firm

rule that they are not to be entertained during the night. Deliberately practised, formal relaxation exercises can also be very helpful. Avoiding a high caffeine intake in the evening, from tea or coffee, will also help.

People who fall asleep easily, but wake repeatedly, may be so exhausted that they go to bed too early, and then awake naturally in the early morning, having had enough sleep. Some people sedate themselves with alcohol every night. This gets them off to sleep quite well but, as the effect is often short-lived, they often wake early. Depression is a common cause of interrupted and restless sleep and often features early waking. Pain is another cause, as is the attempt to give up sleeping tablets to which tolerance has been acquired. When the insomnia is clearly due to any such cause, the right treatment is to deal with the cause. For instance, people who go to bed exhausted may need a short nap in the middle of the day – this can be invaluable.

Depression caused by external misfortune or bereavement will nearly always pass in time, but some depressions require skilled treatment. Pain should be fully investigated and the cause removed, if possible. If this cannot be done, the right approach is to relieve the pain with analgesic drugs, rather than to take sleeping pills.

Sleep-inducing drugs were once prescribed in great quantity, possibly because doctors did not have time to go into the reasons for the insomnia. It is now widely recognized that they are not the real solution for problems of this kind. In selected cases, there is justification for the use of hypnotic drugs, given in the hope that the patient may, thereby, get back into a pattern of normal sleeping. But taking sleeping pills over long periods is bad medicine. Addiction is likely and withdrawal problems inevitable. Tolerance soon develops and the dose will have to be increased steadily to achieve the same effect.

Irregular pulse

Irregularity of the heart rhythm is caused by a defect in the production of the electrical current in the heart that causes the muscular wall to contract. Alternatively, it may result from a defect in the conduction of this current through the heart. Both can be caused by a defective blood supply to the heart muscle from coronary artery disease or by various drugs, the commonest of which is caffeine in coffee.

The pulse may be too fast or too slow, or the regular sequence of beats may be interrupted by occasional extra beats that are followed by a short, but sometimes alarming, pause. In some cases the pulse may be completely irregular both in rhythm and force. Arrhythmias may cause palpitations, faintness, dizziness or angina.

You should never ignore irregularity of the heart action. The commonest cause – premature beats (extrasystoles) – is usually of little importance, but may sometimes indicate organic heart disease. Other causes are nearly always an indication that something is happening which should be looked into. ⚠

Itching

Itching is an awareness of a tickling irritation in the skin which prompts you, almost irresistibly, to rub or scratch. You will do this, although you may be well aware that the relief so obtained is only temporary. Itching is caused by the stimulation of certain nerve endings in the skin, but the reason for this is unclear. The substances responsible may include various enzymes called *endopeptidases*, which occur naturally in the skin and in the bloodstream, and which may be released by some local skin disturbance.

Severe itching is called *pruritus* and this often occurs in and around the anus or the female genitalia and is commonly associated with thrush (candidiasis). Other fungus infections, such as the various forms of tinea, also feature severe itching, and many

fungi contain endopeptidases.

Itching can usually be cured if the cause can be established and treated. Scratching often makes things worse and may even set up a vicious cycle which perpetuates the symptom. Using simple lotions, such as calamine and phenol, is better than scratching. The most important causes of itching are detailed in the following articles. Other less common causes include:

- 'cocaine bug';
- dog and cat fleas;
- Hodgkin's disease;
- hookworm ('ground itch');
- jaundice;
- kidney failure;
- lymphoma tumours;
- neurological disorders such as tabes dorsalis;
- skin bruising (purpura);
- thyroid disorders;
- unduly thick blood (polycythaemia).

Formication is not exactly itching but is a peculiar sensation, as if there are lots of ants crawling under the skin. Formication is characteristic of a number of drug toxic effects or of certain disorders of the nervous system. If you have this symptom you should certainly report it to your doctor.

Itching after heavy sweating

Repeated episodes of heavy sweating in conditions of high humidity and high temperature, as in the tropics, are liable to result in the itchy condition known popularly as 'prickly heat'. This condition, for which the medical term is *miliaria rubra*, arises when the sweat duct is blocked. It may affect people in less extreme conditions, if they are unsuitably dressed. The blockage is thought to be due to excessive sogginess (overhydration) of the skin. In the most severe forms, salt crystals may form in the sweat gland ducts, producing small blisters.

The condition features multiple small red bumps and a constant prickling or itching sensation from overstimulation of the nerve endings. As acclimatization to the ad-verse conditions occurs, prickly heat usually resolves. Air conditioning, wearing suitable clothing to encourage sweat evaporation, and plenty of open-air swimming are all helpful.

Itching anus

Anal itching is common, distressing and embarrassing. There are several possible causes. Apart from those mentioned below, anal itching can be caused, especially in women, by any of the conditions mentioned in the article on **Itching genitals**.

Piles, or haemorrhoids, are varicose veins in the canal of the anus. These are a common cause of anal itching. Persistent constipation, with straining to pass hard stools, can cause damage to the lining of the canal, and if this happens often enough, the veins may lose their normal support and protection. Some people are thought to have veins especially liable to this kind of injury. This is probably just a matter of chance anatomical variation. Anything restricting the free upward flow of blood through the veins leads to an increase in pressure in them. This is why piles are so common in pregnancy.

Protruding piles lead to skin irritation and discomfort and there is usually mucus discharge from the irritated mucous membrane. This adds to the tendency to itching. Discomfort from piles can be relieved by various anaesthetic suppositories and ointments but such measures are purely palliative and do not cure the condition.

Threadworms, or pinworms, are intestinal parasites which commonly infest children in all parts of the world. The threadworm *Enterobius vermicularis* is the commonest worm parasite of children in temperate areas. At least 20 per cent of all children are affected at any one time. Adults are by no means immune. The mature female worm is about 1 cm long, white, and with a blunt head and a fine, hair-like, pointed tail. The male is shorter and is rarely seen. Moving

threadworms produce an intense and unmistakable tickling sensation and one is in no doubt that something is going on down there. You can find out more about them in the article on **Worms in stools**.

Itching between toes

The fungus infection *tinea* is often called 'ringworm', but is not a worm and does not necessarily form rings. It is an infection of the skin by fungi, especially *Microsporum*, *Trichophyton* and *Epidermophyton* species, collectively known as *dermatophytes*. These fungi attack the dead outer layer of the skin, or the skin appendages – the hair and the nails – causing itching and persistent and often progressively extending areas of scaling and inflammation.

The common site of infection is the foot, where the condition is known as *tinea pedis* or 'athlete's foot'. The fungus affects the areas between the toes, usually starting between the third and fourth toe and spreading to the other spaces. You are apt to get this infection if you are not sufficiently careful over personal hygiene, or are unlucky in public swimming pool changing rooms. The fungus is encouraged by hot, sweaty conditions. Once acquired, it tends to be persistent, but responds to prolonged treatment with a suitable antifungal preparation. Regular careful daily washing, drying and powdering of the feet is the best preventive. The imidazole drugs are effective.

Itching elbows and knees

Persistent, long-term itching of the skin in the bends of the elbows and behind the knees is likely to be due to eczema of the type known as *atopic dermatitis*. This kind of eczema runs in families and has an allergic element – it often appears in the first year of life. It is not contagious or infectious unless an area of eczema becomes secondarily infected.

Eczema most commonly affects the elbows and knees but can spread widely to other parts of the skin. It features itching, scaly red patches and small fluid-filled blisters which burst, releasing serum, so that the skin becomes moist, 'weeping' and crusty. Atopic eczema in babies is often caused by allergy to protein in wheat, milk and eggs. In adults, other forms of eczema may predominate and it is often the result of contact with an allergen such as washing-up liquid, biological washing powders, nickel watchstraps or name-bracelets, or other materials to which allergy has developed. Emotional upset and stress may also precipitate the disorder.

The treatment of eczema involves searching for and removing the cause. Local treatment to the skin is secondary to this, but is effective in removing the irritation which so often causes uncontrollable scratching and perpetuates and complicates the condition. Steroid ointments are very effective in relieving symptoms, but have their own disadvantages. In most cases, eczema clears up fully, leaving no sign.

Itching genitals

In women, itching of the external genitalia is usually due to thrush or a trichomonas infection. Thrush, or *candidiasis*, is a yeast fungus infection of warm, moist areas of the body with the common fungus of the genus *Candida*. Most cases are caused by the species *Candida albicans* which can cause thrush of the mouth, vagina or vulva or occasionally take hold elsewhere on the skin. *Candida* thrives best in darkness when the temperatures are right and especially when there is a good supply of carbohydrate for its nutrition. Candidiasis of the female vulva is thus particularly common if there is diabetes, which features sugar in the urine, so a urine test is mandatory in all such cases.

Fungus infections tend to be kept in check by the presence of normal body bacteria (commensal organisms) and if these are too energetically attacked by antibiotics, fungi may get the upper hand and start to spread.

Genital thrush is easily recognized. There is persistent itching or soreness and sometimes a burning pain on contact between urine and affected areas. Inspection shows characteristic white patches, rather like soft cheese, with raw-looking inflamed areas in between. There may be a white, cheesy vaginal discharge. Vulval candidiasis is easily transmitted to a sexual partner, and men, especially if uncircumcised, often develop white patches and inflammation on the glans of the penis. This is called *balanitis* and there is constant discomfort, varying from mild to severe.

Genital thrush infection is encouraged by:

- pregnancy;
- diabetes;
- antibiotics;
- immunosuppressive drugs;
- immunosuppressive diseases;

- tight clothing such as jeans;
- nylon underwear;
- poor hygiene;
- tampons;
- vaginal deodorants;
- bubble baths.

Contrary to widespread belief, the oral contraceptive pill, especially the modern low-dosage pill, does not encourage thrush.

Candidiasis flourishes in people whose immune systems are in any way defective. In AIDS, candidiasis spreads widely both outside and inside the body, extending from the mouth and the anal region well into both ends of the intestinal tract. Even more seriously, it often spreads into the respiratory passages and the lungs. Thrush is treated with clotrimazole (Canesten), miconazole (Daktarin) or a single capsule of fluconazole (Diflucan) by mouth.

Another important cause of vulval itching in women is *trichomoniasis*. This is a genital infection, mainly of the vagina, with the single-celled organism *Trichomonas vaginalis*. The infection is usually transmitted by a male carrier during sexual intercourse. In contrast to other sexually transmitted conditions, this one can be acquired from contaminated objects such as toilet seats. Although it most commonly affects the vagina, it may also involve the urine tube (urethra) in either sex and the prostate gland in men.

Trichomoniasis causes sudden onset of severe genital irritation, burning and itching and a profuse, frothy, yellowish, offensive discharge. It is one of the common causes of vaginal discharge. If the urethra is affected, there is burning on urination and some urethral discharge. Vaginal trichomoniasis often causes discomfort or pain during sexual intercourse. It may affect women of any age and is common during pregnancy. Positive diagnosis is made by spreading a small quantity of the discharge on a microscope slide and identifying the organism.

Men with a prostatic infection can act as carriers of the infection and if one of a pair of sexual partners has the infection, both must be treated or the infection will continue. The drug metronidazole (Flagyl) is the mainstay of treatment and is highly effective.

In men, genital itching is largely confined to those who are uncircumcised and unwashed. Balanitis is inflammation of the bulb (glans) of the penis that usually occurs because personal hygiene has been neglected. Daily washing under the foreskin is mandatory for all men with common sense. Other causes of genital itching in men include thrush (candidiasis) and trichomoniasis (see above). Various other sexually transmitted infections, including syphilis, can cause balanitis.

Itching groin

This condition is usually caused by fungus infection and is dignified by the term *tinea cruris*. The Americans call it 'jock itch' and British soldiers serving in jungle areas used to call it 'crutch rot'. It is a dermatophyte (see **Itching between toes**) or yeast infection, encouraged by tight clothing, obesity and insufficient washing. The irregular brownish edge of the area of inflammation often extends gradually outward from the groin, but the scrotum is not usually involved. It is intensely itchy.

Itchy groin can also be caused, especially in women, by a thrush (Candida) infection spreading outwards from the vulva.

Itching inflamed areas with white patches

This is probably thrush (candidiasis), especially if it occurs in covered areas where skin contacts skin. See **Itching Genitals**. In babies, persistent rashes in the nappy area encourage secondary infection with thrush. *Candida albicans* infection is common in babies and the fungus may be present in the bowel. Rashes lasting for over two weeks, in spite of apparently satisfactory management, should arouse this suspicion and medical advice should be obtained.

Itching mole

Only one skin mole in 1,000,000 turns cancerous so the chances of this happening are small, especially if you are sensible enough to avoid undue exposure to the sun. But if a mole is going to turn into a malignant melanoma, one of the symptoms of this unfortunate occurrence is itching. It is most important to be able to detect malignant change in a mole, as the earlier this is reported the better the outlook.

Such change can be identified by various signs. Apart from itching, these include:

- change in shape, especially increasing irregularity of outline;
- change in size;
- increased projection beyond the surface;
- sudden darkening in colour;
- development of coloured irregularities (different

shades of brown, grey, pink, red and blue);
- pain;
- softening;
- crumbling;
- the appearance of new satellite moles around the original one.

The moles which become nodular are the most dangerous as they tend to penetrate deeply. Melanomas occur most commonly on areas exposed to the sun, but may arise anywhere on the skin. Once suspicion has been aroused, there should be no delay in reporting the condition for an expert opinion. Melanomas are removed with a wide area of normal-seeming tissue around them and skin grafting may be necessary to cover the defect. ⚠

Itching scalp

The commonest cause of scalp itching is dandruff. This condition features scaliness of the scalp from flakes of dead skin, the scales being most conspicuous when loosened and separated by combing or brushing the hair. Significant dandruff represents an increase in the normal rate of scale shedding, often because the skin is mildly inflamed and itchy from various causes.

One of the commonest of these is known as *seborrhoeic dermatitis*. The cause of this condition is unknown but some dermatologists believe it may be due to a yeast fungus *Pityrosporum ovale*. It is usually worse in winter and is often so mild that little is seen except scaling. It may, however, be severe, with yellowish-red, greasy, scaly patches along the hair-line and spreading to other areas of skin such as the eyes or eyelids (causing blepharitis).

Dandruff responds well to the use of medicated shampoos, especially those containing selenium. Selsun shampoo is a popular remedy. Seborrhoeic dermatitis responds well to corticosteroid ointments and, in some sufferers, anti-yeast drugs are effective.

Epidermophyte (skin scale eating) fungus infection of the scalp (tinea capitis) can also cause itching. Kerion of the scalp is an inflamed, boggy circular area caused by a strong immunological reaction to the fungus, which soon brings about healing.

Itching wrists

Persistent itching on the front of the wrists should lead you to look very closely – preferably with a magnifying glass – to see if there are any tiny black dots in the itchy area. If there are, you almost certainly have *scabies*. This is an infestation of the skin with the human mite parasite *Sarcoptes scabiei* which burrows into the skin to lay eggs and feed on dead skin scales. You get scabies by direct close contact often during sexual intercourse. Remember also that scabies in one member of a family is likely to pass quickly to all the others.

Scabies causes intense itching and makes you scratch furiously. This damages the skin and grinds in the mite bodies, causing a severe local reaction. Scabies is usually treated with benzyl benzoate or carbaryl in the form of a lotion. Recently, trials have shown that scabies can be effectively treated with a single oral dose of the anti-worm drug ivermectin. Everyone in the household will have to be treated.

Jaundice

Jealousy in childhood

Joint fixation

Jaundice

See **Yellowing of the skin and eyes**.

Jealousy in childhood

This is a common result of competition, often between brother and sister, or prompted by the arrival of a new baby. The usual signs are bedwetting, a regression to a simpler and more childish mode of behaviour, temper tantrums, or sometimes obvious anxiety.

Children should be warned, well in advance, of an expected addition to the family and should be clearly told that time and attention will have to be given to the new baby. Parents must understand and tolerate the signs of jealousy and should give as much attention as possible to the older children. So far as possible, the baby should not be allowed to intrude into an older child's possessions and living area, as this will make the jealousy worse.

Joint fixation

Total loss of movement in a joint because the bearing surfaces have healed together is known as *ankylosis*. This can happen following joint disease or injury or may be done deliberately as a surgical measure to relieve persistent pain.

L

Lactose intolerance

Lockjaw

Long sight

Loss of appetite

Loss of intelligence

Loss of memory

Loss of movement in a joint

Loss of vision (sparkly-edged)

Loss of voice

Loss of weight (in young girls)

Lumbago

Lump in the throat

Lump under the arm

Lactose intolerance

See **Diarrhoea**.

Lockjaw

See **Pain in the muscles** (muscle spasms).

Long sight

See **Vision worse for distance**.

Loss of appetite

The medical term for this is *anorexia*, which should not be confused with *anorexia nervosa*. Anorexia simply means loss of appetite. It is a symptom of a wide variety of disorders, both minor and major, not only those of the digestive system. It may also accompany minor emotional upsets. Anorexia can occur in almost any acute illness and can result from pain, depression or anxiety. It can occur in people with cancer, heart failure, liver disease and kidney failure. Additionally, it can be caused by various drugs including diuretics, drugs for high blood pressure, narcotics and digitalis. So you will see that loss of appetite, by itself, does not suggest a diagnosis. In most cases temporary loss of appetite is unimportant, but persistent anorexia and loss of weight for no apparent reason should always be investigated. On the other hand, however poor your appetite may seem, if you are *not* losing weight you have no cause for concern.

It is common for young children to go through phases of refusing food and this may be worrying. But even a day or two with little or no food will do no harm so long as fluid is taken. Food refusal is a normal part of a child's development and the child will observe, and may later cash in on, your obvious concern.

Watch out for persistent loss of weight in adolescents. This may be due to anorexia nervosa or to the use of amphetamine or other stimulant drugs.

Anorexia nervosa is a serious psychiatric disorder almost exclusively affecting young woman and with a significant mortality rate. It is a defect in the person's perception of her own body so that, however thin she may be, she perceives herself to be too fat. As a result she starves herself, going to great lengths to avoid food intake and to resist any attempt at treatment.

The condition features:

- gross loss of weight;
- wasting of the muscles;
- tiredness;
- weakness;
- dryness of the skin;
- growth of fine downy hair on the body;
- cessation of menstrual periods;
- real danger of death by starvation or suicide.

Never underestimate the dangers in anorexia nervosa. The affected person will deny that there is anything wrong and will usually refuse to cooperate in treatment. She will hold food in her mouth until she can dispose of it. The condition requires expert treatment in hospital and delay in seeking medical advice can be dangerous. Even after apparently successful treatment and weight gain, relapses are common. The condition has a mortality rate of about 10 per cent. ⚠

Loss of intelligence

In the absence of obvious disorders such as dementia or

Alzheimer's disease in older people (see **Loss of memory**), or meningitis, encephalitis, head injury or other possible causes of brain damage in the young, one must consider the possibility of lead poisoning.

Lead and lead compounds are highly toxic when eaten or inhaled. Small amounts of lead taken in over long periods have a cumulative effect and can be disastrous. Continued exposure to the fumes of leaded petrol, lead paints, pottery glazes, solder or water from lead pipes, causes lead to accumulate gradually in the body especially in the liver, kidneys and brain.

There has been particular concern over the risks from tetra-ethyl-lead used as an anti-knocking agent in petrol. Children exposed to the exhaust fumes from such petrol may suffer chronic lead poisoning and this can cause damage to brain function with headache, loss of physical coordination, loss of intellectual ability and memory, and abnormal behaviour. In the past, large numbers of children have suffered vary-ing degrees of loss of intellectual function – even measurable loss of IQ – as a result of prolonged exposure to atmospheric lead. Public awareness of the problem has, however, led to reduced levels of environmental lead and unleaded petrol is becoming ever more popular.

Loss of memory

The least common cause of loss of memory is *amnesia*. This is the loss of the power to recall from memory or, less commonly, of the power to memorize information. Amnesia may be caused by damage to certain parts of the brain concerned with recalling stored data or registering and storing new data. This damage may result from physical brain injury, disease, the toxic effect of alcohol or the effects of a thiamine deficiency. Often there is loss of memory for events that occurred during a period prior to the start of the trouble. This is called *retrograde amnesia* and some recovery is common. Sometimes there is a defect so that new information is not stored during a period following the event causing the amnesia. This is called *anterograde amnesia* and the effect is usually permanent.

Amnesia may also be a feature of a *fugue*. This is a rare psychological reaction in which the affected person takes on a new identity and wanders away from the old environment, apparently in a state of amnesia for the former life. Such people may take up a new occupation and, indeed, assume a completely new life. They are usually quiet, inoffensive people living a somewhat reclusive existence and they avoid drawing attention to themselves. Fugues occur as a response to an intolerable situation and it is likely that the 'amnesia' is a mechanism allowing the affected person to accept a course of action which would normally be considered outrageous. The amnesia is highly selective and does not preclude use of the previous general education. If there is recovery from the fugue, amnesia for

the period of the fugue occurs. Deserters from military service or from nagging wives are among the ranks of fugue 'victims'. It is apparent that, for some, the fugue represents a reasonable and logical solution to a major life problem.

Dementia is a syndrome of failing memory and progressive loss of intellectual power due to continuing degenerative disease of the brain. This brain damage may occur in several different ways:

- at least 50 per cent of people diagnosed as having dementia are suffering from the brain shrinkage (atrophy) of Alzheimer's disease;
- about 10 per cent are having small repeated strokes with progressive destruction of brain tissue by blood supply deprivation;
- in five to ten per cent the dementia is due to alcoholic damage from long-term overindulgence (this figure varies with the incidence of alcoholism

in the population being considered);

- an important seven per cent are not demented at all, but have psychiatric conditions, such as schizophrenia, depression and hysteria, which mimic dementia and which are susceptible to treatment;
- about five per cent have brain tumours and another five per cent have a form of 'water on the brain' (hydrocephalus);
- in three per cent the condition is due to long-term drug intoxication and in three per cent to Huntington's chorea.

In most of the remaining 15 or so per cent the dementia is either of unknown origin or is caused by one of a variety of other diseases such as liver failure, pernicious anaemia, syphilis, thyroid disease, multiple sclerosis, Creutzfeldt-Jakob disease, epilepsy or Parkinson's disease.

The early signs of dementia are subtle and are likely to be noticed only by close relatives or friends. There may be a loss of interest in work or hobbies, an increase in forgetfulness and easy distractibility. Reasonable discussion of problems becomes impossible. Later it is found that only the simplest of instructions can be followed correctly, orientation in familiar areas becomes defective and the affected person may get lost near home. Judgement is impaired. The main defect is in memory and in the use of language. Nuances of meaning are lost, vocabulary becomes simplified and limited and conversation becomes repetitive and garrulous, full of clichés and stereotyped phrases.

Sudden anger and inappropriate tearfulness are common at this stage and the mood tends towards depression and bad temper. The emotions are abnormally changeable (labile) with quick swings from laughter to weeping. Standards of personal care and hygiene decline. There is indifference to social convention and to the opinions of others. Physical deterioration is a constant feature and there is almost always eventual loss of appetite, emaciation and a high susceptibility to infection.

In the end, the demented person stays in bed, inaccessible to stimuli, incontinent but indifferent to discomfort or pain, mute and mindless. It is a merciful providence of the nature of things that people in this condition are totally unaware of their vegetable state. And it is also in the nature of things that such people often die from infection, usually pneumonia. Few doctors consider it any part of their duty to strive officiously to keep such people alive, by intensive antibiotic treatment.

Probably the commonest cause of progressive loss of memory in elderly people is *Alzheimer's disease*. This condition features loss of all forms of mental function from degeneration and shrinkage of the brain. Alzheimer's disease causes the great majority of cases of dementia. It rarely starts before 60 but is increasingly common in older people. About one third of all people over 85 have the disease. The condition starts with forgetfulness which gradually progresses to severe memory loss, especially for recent events. The loss of memory causes severe anxiety and the personality begins to deteriorate. Confusion and disorientation follow so that the affected person is easily lost, even in long-familiar surroundings, and there may be delusions of persecution. Some become unpleasantly and unreasonably demanding, aggressive or even violent; some just become helpless. Standards of personal hygiene drop and, in the end, full-time care is necessary.

A number of correctable conditions can closely resemble Alzheimer's disease, so full medical investigation is necessary before a positive diagnosis is made.

Loss of movement in a joint

See **Joint fixation**.

Loss of vision (sparkly-edged)

See migraine under **Pain in the head (headache)**.

Loss of voice

The commonest cause of partial loss of voice is inflammation of the vocal cords as part of a severe sore throat. The inflammatory thickening of the cords prevents them from vibrating freely and the voice is affected to a varying degree. When the inflammation settles the voice is restored. Inflammation or other disease of the vocal cords, including nodules on the cords (singer's nodes), causes hoarseness and loss of voice quality but not total absence of sound production. Such persistent affliction of the voice should always be investigated.

Persistent loss of voice may also result from paralysis, partial or total, of the muscles that tighten the vocal cords. This may be due to a cancer in the neck affecting a nerve to the larynx – the recurrent laryngeal nerve. This produces a strange 'cow-cough' type of vocalization. Urgent attention is required. ⚠

Total loss of voice, other than from these causes, is called *aphonia*. This is a psychological, not a physical, condition and usually recovers in time, often as suddenly as it began. Aphonia is rare and is usually caused by emotional stress. There is no organic disorder.

Loss of weight (in young girls)

See **Loss of appetite**.

Lumbago

See **Pain in the back**.

Lump in the throat

The constant feeling of having a 'lump in the throat', which can neither be swallowed nor brought up, is known medically as *globus hystericus*. This feeling often accompanies acute anxiety, sadness or mental conflict and is due to a tight constriction of the muscles placed in a circle around the lower part of the throat (pharynx). Globus hystericus is not caused by any organic defect and, if persistent, requires sympathetic psychiatric management after full physical investigation.

Lump under the arm

See **Enlarged 'glands'**.

Male feminization

Masculinization

ME

Mental blocking

Mental difficulties,
generally

Mental tension

Milk leaking from a
baby's nipples

Mini-stroke

Missed periods

Mole (changes to)

Mongoloid appearance

Mouth-breathing

Mouth drooping

Muscle twitching

Male feminization

There are two ways in which men can come to look like women, the commonest being a shortage of male sex hormones. This can occur from disease or loss of the testicles or because the pituitary gland fails to produce the hormones that stimulates the testicles to produce male sex hormones. These hormones, known as androgens, promote growth and puberty in males. Deficiency starting before puberty prevents the male from having a normal puberty and becoming a fully masculinized person. This misfortune results in the production of a eunuch – a person with a feminine appearance, smooth skin with little body hair, a high-pitched voice, poor muscular development, underdeveloped sex organs and limited sexual drive. Deficiency after puberty has a much smaller effect.

The second way feminization can occur is by taking large doses of female sex hormones – oestrogens. This may be done to help to treat cancer of the prostate gland, or it can be used in the course of sex-change surgery.

Masculinization

Male sex hormones are powerful anabolic steroids which, as a matter of routine, turn girlish little boys into hefty males. Abnormally high production of male sex hormones will cause the male characteristics to be excessively marked. Such excessive output of the hormones usually occurs from a tumour of the cells that produce the hormone, in the testicles or the adrenal glands.

Surprisingly, there are cells of this type also in the ovary and a tumour of these can cause male sex hormone (androgen) excess in women. If this happens before the normal time of puberty, there will be early sexual development and premature body development but the hormones cause fusion of the growing ends of the long bones and this stops body growth prematurely. If it happens in adults, it causes masculinization with increased body hair, muscular development and deepening of the voice. The affected women stop menstruating and have enlargement of the clitoris.

ME

See **Tiredness and weakness**.

Mental blocking

This is the inability to express your true thoughts or feelings, or even to continue with a particular line of thought, as a result of emotional disturbance or conflict in your mind. Severe thought blocking, even to the extent of not being able to recall the thoughts of a moment ago, may occur in serious mental disorders such as schizophrenia. In these cases, thought streams may be replaced by totally different sequences. This will be expressed as wholly disjointed and apparently meaningless speech. The neurologist and psychoanalyst Sigmund Freud (1856–1939) believed blocking to be due to the repressed memory of painful emotions, especially those occurring in early life.

If you suffer blocking you should certainly see your doctor. You may well benefit from some form of psychotherapy.

Mental difficulties, generally

Children vary greatly in intellectual ability and it is impossible to draw a definite line between normality and retardation. There are, however, some whose mental ability is so much below average that, as they grow up, they are unable to perform even simple work or other social functions and need constant supervision and guidance to keep them from distress or danger. Such people are said to suffer from mental retardation. This is the result of brain defect or malfunction and is often present from birth.

Retardation may result from genetic factors directly or indirectly affecting the brain, from injury to the brain before, at, or soon after birth – often from oxygen deprivation – or from later injury or disease of the brain. Infection and poisoning, severe nutritional deficiency, various environmental hazards such as lead poisoning, and severe sensory or emotional deprivation early in life may all affect the structure or function of the brain in such a way as to produce mental retardation.

Mentally retarded people are usually classified by intelligence quotient (IQ). Mildly defective people have IQs from 70 down to about 55; moderately defective people have IQs from 54 to 40; and severely defective people have IQs below 40. People of low mental capacity should be strongly encouraged to try to master some form of useful work under supervision. Work can be a source of pride and satisfaction to the retarded, and training in work activities often reveals higher capabilities than had been expected.

Mental tension

See **Anxiety**.

Milk leaking from a baby's nipples

Don't be alarmed if you see a small leak of milk from your baby's nipples for a few days after birth. This strange phenomenon is well known and for centuries has been called 'witches' milk'. Throughout your pregnancy your pituitary gland produced increasing amounts of a milk-stimulating hormone called *prolactin*, and at the time of your baby's birth there were peak concentrations of this hormone in your blood stream. Some of the hormone got through your placenta into your baby's blood and it is now acting on his or her breasts in exactly the same way as it is acting on yours. However, the small supply of hormone your baby has received will not last long and the milk will soon dry up.

Mini-stroke

See **Vision lost or dimmed for short periods**.

Missed periods

See **Absence of menstrual periods**.

Mole (changes to)

See **Itching mole**.

Mongoloid appearance

Formerly called 'mongolism', Down's syndrome is a major genetic disorder caused by the presence, either in the ovum or the sperm, of an extra chromosome. Every cell in the body of an individual with Down's syndrome has 47 chromosomes instead of the normal 46.

For young mothers, the incidence is about one in 2,000. For mothers approaching menopausal age, the incidence is about one in 40. In about a quarter of the cases, the extra chromosome comes from the father.

A child with Down's syndrome has oval, down-sloping eyelid openings and a large, protruding tongue. The head is short, wide and flattened at the back and the ears are small. The nose is short, with a depressed bridge and the lips thick and turned out. The hands are broad with short fingers, and the skin is often rough and dry. There is slow physical development. Heart and inner ear defects are common and there is a special susceptibility to leukaemia. There is always some degree of mental defect, but this need not be severe and many people with Down's syndrome are able to engage in simple employment.

Those without major heart problems usually survive to adult life, but the processes of ageing appear to be speeded up and most die in their 40s or 50s.

Mouth-breathing

See **Breathing through the mouth**.

Mouth drooping

See **Facial weakness or paralysis**.

Muscle twitching

Known medically as *fasciculation*, these are brief, involuntary contractions of a small group of muscle fibres, causing a visible or palpable twitch under the skin. Fasciculation is very common. Occasional and intermittent fasciculation of the flat muscle around the eye is almost always harmless. Persistent severe fasciculation, however, may imply nerve disease and you should report this to your doctor.

N

Nappy rash

Nasal bleeding

Nasal deformity

Nasal drip

Nasal inflammation

Nasal obstruction

Network pattern on the legs

Nightmares

Night terrors

Night waking

Nipples sore

Noises in the ears

Numbness and tingling in the hand

Nappy rash

See **Skin inflamed under nappy.**

Nasal bleeding

This very common event usually results from minor injury, such as nose-picking or a blow to the nose, but may also result from infection of the mucous membrane, local drying and crusting. Even in adults, nose bleeding should *not* be considered a sign of high blood pressure. A nose bleed can almost always be controlled by leaning forward, pinching the nostrils firmly together for five minutes and breathing through the mouth. Pressure maintained for this length of time will allow the blood to clot and the bleeding is unlikely to recur unless the site is disturbed. If you can't control the bleeding by this method you will need medical attention. The nose may need to be packed with gauze temporarily. Rarely, it may be necessary to cauterize or tie off the bleeding vessel.

Bleeding in children, arising from persistent crusting of the insides of the nostrils, is best treated by using a softening ointment such as petroleum jelly.

Nasal deformity

Noses come naturally in all shapes and sizes and are rather prone to further deformity as a result of trauma. The nose is not only the most prominent feature of the face but is also the most variable, and many otherwise attractive faces are spoiled by noses of inappropriate shape or size. For these reasons the nose has become one of the chief targets of the cosmetic surgeon.

The prominence of the nose also makes it vulnerable to violent injury, as may occur in car crashes, boxing or drunken falls. Inadequately repaired fracture of the nasal bones causes flattening or deflection to one side. Further misfortunes may befall it. The nose is prone to skin cancer – probably more so than any other part of the face – and the result may be a serious loss of tissue. In addition, there are infections, such as congenital syphilis and lupus vulgaris (skin tuberculosis), which may also result in structural loss. Cocaine sniffing commonly leads to perforation of the thin partition between the two sides of the nose. Major deformities of the nose can tax the ingenuity of a skilled plastic surgeon and may require grafting of bone or cartilage or even the use of plastic materials, to provide support, as well as soft tissue grafting.

Rhinophyma, or 'potato nose' is a form of rosacea, occurring almost exclusively in elderly men, in which the sebaceous and connective tissues in the skin of the nose become greatly overgrown so as to produce a bulbous deformity in which the enlarged openings of the skin pores are readily visible. Over-secretion of the sebaceous glands causes the skin to become oily, and wide dilation of small blood vessels produces permanent redness.

In spite of the grotesque appearance, rhinophyma is easily treated. Under anaesthesia, the redundant tissue is boldly pared away until the nose is reduced to an acceptable size and shape. Skin grafting is unnecessary as regeneration readily occurs from residual skin tissue, and healing is rapid.

Nasal drip

Post-nasal drip, popularly known as 'nasal catarrh', is a trickle of watery or mucinous fluid produced in the naso-pharynx in chronic infective, and other forms, of rhinitis (see **Nasal inflammation**). The fluid passes down the back wall of the throat, some-times with difficulty because of its stickiness, causing an un-comfortable awareness of its presence. When infection is ac-tive, the post-nasal drip fluid contains pus as well as mucus.

Post-nasal drip is also a feature of the condition of *vasomotor rhinitis* in which the mucous membrane of the back of the nose and throat becomes overactive and secretes excessively. This may be due to allergy, stress, infection, sexual excitement ('honeymoon rhinitis'), drugs for high blood pressure or the overuse of decongestant nasal sprays and drops, which pro-duce a rebound congestion of the mucous membrane.

Nasal inflammation

Inflammation of the mucous membrane lining of the nose is called *rhinitis*. This causes swelling, so that the air flow is partly or wholly obstructed, and overactivity of the glands in the mucous mem-brane which causes excessive mucus production and a watery discharge.

Rhinitis is a feature of the common cold and of hay fever (allergic rhinitis), which is not caused by hay and is not a fever. It is an allergy to grass, weed and tree pollens, moulds, hair, feathers, skin scales (dander), house mite droppings, house dust or other airborne substances. It causes sneezing, stuffiness and a watery nasal discharge.

Vasomotor rhinitis is an in-termittent condition due to disturbance of the function of nerves controlling blood vessels that supply the mu-cous membrane. The mem-brane becomes over-responsive to stimuli, which may be psychological, hormo-nal, or climatic, and there is sneezing and a watery dis-charge. It is common in im-migrants from the tropics and in those taking oestrogens, including the oestrogen-pro-gestogen contraceptive pill. It may be brought on by sexual arousal or by eating highly spiced foods.

Hypertrophic rhinitis is the result of long-term inflammation or repeated infection. There are persistent symptoms and the lining becomes thickened and congested. *Atrophic rhinitis*, in which there is shrinkage and loss of the mucous membrane, can result from sarcoidosis, tuberculosis or excessive surgery to the nose. There is dryness, crusting, loss of the sense of smell, and an unpleasant odour (ozaena) of which the affected person is often unaware. See also **Chills**.

Nasal obstruction

Obstruction of the air passages through the nose can occur in several ways. Nasal congestion is due to inflammation of the mucous membrane lining of the nose, usually as a result of an allergy or a virus infection. The mucous membrane of the nose swells very readily and because the air passages are narrow they are easily closed off on one or both sides. Some people have narrower passages than average and these may be unusually prone to nasal blockage. A swollen lining is often accompanied by excess mucus production, which doesn't help. Most cases are caused by colds or hay fever, persistent sinusitis or polyps in the nose. Polyps are narrow-necked, bulbous protrusions from the mucous membrane and can be surgically removed if necessary.

Various decongestant nose drops or sprays can often be used to relieve nasal congestion. Decongestants containing ephedrine or ephedrine-like substances should not be used in young children. They may be dangerous and the 'rebound' effect leads to increased congestion.

A permanent blockage on one side may be due to the central partition of the nose being too much off centre (deflected septum) and this can be corrected surgically.

Network pattern on the legs

A prominent reddish-brown network pattern, like wide fishnet tights, used to be very common in the days of coal fires when people sat close in order to keep warm. This was known as *erythema ab igne* ('redness from fire'), and the pattern is actually that of the blood vessels under the skin. A very similar condition, which appears spontaneously and is unconnected with heat, is known as *livedo reticularis*. This is a feature of the disease Cushing's syndrome, in which there is an excess of steroid hormones, and of various collagen diseases such as lupus erythematosus. Recent research has shown that the pattern is associated with certain circulating antibodies – antiphospholipid antibodies – which can sometimes produce rather unpleasant effects. So if you think you have developed livedo you should see your doctor. ⚠

Nightmares

Intensely vivid and unpleasant dreams are suffered more by children than by adults. Nightmares are often connected with some prior event of a highly traumatic nature such as an assault, a serious accident or injury, severe frights or fears. They may be caused by the withdrawal of sleeping pills. Nightmares are anxiety dreams and occur during the periods of rapid eye movement (REM) sleep. They are distinguished from night terrors which occur in the early part of the night during the period of deep, non-REM sleep. See **Night terrors**.

Night terrors

These produce much more powerful physiological effects than nightmares – the heart rate accelerations have been among the highest recorded, the respiratory rate is very high and there is marked sweating. There is often loud screaming. The deeper the non-REM sleep, the more severe the night terror tends to be. The content of the night terror is usually a conviction of suffocation, choking, entrapment in a small space or impending

167

death. Night terrors are commonest around the age of five or six and tend to stop in adolescence.

Night waking

About a quarter of all British children, aged one to two, regularly disturb their parents' sleep during the night. This is a difficult problem, and a variety of approaches have been recommended – a clear indication that none is completely satisfactory. They include:

- changing the domestic routine so as to reduce daytime naps;
- sedatives for the child and/or the parents;
- leaving the child to cry;
- attempts at behaviour modification.

Trying to modify behaviour involves methods such as rewarding the child for not disturbing the parents or introducing a fixed bedtime ritual which conditions the child to stay quiet. Rituals are effective with children and, preferably, both parents should participate in them. They might include an agreement not to cry during the night.

Sedatives are widely used but they work only while they are being given. They cannot be relied on to induce habits of all-night sleep. The antihistamine drug Vallergan (trimeprazine) has useful sedative properties and is widely used in children.

Nipples sore

See **Pain in the breast**.

Noises in the ears

Hissing, whistling or ringing sounds heard in one or both ears, or in the centre of the head, are described medically as *tinnitus*. In most cases, the sound is continuous, but awareness of it is usually intermittent and the degree of distress it causes depends on the personality. Tinnitus is almost always associated with some degree of deafness and is caused by the same kind of damage that causes deafness – damage to the hair cells of the cochlea of the inner ear. The reason for the damage is not always apparent.

Tinnitus often starts spontaneously, but it may be brought on by any of the factors known to cause deafness, such as nearby explosions, prolonged loud noise, aminoglycoside antibiotics and various ear disorders such as Ménière's disease, otosclerosis and presbyacusis.

Tests have shown that the impression of how loud the tinnitus is, as experienced by sufferers, is misleading, and that the actual levels, as judged by comparison with external sounds, are, in fact, very low. Nevertheless, tinnitus can be very trying, especially in quiet conditions, and sufferers often resort to external sounds to cover it. Personal headphones may be useful and white noise generators, known as tinnitus maskers, have been found useful by some.

Certain drugs, such as local anaesthetics and others which interfere with nerve conduction, have been found to have an effect on tinnitus and some patients have been greatly relieved by the use of the drug carbamazepine (Tegretol). Such measures do not, however, have a major part to play in the management of the disorder. The majority of tinnitus sufferers soon become used to the problem and learn to live with it without too much distress.

Numbness and tingling in the hand

See **Pain in the hand**.

Obesity

Obesity

Fat mothers usually have fat babies and these tend to turn into fat adults. Patterns in eating may well be established early in life and it is probable that fat mothers unconsciously encourage habits of excessive intake in their children. This is more plausible than the suggestion that obesity – which is essentially an acquired characteristic – is hereditary. It has also been suggested that infant obesity, from excessive intake, leads to the production of an increased number of fat cells in the body and that the number of fat cells remains constant after childhood. If this is true, the obese have more cells to fill than the non-obese and are faced with an almost insuperable problem in keeping to their ideal weight. This idea has been disputed by some experts. Although body weight varies with height and with skeletal shape and bulk, the largest variation in body weight in Western societies is the amount of fat storage.

Obese people suffer from:

- high blood pressure;
- diabetes in maturity;
- in women, an increased incidence of cancers of the breast, womb, ovaries and gall-bladder;
- in men, an increased incidence in cancer of the colon, rectum and prostate gland;

- orthopaedic problems, such as osteoarthritis and foot trouble;
- depression.

The health implications of obesity are serious. Repeated surveys of the fate of obese people have confirmed that a significant excess of illness occurs in those whose body mass index (the weight in kilograms divided by the square of the height in metres) is greater than 27. About one fifth of the men and about a quarter of the women in Britain have a body mass index higher than 27. Efforts should therefore be made, at all costs, to avoid obesity, and the time to start is in infancy. Mothers should never inflict their own eating habits on children and should never use food for any purpose other than nutrition. Children should be allowed to eat only at meal times.

Obesity is defined as the excessive storage of energy in the form of fat. This can only result from a lack of balance between food intake and energy expenditure. Whatever other factors apply, obe-

sity cannot occur unless more food is eaten than is used. All excess of intake over expenditure is laid down as fat – a collection of thin-walled, oil-filled cells situated mostly beneath the skin. Surprisingly, most adults manage to achieve a reasonable balance between intake and energy output and remain roughly the same weight. This applies as much to very fat people as to the thin. Obesity is not a simple eating disorder resulting from uncontrolled greed. There is evidence that some obese people may have the same metabolic rate as thin people, but that their energy expenditure is less. The food intake tends to be proportional to the weight so those with a low energy expenditure get heavier.

All this makes life very hard for the overweight person. Regrettably, there is no magic cure. Reduced calorie intake is a far more efficient way of reducing weight than taking exercise. But regular exercise is an essential part of the process of weight reduction. Contrary to expectation, exercise helps to limit food intake. However, weight cannot be lost in a healthy person, without reducing intake. New, smaller eating habits must be established. 'Crash' diets, or those involving non-nutritious food substitutes, are generally pointless, as they do not get at the basic requirement of trying to amend a years-long habit of putting too much in the mouth. Effective weight reduction must also be sustained over a long period so that it becomes permanent. For this reason, would-be weight reducers who spend money on health farms, proprietary diets, books and magazines on dieting, and expensive exercising equipment are wasting time and money. The diet should be normal, but must be in quantities so small that they inevitably cause hunger until the body adapts. It may be a miserable prospect, but in the end it can come to seem normal.

Pain

Pain in the abdomen

Pain in the ankle

Pain in the back

Pain in the big toe

Pain in the bones

Pain in the breast

Pain in the chest

Pain in the ear

Pain in the elbow

Pain in the eye

Pain in the face

Pain in the foot

Pain in the hand

Pain in the head
(headache)

Pain in the hip

Pain in the joints,
generally

Pain in the joint of the jaw

Pain in the knee

Pain in the muscles

Pain in the neck

Pain in the shoulder

Pain in the temples

Pain in the testicle

Pain in the throat

Pain in the wrist

Pain on bowel movement

Pain on deep breathing

Pain on menstruation

Pain on sexual
intercourse

Pain on urination

Pale stools

Palpitations

Panic attacks

Penis problems:
ballooning

Penis problens: bending

Penis problems: discharge

Penis problems: early
orgasm

Penis problems:
inflammation

Penis problems: itching

Penis problems: outlet
displacement

Penis problems: persistent
erection

Penis problems: shrinkage

Penis problems: ulcer

Penis problems: unresponsiveness

Penis problems: warts

Period pains

Pins and needles

Potato nose

Pounding headache, disturbance of vision and weakness

Premature ejaculation

'Prickly heat'

Protruding teeth

Pain

Pain is the commonest of all symptoms so this section – comprising a sequence of articles dealing with various sources of pain – is necessarily the longest in the book. Before looking through it to find the particular pain you are interested in, however, you will probably find it helpful to get a general idea of the nature of pain and of some of its features.

The term 'pain' comes from the Latin *poena* meaning 'punishment', and there are some people who are convinced that all pain is deserved. This is not a particularly logical response

and most people take a less pessimistic view. Pain is a sensation which nearly everyone finds unpleasant. It is usually localized and felt in the area of the body in which its cause occurs. However, this is not necessarily the case, and many pains are felt in areas remote from the cause. This is called *referred pain*. Pain is caused by strong stimulation of sensory nerve endings by an event or process that is damaging, or is liable to damage, body tissues of any kind. Unless it is very persistent (chronic), pain commonly serves as a warning of danger and leads to action that, hopefully, will end it. Such action may be reflex, involuntary and very rapid – as when a hand is pulled away from a hot object – or conscious, deliberate and purposeful – as when you read this book and then consult your doctor.

Pain causes distress, anxiety and sometimes fear, and the psychological and physical changes associated with it may be similar to those you experience during anger and aggression. The significance you attach to the pain depends more on the degree and quality of these secondary effects than on the actual intensity of the pain itself. The psychological reaction to pain is often modified by past experience. If pain is separated from its mental reaction, as happens when you are given drugs like morphine, it may still be felt but you may no longer consider it unpleasant and may even be indifferent to it. The distress caused by pain depends also, to a large extent, on your awareness of the cause. If you were being tortured, you would probably react more strongly to a minor pain than you would if the same pain were the result of an innocent cause such as an accident. Similarly, if you think a pain is due to cancer, you will suffer much more from it than you would if you know that it is due to a completely remediable condition like a broken leg.

The nerve endings for pain are called *nociceptors*. These are stimulated into sending pain messages to the brain by the chemical action on them of substances, such as prostaglandins, released from local tissues damaged by the injury causing the pain. Different nociceptors show different sensitivities, some being stimulated by low-grade 'warning' events, such as firm pressure or temperatures not high enough to burn. These cause a sensation of threat rather than pain. Other pain nerve endings respond only when strongly stimulated, as by skin cutting, pricking or burning. In both cases, the stronger the stimulus, the more powerful the nerve impulses sent to the brain.

Pain impulses can also arise from stimuli affecting the

nerve fibres at a point nearer the nervous system than the remote nerve ending. Stimuli of this kind occur in diseases such as shingles and are also responsible for one form of referred pain.

Although the nerves carrying pain impulses terminate in the brain, and give rise to neurological activity there, the pain is usually felt in the region in which the nerve endings are situated. Nerve impulses passing to the brain may be blocked by local anaesthetics, by electrical stimulation applied through the skin, by acupuncture, and by the inhibitory action of other nerve fibres coming down from the brain. The latter are believed to release blocking substances called *endorphins* and *enkephalins*. Morphine and other similar drugs are believed to relieve pain by acting on nerve receptor sites in a manner similar to that of endorphins. Pain control can also be effected by hormones – removal of the pituitary or adrenal glands increases sensitivity to pain. The hormones involved have

not been positively identified, but are believed to be endorphins.

Pain impulses travelling up the spinal chord pass through neurological 'gates' similar in function to the electronic logical gates in computers. These impulses can be blocked by signals coming from elsewhere. This provides an explanation for some of the physical methods of pain control. Many of these methods are effective, and include skin rubbing with a soft cloth, electrical stimulation of the skin (TENS) using a variety of machines, acupuncture or acupressure, massage, or cold sprays to the skin.

Experts on pain control emphasize that pain should be treated by the simplest and safest available means, but that attempts should always be made to relieve it, once the cause is clearly known. Prolonged pain is demoralizing and debilitating and should be controlled as early as possible. Neglected pain becomes more difficult to control. Pain-controlling drugs work best if they are used as soon as the pain reappears, and they should not be withheld until pain becomes unbearable. Different forms of pain control, used in combination, are more effective than methods used in isolation. Authoritative reassurance by a doctor, when appropriate, increases the effectiveness of pain control measures.

Local anaesthetic injections can control pain, but the effect is brief and this is not a practicable method. They may, however, be useful as a preliminary trial before resorting, in extreme cases, to permanent nerve destruction by alcohol injection or by severing them surgically. In general, surgical methods of pain control should be avoided. They inevitably involve unpleasant permanent loss of sensation and, even when the pain fibres are cut in the spinal chord, do not necessarily succeed in controlling the pain.

Pain in the abdomen

There are many causes for pain in the abdomen and – unless there is an obvious explanation, such as indigestion from greedy overeating – you should always take such pain seriously. It's not a bad idea, also, to take greedy overeating seriously. The most important causes of tummy pain are:

- colic from dietary indiscretion;
- food poisoning;
- gastroenteritis;
- irritable bowel syndrome;
- appendicitis;
- dysentery;
- bowel obstruction;
- duodenal ulcer;
- stomach ulcer;
- gall bladder colic;
- peritonitis;
- pelvic inflammatory disease;
- adhesions;
- amoebiasis;
- liver abscess.

If your abdomen hurts when you press on it and you are fevered, vomiting and feel ill, you may have food poisoning or gastroenteritis, appendicitis, bowel obstruction or peritonitis, possibly from a perforated duodenal ulcer. ⚠

Food poisoning is a group of disorders featuring nausea, vomiting, loss of appetite, fever, abdominal pain and diarrhoea. It is caused either by living germs present in food, which incubate and reproduce in the body until enough are present to cause illness; or by contamination of food by the poisons (toxins) from germs which have incubated outside the body. In the former, there is usually a delay of a day or two before symptoms occur; in the latter, symptoms come on within hours. Food poisoning can also be caused by inorganic or organic poisons such as metal salts or plant or animal poisons. Naturally occurring poisons include those in mushrooms, such as Amanita phalloides.

Germ toxins are very powerful and produce acute, but usually short-lived effects. A common cause of toxin contamination of food is the presence of septic spots on the skin of food-handlers. In this case the staphylococcal toxin is the cause of the illness. Living staphylococci also con-taminate the food and these may incubate to produce further toxin. The commonest bacterial contamination of food is by *Salmonella typhimurium*, which is commonly found in meats and eggs. Food handled by people careless about washing is often contaminated by human faeces.

The organism *Clostridium botulinum* can survive in canned or bottled foodstuffs. It is most commonly found in meat pastes and other processed animal products and the great majority of cases have arisen from food prepared in the home and inadequately sterilized. The result is the dangerous condition of botulism, which is fortunately rare. This word comes from the Latin *botulus* meaning 'a sausage'. The condition, which is grave and often fatal, was first observed in Germany and rightly attributed to eating contaminated sausage. Botulinum toxin is one of the most powerful poisons known to man. It operates by interfering with the release of an essential neurotransmitter – acetylcholine – at nerve endings. The effect of this is that nerves are unable to pass on their impulses to make muscles contract. A dose, measured in thousandths of a gram, is sufficient to kill.

The onset of symptoms is abrupt and occurs from four hours to a week after eating the contaminated food. The mouth becomes dry and the vision blurred and doubled; the upper lids droop; there is sickness, vomiting and diarrhoea with cramping pain in the abdomen. Soon swallowing becomes impossible and the muscles of the limbs become weak, almost paralysed. The gravest danger is that the breathing might become paralysed. In this event, death is certain unless respiration can be maintained artificially. ▲

Gastroenteritis is inflammation of the stomach and intestine. There is fever, abdominal pain, diarrhoea and vomiting. Every year, 10,000,000 people, mostly babies and infants, die from acute gastroenteritis. Most of these deaths occur in tropical and backward areas and most of the children die from dehydration and malnutrition. Given adequate medical resources, all are preventable. Gastroenteritis is caused by bowel germs, such as *Escherichia coli, Salmonella, Giardia lamblia*, rotaviruses, coronaviruses and other enteroviruses. In most cases, infection is the result of poor hygiene, especially in bottle-feeding. Breast-fed babies are seldom affected. Most attacks clear up on their own, but if the diarrhoea and vomiting are severe, death can occur from simple loss of fluid. Babies can often be saved merely by forcing fluids by mouth, but, in many cases, they are too weak to swallow and their only chance rests in rehydration by intravenous fluids. Training doctors in underdeveloped countries in the skills of inserting a scalp vein cannula and setting up a glucose-saline drip leads to the saving of hundreds of lives and the prevention of an enormous amount of human distress.

In the Western world, probably the commonest cause of abdominal pain is irritable bowel syndrome (see **Diarrhoea**).

If your abdominal pain is associated with blood and mucus in the stools, you probably have dysentery. This is an inflammation of the bowel resulting from infection either with shigella organisms (bacillary dysentery or shigellosis) or with the amoeba *Entamoeba histolytica* (amoebic dysentery). You get shigellosis by taking food contaminated with the excreta of infected people or carriers. It may be transmitted by flies. It affects children more severely than adults, and causes inflammation, swelling and ulceration of the large intestine and the lower part of the small intestine. There is abdominal pain, fever, nausea and diarrhoea of increasing frequency, up to 20 or more bowel actions a day being common. The stools are characteristically streaked with mucus and blood.

In small children, the chief danger is again from dehydration as a result of excessive water loss. Babies may die within a week of onset unless effective fluid replacement is achieved. This is the most important element in the treatment of all cases and often antibiotics are unnecessary. Many strains of shigella species have already become resistant to several antibiotics.

Amoebic dysentery is caused by the ingestion of the cystic form of the amoeba on fruit and vegetables contaminated by human faeces. This is especially common in parts of the world where human excreta is used as fertilizer. Amoebic dysentery can also be spread by male homosexual intercourse or directly from person to person when personal hygiene is poor. The cysts turn into the active form in the intestine and the amoebae burrow into the wall of the colon to cause small abscesses, then ragged, undermined ulcers. The amoebae then enter the veins of the intestine and are carried to the liver where, if sufficiently plentiful, they may cause large abscesses full of a chocolate-brown or yellow fluid consisting of broken-down liver tissue.

Symptoms are often mild and vague, but the abdominal pain is persistent although usually low grade. There is also abdominal discomfort and a feeling of sickness, mild diarrhoea with blood and mucus and sometimes tenderness over the liver. Liver abscesses may cause referred pain in the right shoulder, fever, shivering, weakness, nausea, jaundice, loss of appetite and loss of weight. Sometimes an abscess may burst through the diaphragm into the lung and the contents – said to resemble anchovy sauce – may be coughed up. Amoebic dysentery is more difficult to treat than shigellosis, but the drug metronidazole (Flagyl) is effective. Stool examination under a microscope can show the amoebae.

Appendicitis is inflammation of the blind-ended, worm-like appendix which hangs from the large intestine in the lower right corner of the abdomen. The condition is commonest in adolescents and young adults but can occur in small children. It is much less common than it was a few decades ago – the reason for this is unknown. The symptoms begin with pain in the region of the navel which soon moves to the lower right corner. Pressing here is very painful, and body movement, deep breathing and coughing cause distress. There is usually slight fever, constipation, nausea and occasionally vomiting. Perforation of the appendix leads to the even more serious condition of peritonitis. ⚠ Often an appendix abscess forms around the leaking organ and the mass becomes walled off by fibrous tissue from the rest of the abdomen. An operation to remove the appendix (appendextomy) cures the condition in almost all cases.

Bowel obstruction may occur in a number of ways. The bowel may become:

- twisted (volvulus);
- strangulated by its own swelling if stuck in a hernia;

- 'telescoped' into itself (intussusception);
- blocked by impacted faeces, especially in the elderly;
- blocked by an internal tumour;
- blocked by a tumour encircling the bowel wall;
- obstructed by a failure of the normal mechanism (peristalsis) which carries the contents along (ileus, adynamic).

Bowel obstruction may even be present at birth (congenital) as a result of a narrowing at the outlet of the stomach, or of a failure of part of the bowel to form a tube.

Obstruction causes pain in the abdomen which repeatedly rises to a peak and then subsides (colic) as the bowel stretches in trying to overcome the obstruction. Gas forms in the intestine and may cause distention. There may be a visible 'ladder' pattern on the wall of the abdomen caused by prominent loops of small bowel. If the obstruction is near the upper end of the intestine, vomiting occurs early and is stained with bile. Lower obstruction may not cause vomiting. Because the rectum is below the obstruction, stools may be passed until the bowel below the point of obstruction is empty. Thereafter, there is total constipation. ⚠

There must be no delay in seeking medical advice, so that prompt diagnosis and surgical treatment may be given before serious complications occur. The operation will be designed to remove the cause of the obstruction and restore normal bowel function. This may involve removing a loop of bowel and a colostomy or ileostomy.

Duodenal and stomach ulcers are classified together as peptic ulcers. These may occur in the lining of the stomach, duodenum or at the lower end of the gullet (oesophagus). Peptic ulcers involve local loss of the mucous membrane lining, with some penetration into the underlying muscular layer. The condition is common, affecting about 10 per cent of all adult males and two to five per cent of women. Cigarette smoking interferes with the healing of ulcers and may contribute to their occurrence.

Ulcers result when the stomach juices, which are highly acid and contain a powerful digestive enzyme called *pepsin*, succeed in digesting a part of the bowel wall. Normally, they are prevented from doing this because they are present in insufficient quantity and because the lining is protected by mucus and neutralizing bicarbonate secreted by the lining cells. A number of factors interfere with the ability of the lining to resist digestion. These include the taking of certain drugs, especially aspirin and alcohol, and the reflux of bile and secretions from the small intestine into the stomach. The organism *Helicobacter pylori* is closely associated with peptic ulceration (see below). Severe head injury, burns, major operations and severe infections are all known to promote peptic ul-

cers. Ulceration of the lower oesophagus occurs only when there is reflux of acid from the stomach.

The duodenum is the C-shaped tube which constitutes the first part of the small intestine. The stomach contents empty directly into the duodenum, and the first 3 cm take the brunt of this highly irritating mixture. Soon, however, the acid is neutralized by the alkaline secretions from the pancreas, which enter the duodenum about its mid point. Duodenal ulcers are usually found within 3 cm of the stomach outlet and are local areas in which the bowel wall is being digested by the acid and the pepsin. Ulcers do not occur in people who do not secrete stomach acid.

Duodenal ulcers are usually single, but two or more may occur simultaneously. They are usually about 1 cm in diameter and penetrate the wall at least as far as the muscular coat immediately under the lining. In severe cases they may pass right through (perforating ulcer), leaving a hole through which the contents of the bowel can escape into the sterile peritoneal cavity of the abdomen. This causes the serious condition of peritonitis.

As in gastric ulceration, causal factors include the amount of acid secreted, the efficiency of the mucus, secreted by the lining, in protecting its own surface from digestion and the presence of *Helicobacter pylori*. To what extent, and by what means, these and other factors are influenced by the psychological or emotional state of the affected person, or by life stress, is not entirely clear, but it is common experience that some forms of stress make symptoms worse.

Peptic ulceration causes a burning, boring, gnawing pain high in the abdomen, in the angle between the ribs. The pain usually comes on about two hours after a meal. Duodenal ulcer pain is characteristically relieved by taking a small amount of food. This causes the stomach outlet to close, temporarily, so that the new food can be retained for digestion. The pain is not present on waking in the morning but tends to come on around the middle of the morning. It is also common for duodenal ulcer pain to wake the sufferer two or three hours after falling asleep. The diagnosis is often apparent from the history but may be confirmed by a barium meal X-ray and by endoscopy (examining the inside of the body using an endoscope).

The great majority of gastric and duodenal ulcers heal in four to six weeks, but a neglected ulcer may perforate, causing peritonitis (see below) with very severe, widespread pain and an abdominal wall that is as hard as a board. A range of treatments is used, including the eradication of *Helicobacter pylori* organisms with antibiotics and bismuth, antacid drugs to neutralise stomach acid, histamine H_2 blockers to reduce acid secretion, proton pump inhibitor drugs such as omeprazole (Losec), drugs which form a protective coating on the base of the ulcer and promote healing, drugs which reduce painful spasm, and certain prostaglandin drugs which reduce acid. In addition, treatment with tranquillizing drugs may help by relieving anxiety or depression. In spite of great advances in drug treatment, surgical operation is necessary in some cases.

Unfortunately, chronic peptic ulceration often persists for life, with relapses every two years or so. Relapses are said to be less common if *Helicobacter pylori* organisms are eliminated. You can greatly improve the outlook by giving up smoking, throwing away your aspirin tablets, taking alcohol only in moderation and in reasonable dilution, and reducing your dietary intake. The nature of the diet seems to be relatively unimportant so long as it is nutritious. Strict diets are not required, only common-sense avoidance of items known to cause symptoms.

Biliary colic is the name given to severe, intermittent pain in the upper right corner of the abdomen caused by powerful contractions of the gall bladder in an attempt to push a gallstone along the bile duct. The pain may be shockingly severe and lasts for up to an hour at a time. It can spread up into the chest and you may think you are having a heart attack. It can be relieved by drugs that control muscle spasm, but full investigation is essential and surgery may be necessary to remove the gall bladder.

Peritonitis is an acute inflammation of the membrane which lines the abdominal cavity and forms the outer coating of the abdominal organs (the peritoneum). By contrast with the contents of the bowel, this membrane is sterile and is very susceptible to infection. Peritonitis usually results from perforation of some part of the intestine so that the contents are able to gain access to, and infect, the peritoneum. Perforation of an inflamed appendix, or of a gastric or duodenal ulcer, are the commonest causes of peritonitis, but it can also result from perforating injury as may occur in a stabbing assault or a criminal abortion.

Peritonitis causes paralysis of peristalsis (paralytic ileus) and this effectively blocks the bowel. Fluid from the blood accumulates in the abdominal cavity and the loss of fluid from the circulation may cause shock. There is severe abdominal pain, board-like rigidity of the abdominal muscles and high fever. Unless effectively treated, peritonitis is rapidly fatal. Treatment involves fluid infusion to control shock, surgery to drain the peritoneal cavity and repair the cause, and antibiotics to deal with the infection. ⚠

In women, pain deep in the abdomen may suggest pelvic inflammatory disease, including inflammation of the fallopian tubes (salpingitis) or premenstrual syndrome. Pelvic inflammatory disease is often a consequence of an earlier sexually transmitted infection and this may not have been detected at the time. Spread into the pelvic cavity occurs by way of the fallopian tubes. Pain in the lower abdomen associated with burning on passing urine suggests a urinary infection, probably cystitis.

Adhesions may also cause abdominal pain. These are abnormal connections between parts of the body that have been inflamed and have lost their 'non-stick' coverings. They occur mainly inside the abdomen after severe internal infections, injuries, operations, or after certain diseases that attack the membrane that covers the abdominal organs (the peritoneum). Internal adhesions may cause pain by obstructing the intestines.

Other causes of abdominal pain include:

- heartburn;
- gastritis from alcohol irritation to the stomach lining;
- hiatus hernia;
- shingles;
- acute pancreatitis;
- diverticulitis;
- bowel or stomach cancer;
- irritable bowel syndrome;
- ulcerative colitis.

Sometimes upper abdominal pain is caused by a heart attack. If you are in any real doubt as to the cause of the pain, take nothing by mouth and call a doctor. See also **Colic**.

Pain in the ankle

The commonest cause of pain in the ankle is stretching or tearing of the ligaments that help to hold the foot onto the bones of the lower leg. You will be in little doubt of the cause if this is the source of your ankle pain, as you will be unlikely to have forgotten that you 'twisted' your ankle recently. The deltoid ligament is the strong triangular ligament, on the inner side of the ankle, which helps to bind the foot to the leg. This, and the corresponding ligament on the outer side, can be stretched or even torn by sharply turning the sole of your foot outwards or inwards. If you do this repeatedly the ankle may become less painful but it will be more unstable and you should try to avoid this. Tight strapping that pulls the foot up onto the leg may be needed.

Other causes of pain in the ankle include the effects of old fractures and various forms of arthritis.

Pain in the back

There are many causes of this and it is not always easy to distinguish between them. They include:

- obesity;
- injudicious lifting (bending the spine instead of the knees);
- slipped disc;
- fibrositis;
- tail (coccyx) pain;
- arthritis;
- spinal cancer.

You are most likely to suffer from back pain if you are overweight; if you spend a lot of time sitting in one position; or if your job involves heavy lifting and carrying. The pain in backache may come from:

- spasm of the muscles around the spine;
- a stretched or torn ligament;

190

- actual damage to one of the many joints between the vertebral bones;
- pulpy material that has been squeezed (prolapsed) from a disc between the bones (an intervertebral disc) and is pressing on spinal nerve roots.

Fibrositis is a medically vague term often used by doctors to describe muscle pain and tenderness when they are uncertain of the cause. It is not, as the name implies, inflammation of fibrous tissue. Whatever it is, it can affect the back muscles. It is often worse in cold and damp weather and may make you feel generally rotten. However, there is no real stiffness or muscle spasm and movement is unrestricted. Simple pain-killers, such as the non-steroidal anti-inflammatory drugs (NSAIDs) are often effective.

If the pain is right down at the base of your spine and came on after a fall onto your bottom, the chances are that you have a problem with your coccyx – the little tail of four fused bones. This is called *coccydynia* and it sometimes occurs without trauma, often during pregnancy. There is also usually tenderness on pressure with coccydynia. Tail pain may even imply a fracture of the coccyx.

Disc pulp prolapse, commonly called 'slipped disc', can cause pain, numbness and tingling running down your leg as far as the foot, as well as backache. You may find that you get a stab of pain when you cough or sneeze. Spread of the symptoms to the leg is often a fairly serious matter as it implies possibly damaging pressure on the spinal nerve roots leading to weakness in muscles activated by the nerve, so you should not delay reporting any such complication of backache. ⚠ See also **Pain in the neck**.

Various forms of arthritis of the spinal joints can cause long-term back pain. This group of causes includes osteoarthritis and ankylosing spondylitis. Kidney trouble, especially infection of the urine drainage system (pyelonephritis) can cause severe back pain with tenderness to touch on one side of the spine. But this cause will almost always be associated with fever, shivering and pain on passing urine. Osteoporosis of the spine may lead to unsuspected fractures and severe back pain. X-ray will immediately show the cause of the pain. A fortunately rare cause of back pain is secondary cancer that has spread to the spine. This gives a constant, boring type of pain that keeps you awake and is not relieved by rest. Any back pain associated with other symptoms calls for immediate medical attention.

Most forms of back pain respond to rest, but it is important not to lie on a sagging bed. You can get a lot of help from boards or planks slid under the mattress so that you are lying on a really firm support. So long as there is no hard pressure on your bony points you will soon come to appreciate this way of resting and this may be all you need to cure your backache. But do remember the importance of keeping your back muscles in good shape by regular exercise.

Pain in the big toe

See **Pain in the foot**.

Pain in the bones

Occasional aches and pains may seem to be situated in the bones, but fleeting pain of this kind is unlikely to indicate any real bone problem. Persistent boring pain in a constant site in a bone is a different matter. Most bone cancers start somewhere else in the body and reach the bone as part of a general spread of the cancer. Regrettably, by the time this has happened, the trouble is often far advanced. This kind of bone cancer may announce itself by a sudden, unexpected break in a bone that has been weakened by the tumour. Often there is bone pain and a hard swelling. Sometimes a single bone secondary is the only sign of spread of a cancer. In this case treatment may be effective.

Cancer that starts in the bone, although rare, usually

affects young people. If it does occur, early diagnosis is critically important, so there are a few things you should know about it. The most frequent sites are at the lower end of the thigh bone or the upper end of the lower leg bone. There is pain, tenderness to the touch and swelling. If this happens for no apparent reason in a child or young adult, the matter should be reported at once and an X-ray taken. Bone cancer shows up readily on X-ray. Remember that there are many more common causes of such symptoms and that bone cancer is somewhere near the bottom of the list, but one cannot take chances with such a dangerous condition. In recent years there have been remarkable advances in the treatment of primary bone cancers, but early diagnosis is usually essential if life is to be saved. **⚠**

Pain in the breast

Mastitis is inflammation of the breast. This nearly always affects women but may rarely occur in men.

Mastitis is nearly always an acute condition but it may rarely be persistent (chronic). Breast inflammation sometimes occurs as a result of infection elsewhere in the body, with spread by way of the blood, but a woman affected in this way will be obviously very ill. Acute mastitis can also occur as part of a mumps infection, from spread of mumps virus to the breast. This is uncommon. Chronic mastitis is rare and can result from infection with tuberculosis, syphilis and actinomycosis. The term 'chronic mastitis' is sometimes wrongly applied to a condition in which the breasts are of an irregular rubbery consistency and contain painful or tender nodules or cysts. This is not an inflammation and the condition, which is common, is not a mastitis. It is caused by an upset of the balance of the hormones that control the menstrual cycle and does not normally require treatment.

The common form of acute mastitis occurs during breast-feeding and is caused by infection that gains access through a crack or an abrasion in a nipple. The germs most commonly involved are *Staphylococcus aureus* – the same as those that cause boils and impetigo. The pain of acute mastitis may be quite severe, and it may be accompanied by high fever and, in the affected breast, localized redness, hardening and severe tenderness to touch. The 'glands' (lymph nodes) in the armpit swell up so that they can be felt, and become tender. Unless the infection is quickly controlled by effective antibiotic treatment, a breast abscess may form which will have to be opened and drained surgically.

Breast abscesses rarely occur except during breast feeding. The first stage in the development of an abscess is softening and local tissue death in one or more areas of the breast. Soon a collection of pus forms, surrounded by hardened and inflamed tissue. Such an abscess must be drained surgically. Milk production must be stopped by giving hormones or other drugs.

General breast tenderness and tension are normal features of breast feeding but there should never be pain. Any local tenderness, redness or pain must be reported at once. ⚠

Pain in the chest

Chest pain is a major source of concern to many people, especially to middle-aged men who are aware that central chest pain may signal heart trouble and quite rightly fear that this symptom may be of serious import. Chest pain, however, has many causes and the characteristics and quality of the pain differ in these different conditions. The most important causes of chest pain are:

- angina pectoris;
- heart attack;
- pleurisy;
- heartburn;
- duodenal ulcer;
- bronchitis;
- lung cancer;
- tuberculosis;
- shingles;

- chest wall injuries;
- Bornholm disease;
- secondary cancer, affecting the ribs.

Angina pectoris and the pain of heart attack (coronary thrombosis) are the most feared, but, contrary to the general belief, these are not identical. Anginal pain is always related to exercise and usually comes on after a fixed amount of exertion, such as walking a predictable distance. It is the result of heart muscle trying to work with an inadequate supply of blood because the arteries that supply the muscle – the coronary arteries – have become too narrow. It is of very variable intensity, even in the same person, and may be affected by the temperature, the weather, the state of mind and the condition of the digestion. The pain may be so mild as to be hardly a pain – more a feeling of uneasiness or pressure in the chest – or so severe as to arrest all action. It often causes breathlessness and belching. When the exertion ceases, the angina soon settles. Severe angina is very frightening. One medical sufferer commented that it was the only pain that made him fear he was going to die, or, if severe enough, that he was not going to die.

Angina can also be caused by brief periods of tightening (spasm) of the coronary arteries, irregularities in the heart beat or narrowing of the main outlet valve of the heart. It can also result from severe anaemia, which prevents the blood from carrying its full complement of oxygen, or from abnormal thickening of the blood.

Angina *never* lasts for more than a few minutes and is relieved by rest or by medication that widens the coronary arteries. If the symptom persists and you feel you are going to die, the chances are that a heart attack has occurred. In this case, a branch of a coronary artery has probably been closed off completely by blood clotting (coronary thrombosis) or by prolonged spasm. In a heart attack, the part of the heart muscle normally supplied with blood by the affected artery actually dies. If the area concerned is fairly small, the rest of the heart muscle can go on working and recovery is possible. The pain of coronary thrombosis may also sometimes be mild, but is usually a crushing agony which goes on and on and is accompanied by a conviction of impending death. It often radiates up into the jaw, through to the back and down the left arm. It is associated with severe restlessness and distress and there will seldom be any doubt that something serious has happened. These symptoms are an indication for the most urgent medical attention. Call an ambulance immediately and tell the operator that it is a case of heart attack. ⚠

Pleurisy causes a characteristic stabbing pain brought on by deep breathing. The pain is sudden and sharp and occurs at a certain point during breathing in at which the inflamed areas of the two surfaces of the pleura rub together. You may have a sense of something rubbing

and may be able to relieve the pain by changing position. There will usually be other signs of chest infection such as fever, cough and sputum.

The burning pain caused by *reflux* of stomach acid into the gullet (heartburn) may be felt in the centre or lower part of the chest and can be intense. It is unrelated to exercise but may be related to emotion or dietary indiscretion. It rises slowly to a peak and then usually subsides after a few minutes. It, too, may be associated with belching.

Duodenal ulcer causes chest pain, usually in the angle between the lower ribs. This pain is absent on waking, comes on in the middle of the morning and is relieved by food. It is depressing in the regularity of its recurrence, coming on again, with characteristically accurate timing, two or three hours after a meal. It often wakes you at one or two o'clock in the morning. The pain of a stomach ulcer differs in that it is caused – rather than relieved – by food.

Bronchitis is inflammation of the lining of the air tubes of the lungs (bronchi). Acute bronchitis generally follows a cold, sore throat, or influenza, usually in winter, and is very common in people with chronic bronchitis. It may also be brought on by smoking or by breathing a polluted atmosphere. There is a cough, at first dry but later with increasing amounts of sputum, fever for a few days, breathlessness and wheezing. There is commonly pain in the chest but the other symptoms are more prominent. In most cases bronchitis settles within a week or two, but there is always the risk, especially in cigarette smokers, that it may progress to chronic bronchitis with inevitable winter flare-ups. Chronic bronchitis is one of the forms of obstructive lung disease and is liable to become permanent with age and lead to progressive disablement. Recurrent attacks of bronchitis should always be taken seriously and properly treated, and the cause identified and avoided. Smoking is espe-cially dangerous in people with a persistent, productive cough.

Lung cancer nearly always starts on the lining of one of the air tubes (bronchi). It is one of the commonest forms of cancer and accounts for more than half of all male deaths from cancer. The enormous increase in the frequency of this kind of cancer is entirely attributable to the increase in cigarette smoking since the middle of the 20th century.

The cancer may take various forms and these offer different degrees of danger. The tumour may grow within the bronchus until it causes obstruction and collapse of the part of the lung beyond it, or it may eat its way through the wall to invade the surrounding lung tissue and even the chest wall. When this happens, the involvement of the nerves between the ribs, or of the ribs themselves, causes great pain. The tumour may spread into the partition between the lungs to involve the heart, the gullet, the trachea, the great veins returning blood to the heart, or the nerves to the voice box (larynx). The latter complication causes severe loss of the voice, and this may be the first sign of lung cancer. Spread also occurs to local lymph nodes and, by way of the bloodstream, to the bones, brain, skin, liver and other organs.

The presenting sign of lung cancer is usually a productive cough and there is often a little blood in the sputum. When a segment of a lung or a whole lung collapses there is breathlessness. Pain in the chest is common, especially if the cancer has spread to the lung lining (pleura) or the chest wall. Often the tumour is initially silent and the first indications are due to remote spread to other parts of the body. Spread to the brain can cause fits, paralysis, personality changes and speech problems. Spread to the liver may cause jaundice and loss of weight. Tumour spread to bone (secondaries) may cause a deep boring pain in the bones, sometimes even a spontaneous fracture. No-

dules of secondary cancer may occur in the skin.

X-ray examination usually shows a dense shadow corresponding to the solid tumour or an opaque segment corresponding to a collapsed lobe of the lung. Sometimes the diagnosis can only be made by examining the inside of the bronchi with a bronchoscope. If a tumour is seen, a sample (biopsy) is usually taken for examination. Cancer cells can sometimes be found in the sputum.

If the tumour is localized to one lobe or one lung, removing the lobe or lung by surgery offers the best chance of survival. Unfortunately, this applies only in about one case in five. Even in these cases, the five-year survival rate is only about 30 per cent. If there has been further spread, the outlook is poor and most patients can expect only a few months of life. Chemotherapy and radiotherapy may sometimes prolong life a little, but cannot cure the condition.

Tuberculosis, once a common cause of serious illness

and death is now largely restricted to the Third World and to people with AIDS. It is caused by the germ *Mycobacterium tuberculosis*, often called the tubercle bacillus. Tuberculosis can affect the lungs (pulmonary tuberculosis) or other parts of the body, such as the lymph nodes (tuberculous adenitis or scrofula), the skin and the bones. Lung tuberculosis is, in general, contracted from other people who cough out tubercle bacilli, while general (systemic) tuberculosis is usually derived from infected milk from cows with bovine tuberculosis. In most cases human lung infection is well localized, controlled by the immune system, and is symptomless. Active lung disease occurs if immunity drops.

The great majority of people have had a primary infection with tuberculosis, as is shown by a positive tuberculin skin test. Those who are tuberculin negative are more susceptible and may benefit from BCG inoculation. Tubercle bacilli can remain dormant for years before producing active disease.

Symptoms of pulmonary tuberculosis include chest pain, fever, fatigue, loss of appetite and weight, night sweats and persistent cough. Sputum may be streaked with blood. Tuberculous pleurisy leads to an accumulation of fluid in the pleural cavity and partial collapse of the lung. Occasionally, the destructive process in the lung may involve a large artery, causing massive haemorrhage. Tuberculosis may spread widely throughout the body (miliary tuberculosis). Tuberculous meningitis is another dangerous complication.

Tuberculosis is treated with various regimens of drugs in combination. Isoniazid, para-aminosalicylic acid (PAS), rifampicin, ethambutol, pyrazinamide and streptomycin all have their place in the now highly effective management of this disease. Treatment is generally needed for 9 to 12 months.

Shingles is an important cause of chest or abdominal

pain. It has special features that make it easy to distinguish from other causes of pain (see **Skin tingling and with painful blisters around the flank**).

Bornholm disease, also known as epidemic pleurodynia, epidemic myalgia, or the 'Devil's grip', is caused by a *coxsackie* virus. The condition was first described after an outbreak on the Danish island of Bornholm. It causes sudden attacks of severe pain in the central lower chest and upper abdomen, with headache, fever, sore throat and general upset. These attacks may occur repeatedly over a period of several weeks, causing much anxiety. Bornholm disease is commonest in children and tends to occur in epidemics. Isolated cases, however, often cause much concern for the symptoms may be severe and may mimic more dangerous conditions. The virus can be obtained and identified from the throat or from a stool sample. There is no specific treatment but recovery is eventually complete.

Chest pain may also be caused by secondary deposits of cancerous tissue in the ribs from a primary tumour elsewhere in the body. The primary tumour is most commonly in the breast, womb, colon or prostate gland. Cancer that has spread remotely to bone is, of course, a very serious matter but, even so, the earlier it is diagnosed the better. Life can often be considerably prolonged by treatment.

You should always ensure that unexplained chest pain is investigated. The majority of cases are not due to serious causes, but unless the cause is obvious, it is not a symptom you can safely ignore.

Pain in the ear

Earache is very common, especially in children. There are several possible causes and these include:

- middle ear pressure problems;
- middle ear infection (otitis media);
- external ear infection (otitis externa).

200

Pain in the ear is most commonly caused by an alteration in the pressure in the middle ear due to failure of the normal pressure equalizing mechanism. This mechanism relies on the free movement of air in and out of the middle ear, by way of the eustachian tube which runs from the back of the throat to the middle ear on each side. This painful, and sometimes damaging, alteration in pressure is called *barotrauma* and it usually relates to a change in atmospheric pressure. This can occur during flying or scuba diving or sometimes when passing through a tunnel in a car. The eustachian tube normally allows the pressure in each middle ear to equalize with the external air pressure. Opening of the tubes is actuated by swallowing. But if the eustachian tubes are blocked as a result of a cold, or are obstructed by adenoids the valve will not work. In this case a drop in the atmospheric pressure will cause the ear drum to bulge painfully outward, and a rise will force it inwards. Baro-

trauma can also affect the sinuses around the nose, causing persistent pain if their drainage channels are blocked.

If you have a bad head cold try to avoid flying if possible. If you experience barotrauma, try vigorous swallowing. If swallowing doesn't work you can try breathing out while closing your mouth and pinching your nose. A nasal spray or nose drops containing a decongestant drug may help. Most cases, although unpleasant, are not dangerous and the symptoms will usually pass within a matter of hours. If they do not, see a doctor.

If a child has swollen adenoids or inflammatory swelling of the nose lining, the tube may become temporarily blocked and air cannot pass into the middle ear. When the middle ear is closed off in this way, the air within it is soon absorbed into the blood circulating in its lining walls. The higher external atmospheric pressure then forces the ear drum painfully inwards. Earache from this cause can be relieved by any measure that relieves eustachian obstruction. Nasal decongestants can help, but it may sometimes be necessary to remove the adenoids or tonsils.

Eustachian obstruction also interferes with fluid drainage of the middle ear and may lead to infection of the middle ear (otitis media). This is another common cause of earache resulting from pressure effects on the drum but, in this case, the drum is forced outward by the accumulation of pus and watery discharge in the middle ear.

Pain in the ear also commonly results from inflammation in the external ear passage (otitis externa). Here, the skin is tightly bound down to the underlying tissue and there is little room for expansion. A small boil in the external passage is exquisitely painful. Infection of the skin of the passage, by viruses, bacteria or fungi is a frequent cause of earache. Most cases of otitis externa are caused by injudicious poking with hairpins,

matches or paperclips, so that the skin surface is damaged and infection introduced.

Pain in the elbow

Tennis elbow is the term generally given to inflammation in the region of the bony prominence on the outer side of the elbow from which several forearm muscle tendons arise. Excessive use of the muscles which extend the wrist causes trauma at this point. There is pain and tenderness in the elbow, on the thumb side, and in the back of the forearm, made worse by use of the elbow and hand. Inflammation of the corresponding bump on the inner side of the elbow is called *golfer's elbow*. The treatment involves avoiding the activity (tennis or whatever) which caused the problem for a while plus rest, support, painkillers and anti-inflammatory drugs. If the inflammation resulted from playing sport, professional advice on technique may be necessary.

Elbow pain can also be unrelated to any elbow problem

but may be pain referred from a disorder of the neck part of the spine called *cervical spondylosis*. This is a degeneration of the neck bones with lipping of the edges that may be so extreme as to press on the nerves coming out of the spinal cord. If a nerve affected in this way goes to the elbow, pain will be felt there. Cervical spondylosis can also cause wrist pain.

Other causes of elbow pain include rheumatoid arthritis (see **Pain in the joints, generally**) and inflammation of the fibrous capsule of the joint. This is called *olecranon bursitis*. Septic arthritis must be drained surgically and sometimes an enlarged bursa (lump) will need to be removed.

Pain in the eye

You should remember that while a simple pink eye (conjunctivitis) can cause quite severe irritation, it never causes actual pain. Real eye pain – usually a dull ache felt within the eye – must always be taken seriously and investigated. This is especially so if the pain is associated with any disturbance of vision.

Eye pain may be caused by a range of conditions. All are important. They include:

- foreign body in the eye;
- corneal abrasion;
- other corneal injuries;
- corneal ulcer;
- internal inflammation (uveitis);
- acute glaucoma.

If you have a foreign body in your eye, you will probably be aware of the cause of the pain. Remember, however, that foreign bodies often lodge high under the upper lid and press painfully on the cornea. Such a foreign body may be revealed if you look down while pulling up the lid. You will probably need help. If this relieves the pain, the chances are that a foreign body is present. Your upper lid can be folded up over a matchstick but only if you continue to look down while this is being done. If a foreign body is present it can usually be picked off with the corner of a folded piece of paper or a clean handkerchief. Never let anyone use a needle or other sharp or hard object. Don't try to remove a foreign body from the cornea. See your doctor as soon as possible. ▲

The cornea is the clear outer lens of the eye. It has a thin outer skin, the epithelium, that covers the many sensitive nerves in the cornea. Loss of this epithelium layer is called a *corneal abrasion.* This exposes the sensory nerves to strong stimulation by every movement of the lids. Even gentle blinking may be extremely painful. The sensation is almost indistinguishable from that of having a sharp piece of grit under an eyelid and you may be convinced that there is a foreign body in the eye. Abrasion may be caused by any mechanical trauma, such as a scratch by a baby's fingernail, or by ultraviolet light (UVL) radiation, whether from an electric arc lamp, a sun-tan lamp or excessive sun at high altitudes. Such UVL can damage the outer layer of the cornea. This layer tends to strip off, exposing the nerve endings and causing severe pain. This may affect unprotected amateur welders, some hours after exposure. Skiers or mountaineers may suffer a similar effect – in this case, the condition is known as 'snow blindness'.

Most cases of abrasion occur, however, because of lack of oxygen to the cornea as a result of overwear of hard contact lenses. You may be unable to avoid tight spasm of the lids, which makes the pain worse, and there will be copious weeping. A neglected abrasion may become infected and progress to ulceration. Corneal abrasions are treated by padding the eye for two or three days and by using antibiotic drops to prevent infection. You should stop wearing your contact lenses for two or three weeks.

If your cornea is deprived of the normal protection of the blink reflex it soon becomes severely damaged. This occurs in any condition in which the lids cannot close to cover the cornea. Corneal exposure is always serious and leads to rapid drying and opacification with severe loss of vision.

Chemical injuries to the cornea can result from acid or alkali splashes. Alkali on the cornea is especially dangerous as it rapidly sinks in, causing massive and spreading tissue destruction. Many have been permanently blinded by accidental or deliberate spraying with ammonia and other alkalis. Only immediate and prolonged flushing with large volumes of water is likely to save sight in such cases. ⚠

If the cornea becomes infected a crater (ulcer) will form. This is very painful because the nerves are stimulated. An ulcer that is central can damage vision, and an ulcer that goes deep may penetrate the cornea. This is a serious and sight-destroying complication. One of the commonest infecting organisms is the cold sore or genital herpes virus, herpes simplex. This is acquired by kissing and contact and, once established in the cornea, is probably present for life.

Herpes simplex causes the characteristic branching *dendritic ulcer* with pain, watering and foreign body sensation. Properly treated within a few days of onset, the condition can be cured, but if such an ulcer is treated with steroid eye ointments or drops, it may become established and cause years of distress.

Gonorrhoea can cause a dangerous corneal ulcer, liable to perforate rapidly. Similarly, various fungi can lead to very persistent ulcers. These are uncommon and the diagnosis may be missed unless the condition is suspected and scrapings are examined. Contact lens wearers sometimes develop corneal infection and ulceration from an organism called *Acanthamoeba* which grows in contact lens solutions and containers not properly sterilized.

Uveitis is an inflammation of the eye's iris, the surrounding focusing muscle and sometimes the layer under the retina. Uvea is the Greek word for a peeled black grape and this is what the eye looks like with the white outer coat (the sclera) removed. Acute uveitis is not an infection, but usually an immunological problem. The pupil on the affected side is smaller than on the other and often has an irregular outline. The iris may appear to be a slightly different colour from the healthy one. Vision is blurred or misted and there is, almost always, a dull to severe aching pain in the eye itself.

Treatment is urgent because in uveitis the iris forms adhesions to the front surface of the crystalline lens behind it and if these become firm, permanent damage will result. Such adhesions can cause the serious condition of acute glaucoma and must be avoided at all costs. ▲ Glaucoma is an eye disorder in which the pressure of the fluid within the eyeball is too high.

The commonest glaucoma – chronic simple glaucoma – does *not* cause pain (see **Vision lost to the sides**). There is, however, another kind of glaucoma in which the outlet obstruction is caused by mechanical or disease processes in the eye. In this type the effects may be much more sudden and severe, with great pain and sudden loss of all vision. This is the case in acute congestive glaucoma or in glaucomas caused by inflammatory eye disease with adhesions (see **Vision lost in a painful red eye**). The symptoms of acute glaucoma are very severe and you are unlikely to be in any doubt that a serious condition has arisen. The affected eye is acutely painful, intensely red and congested, and very hard and tender to the touch. The pupil is enlarged and oval and the cornea steamy and partly opaque. The vision is grossly diminished. There is shock and sometimes pain in the abdomen. Urgent treatment, to reduce the pressure is needed, so no time must be wasted. ▲

A less severe, but commoner form – sub-acute glaucoma – causes symptoms which you should know about. These usually occur at night when the pupils are wide. There is a dull aching pain in the eye, some fogginess of vision, and, characteristically, concentric, rainbow-coloured rings are seen around lights. You should never ignore these symptoms, for repeated sub-acute attacks can damage the eye and there is always the risk of a devastating attack of acute glaucoma. The condition can easily be prevented by using eyedrops and cured by a simple operation or outpatient laser procedure.

Pain in the face

Excluding toothache, facial pain is usually due to one of the following causes:

- sinusitis;
- a disorder of the nerves of the face (neuralgia).

Sinusitis is inflammation, almost always from infection, of the linings of the bone cavities of the face (the sinuses). This is often a complication, due to secondary bacterial infection, of the common cold. The inflammation of the mucous membrane lining causes swelling and this may lead to obstruction of the narrow outlet so that mucus and pus cannot easily escape. The result is a feeling of fullness or even pain, which is felt in the forehead, cheeks or between the eyes, depending on which sinuses are affected. Severe sinusitis causes fever and general upset. The symptoms are usually compounded with those of the associated common cold.

Complications of sinusitis are rare and any tendency for the infection to spread to adjacent bone can usually be easily controlled by antibiotics.

The most severe and distressing form of facial pain is called *trigeminal neuralgia*. This is a poorly understood disorder in which sudden nerve impulse discharges occur in the sensory nerve of the face – the fifth, or trigeminal, cranial nerve – on one side. These discharges cause episodes of excruciating stabbing pain in the cheek, lips, gums, chin or tongue lasting for only a few seconds or, at the most, a minute or two, but usually so intense that the affected person has to stop whatever he or she is doing. The severity of the pain causes the muscles of the face to wince, hence the earlier name of *tic douloureux* meaning 'painful twitch'.

The condition affects middle-aged and elderly people, almost exclusively, causing repeated attacks over periods of several weeks. During these periods, the affected person may be constantly 'on edge' in anticipation of the next stab of pain. There is a tendency for the periods of freedom between series of attacks to become shorter with time.

A feature of the condition is that it may be brought on by touching a particular part of the face or any other area supplied by the trigeminal nerve, such as the lips, gums or tongue. It may thus be precipitated by chewing, swallowing or even speaking.

The cause of trigeminal neuralgia is uncertain and treatment is difficult. The drug carbamazepine (Tegretol) is effective in most cases, but about 20 per cent of sufferers develop resistance and some are unable to tolerate a high enough dosage to relieve the pain. When drug treatment fails, an injection to destroy the root of the nerve, or even cutting the nerve surgically, may be necessary. These procedures cause permanent numbness of one side of the face and complications are common. See also **Pain in the joint of the jaw** and **Pain in the head (headache)**.

Pain in the foot

There are several causes of foot pain. Some of them are obvious. They include:

- bunion;
- march fracture;
- fallen arches;
- rigid toe;
- nerve entrapment;
- gout;
- heel problems;
- soft tissue problems.

One of the commonest causes of foot pain is bunion. The medical term for the condition that leads to bunion is *hallux valgus*. This is a very common deformity, caused by unsuitable footwear, in which the big toe is angled outwards away from the midline of the body (this is what valgus means), so that the head of the nearer toe bone forms a prominent bump on the inner edge of the foot. Sometimes the deflected toe rides over or under the other toes.

Hallux valgus leads to the formation of an inflamed pressure swelling (bursitis) over the prominence – the condition known as a bunion. Although some feet are so shaped as to be more prone to this than normal, most cases are the result of a triumph of fashion over common sense – unsuitably pointed footwear. Continued pressure on the bursa will cause the bunion to become inflamed and very painful and without treatment the condition can only get worse.

Don't neglect bunions. A change to sensible shoes, and a toe pad to straighten the big toe, may be all that is necessary. Removing a bunion doesn't help as a new one will soon form. In cases

of severe hallux valgus, surgery is usually necessary to correct the deformity.

Bunion is fairly obvious, but you may not be aware of the cause of pain that results from a hairline 'march' fracture of one of the long bones of the foot (metatarsal bones). This may be caused, as the name implies, by excessive trauma in walking.

Another common cause of foot pain is 'fallen arches' – a lay term for a flat foot or *pes planus*. There are two arches in each foot – from toe to heel and from side to side. Loss of these upward curves does not necessarily cause symptoms, but many people with fallen arches have hot, stiff, uncomfortable and painful feet, especially on prolonged standing or walking. The elastic 'heel then toe' gait is lost and, eventually, walking becomes an inelegant, awkward and painful stamping process.

Flat feet are due, essentially, to a relative weakness of the muscles of the lower legs which, by way of their tendons, support the upwardly curved arches of the bones of the feet. Insufficient upward pull on the arches throws the full strain on the foot ligaments and these soon stretch. Excessive muscular fatigue and overweight contribute to the problem. So long as the arches of the feet remain flexible and mobile, much can be done to control the condition – wearing suitable footwear, exercises, arch supports, weight control and avoiding undue strain. Rigid fallen arches, with secondary damage to the joints and the bones, is beyond redemption, but the feet can be made more comfortable by surgical fusion of painful joints.

Foot and ankle pain are often caused by rheumatoid arthritis and osteoarthritis. Rheumatoid arthritis will often lead to severe foot deformities.

Hallux rigidus is a form of osteoarthritis in which the big toe joint cannot bend backwards properly during walking. This arthritis may be the result of injury, gout or the cartilage disorder osteochondritis dissecans. This condition leads to the release of small fragments of cartilage or bone (loose bodies) into the interior of the joint, causing swelling, pain and restriction of movement. Because the toe cannot bend back, walking is very painful. Joint replacement may be needed.

Morton's metatarsalgia is a cause of foot pain, especially in women of 40 to 50. There is sharp pain in the forefoot that extends forwards to the toes. The trouble is caused by a nerve being trapped between the long bones of the foot, usually between the third and fourth space from the big toe side. The affected nerve becomes thickened and surgery may be necessary.

Gout is an acute joint disease caused by monosodium urate monohydrate crystals desposited around the joints, tendons and other tissues of the body. This affects the joints of the big toe more often than any other joint, and is an important cause of acute foot pain. The crystals in the joint cause severe inflammation and tissue damage. Crystal deposition occurs when the levels of uric acid in the body are abnormally high. The commonest cause for this is that the kidneys fail to excrete uric acid fast enough. The reason for this is still unclear, but seems to be genetically determined – 75 per cent of cases are caused in this way. In about 20 per cent of cases gout is caused by excessive production of uric acid. A relatively rare cause is a sex-linked genetically determined error of metabolism of a group of substances found in the nuclei of cells called *purines*. Uric acid is a purine and is relatively insoluble in water. Any excess, therefore, tends to lead to the formation of crystals.

Gout usually begins with excruciating pain and inflammation of the innermost joint of the big toe. Less often, it starts in the ankle, the knee joint, a joint in the foot, hand, wrist or, least often, an elbow. If untreated, the attack lasts for days or weeks but eventually subsides. Some people have one attack only, or attacks at intervals of years. More commonly, attacks are recurrent with increasing frequency until the condition is constantly present.

Full investigation to establish the cause is important. The mainstay of treatment is non-steroidal anti-inflammatory drugs (NSAIDs), such as indomethacin or naproxen, used at the earliest possible stage and continued until the attack subsides and for a week or so afterwards. Colchicine, extracted from the crocus, is a highly effective drug but may cause side-effects. Gout can be prevented long term by the use of the drug allopurinol which lowers the levels of uric acid in the blood. This must not be used until several weeks after an acute attack.

Pain in the heel may be due to a prominent bony knob on the back of the heel bone causing pressure against the shoes. If necessary, this knob can be chiselled off. Heel pain may also occur from traction strain at the point at which the Achilles tendon is fixed to the bone. This is common in athletes. Rupture of the Achilles tendon is fairly common. Foot pain may also result from inflammation of the sheet of tendon under the skin of the sole of the foot. This is called *plantar fasciitis*.

Pain in the hand

Hand pain may result from obvious causes such as fractures of the palm bones (metacarpals) or from deep infection of the soft tissues. If the palm of your hand becomes inflamed, swollen and red, you need urgent treatment if permanent damage is to be avoided. ⚠ Hand pain is also commonly caused by osteoarthritis or rheumatoid arthritis or by cervical spondylosis (see **Pain in the neck**).

The carpal tunnel is a restricted space at the front of the wrist, bounded by ligaments, through which pass the tendons that flex the fingers and wrist. This space is roofed over by a tough ligament, called the *flexor retinaculum*, which prevents the tendons from pulling away from the wrist when it is bent. One of the two sensory nerves to the hand, the med-

ian nerve, also passes through the carpal tunnel and there is little or no room for expansion. Any swelling in the region, from any cause, will, therefore, tend to compress the median nerve and interfere with the conduction of nerve impulses. The result is numbness, tingling and sometimes pain in the half of the hand on the thumb side which is supplied by the nerve. This is called *carpal tunnel syndrome* and it may be associated with excessive occupational use of the wrist. In rheumatoid arthritis, pituitary gland growth hormone overproduction (acromegaly) and underaction of the thyroid gland (myxoedema) it is thickening of the overlying ligament which causes the problem. There is also a familiar variety, for some reason mainly affecting large numbers of people of Swiss origin living in Indiana, in which a substance called *amyloid* is deposited in the tunnel.

The syndrome often occurs for no obvious reason but is commonest in women, especially in pregnant women or those taking oral contraceptives. It is also associated with the premenstrual syndrome. When severe, it may be relieved by a surgical operation to cut the ligament overlying the tunnel. Surgical inspection of an opened carpal tunnel often shows a deep compression mark on the median nerve.

Pain in the head (headache)

Headache is one of the commonest of all symptoms. Most headaches are stress-induced and arise from mental tension reflected in long-sustained tightness (spasm) of muscle in your scalp or neck. Many are due to migraine, some to fatigue, emotional upset or alcohol and a few to allergy. Eye strain is not a frequent cause of headache, as many people seem to think. Very few headaches are due to organic diseases like brain tumours or aneurysms (see below), high blood pressure, sinus infections, encephalitis or mastoiditis. Put all together, this latter group con-

stitutes only about one per cent of all headaches.

Headaches must be taken very seriously, however, if they are accompanied by any of the following signs or symptoms:

- fever;
- neck stiffness;
- a change in the clarity of your vision;
- loss, for more than 20 minutes, of part of your field of vision;
- a recent drooping eyelid;
- a painful red eye with blurred vision;
- sudden projectile vomiting;
- tenderness and redness in either temple;
- weakness in any part of your body.

You must also be concerned if the headache came on suddenly, is very severe and persistent and you can think of no obvious cause. Take this very seriously and get urgent medical advice if you have had a recent head injury, however minor, and you feel unusually drowsy. People with high blood pressure should be particularly wary of new and severe headaches. ▲

If you are having trouble with your vision, see an optician. If you think you have sinusitis or if the pain is really in an eye rather than in your head, see your doctor.

Migraine is not so common as the usage of the term would suggest. Many headaches so described are not migraines. The term comes from the words 'hemicranial', meaning 'half-head' so if the pain is all over your head, it isn't a classical migraine. Typically, a migraine starts with sparkly edged loss of vision affecting part of the field of vision and lasting for about 20 minutes. After that, you may get a nasty headache on one side and will probably want to lie down in a dark room. You may feel very nauseated and might vomit. The headache may last for hours or, rarely, days.

Migraine can also feature more alarming symptoms such as weakness on one side of your body, difficulty in speaking or in understanding what words mean. If you get symptoms of this sort you shouldn't worry too much, but you should certainly consult your doctor. In fact, it is probably a good idea to do so anyway – there are some very effective migraine remedies and you are probably suffering more than you need. Also, your doctor may well give you advice on how to avoid attacks.

Tumours originating in the brain are rare. The majority of brain cancers arise elsewhere in the body and spread to the brain in the bloodstream. These are called secondary tumours. Primary brain tumours start in the brain or in its surrounding membranes. Tumours that have spread from primary cancers elsewhere – such as in the breast, colon or prostate gland – imply fairly advanced disease, so that the brain tumour is not necessarily the main problem. In such cases, body scanning will usually show that the cancer has also spread to other parts of the body, such as the bones.

Tumours originating in the brain or its coverings are often

non-malignant and do not actually invade the tissues. But they are always serious because there is no room for expansion inside the skull, and any expanding process will compress, and probably damage, essential brain substance. Malignant tumours are even more dangerous because of the way they spread into, and destroy, brain tissue. This makes them very difficult to remove without the sacrifice of much brain substance.

The symptoms of brain tumours include headache, loss of part of the field of vision, weakness, speech difficulties, loss of sensation in various parts of the body, loss of the mental powers and epileptic seizures. If a brain tumour is growing rapidly there may be very severe headache and an unusual kind of sudden, unexpected, violent vomiting called *projectile vomiting*. Any such symptoms should, of course, be reported immediately. ⚠

An aneurysm is a swelling bulge on an artery. This can occur in the network of arteries on the underside of the brain. Aneurysms on the brain vessels are often the result of a weakness present at birth. Typically they cause no symptoms for years, but if they start to enlarge or if they rupture the effects are very serious. Pressure on nearby nerves may cause double vision from paralysis of the eye-moving muscles, widening of the pupil or drooping of the upper eyelid. A ruptured brain aneurysm causes severe headache and damage to nearby brain structures with resulting severe loss of function, unconsciousness and even death. The bleeding from a ruptured aneurysm is called a *subarachnoid haemorrhage* and this is the main cause of stroke in young adults.

Encephalitis is inflammation of the brain. Most cases are caused by infection, especially by viruses such as herpes simplex, herpes zoster, polioviruses, echoviruses or coxsackie viruses. Herpes encephalitis is rare except in the case of children whose immune systems have been compromised by natural immune deficiency, by AIDS or by

215

necessary medical treatment. The other forms tend to occur in epidemics and may follow mumps, measles, rubella and chickenpox.

Encephalitis causes severe headache, fever, vomiting, sickness, often a stiff neck and back, and epileptic fits, and may progress to mental confusion and coma. A fatal outcome may occur within hours of onset, but even gravely ill patients may make a full recovery. Drugs like acyclovir have changed the outlook in cases of herpes simplex encephalitis. Long-term effects are sometimes serious and may include mental retardation, epilepsy and deafness.

Most headaches may safely be self-treated, but do read the above exceptions first. Don't just take painkillers as a substitute for taking the trouble to try to find and remove the cause. Consider the possibility of obvious causes like:

- neck strain from poor posture;
- tension from unnecessary long concentration;

- poor lighting conditions at work;
- an unsuitable job;
- hatred of your boss.

Try to analyse the cause of your headache and take appropriate action. Check, if you can, whether you can detect factors or foods that bring on a headache. Learn to relax. Avoid excessive fatigue but don't sleep too much either. Biofeedback is one way of learning how to relax and prevent the muscle spasm that causes the pain.

Simple over-the-counter painkillers comprising aspirin, paracetamol, and ibuprofen may, in general, be safely used, in moderate dose, for headache. Don't give aspirin to children and don't take it if there is any risk of bleeding anywhere. Paracetamol, in excess, is a killer. Tension headaches don't respond well to simple painkillers as they are often a feature of depression or other emotional problems. If you think your headaches are of this kind, see your doctor as you may need antidepressant drugs or psychotherapy.

Pain in the hip

Hip pain in young children may be due to the condition of *Perthes' disease*. This is a degeneration of the head of the thigh bone (femur) caused by a loss of its blood supply so that part of the head of the femur dies. Boys are affected much more often than girls and the condition usually affects children aged 4 to 8 years. There is complaint of pain and obvious limping and the child is reluctant to move the hip joint. This condition requires careful medical management.

In adults, a slipped disc can cause nerve root pressure that is referred to the hip. There will, however, usually be back pain also and there may be pain down the back of the leg on the affected side (sciatica). Hip pain may also be due to osteoarthritis or rheumatoid arthritis or to inflammation of the tendons or the fibrous capsule surrounding the hip joints. It may be due to a nearby hernia.

One of the commonest causes of hip pain in older people is osteoarthritis of the hip joint. Rheumatoid arthritis also commonly affects this joint. These two conditions are usually so severe and disabling that they justify total hip replacement (see **Pain in the joints, generally**).

Another common cause, especially in elderly women, is a fracture of the neck of the thigh bone. This is very commonly due to osteoporosis (see **Brittle bones**). There should be no avoidable delay in getting expert treatment to fix the fracture. Hip replacement may be necessary if the blood supply to the head of the femur is lost as a result of the fracture.

Pain in the joints, generally

Several general conditions cause joint pain, the most important being:

- osteoarthritis;
- rheumatoid arthritis;
- rheumatic fever;
- gout.

Osteoarthritis is a degenerative joint disorder involving

damage to the cartilage-covered bearing surfaces and sometimes widening or remodelling of the ends of the bones involved in the joint. Osteoarthritis is the commonest form of arthritis and the cause is unknown. It is, however, commonly associated with injury or deformities of the skeleton which disturb the normal mechanics of the joints and the relationships of the joint surfaces. Obesity is an important aggravating factor. Although 'arthritis' in the name suggests inflammation, there is little of this. Bony spurs often develop at the margins of the affected joints.

Osteoarthritis is closely related to ageing and many people of 30 show early osteoarthritic changes. By age 65, about 80 per cent of people have some objective evidence of the disorder, but only a quarter of these have symptoms. In the elderly, women tend to be more severely affected than men. Osteoarthritis most commonly involves the spine, the knee joints and the hip joints. Symptoms come on gradually, with pain which at first is intermittent and then becomes more frequent. Joint movement becomes progressively more limited, at first because of pain and muscle spasm but later because the joint capsule becomes thickened and less flexible. Movement may cause audible creaking, and swelling results from quite minor injury.

Short of joint replacement, there is no specific remedy for osteoarthritis, but much can be done to relieve the symptoms. It is important to avoid undue stress or injury to the joints. Losing excess weight is also very helpful. Rubber heels can reduce jarring and a walking stick can be valuable. A change of occupation may be necessary. In some cases, injection of corticosteroids into the affected joint can markedly reduce pain and disability.

Rheumatoid arthritis is a general disease of unknown cause that affects one to three per cent of the population. The usual age of onset is between 30 and 40, but the disease may start at any age and may even involve children (juvenile rheumatoid arthritis or Still's disease). Women are affected three times as often as men and about 16 per cent of the female population over 65 have the disease. The cause remains unclear, but there appears to be a genetic predisposition and an immunological disorder, probably triggered by an infection. No causal organisms have been identified, but all sufferers have antiglobulin antibodies circulating in their blood. These are called *rheumatoid factors* and are important in making the diagnosis. The great majority of people with swollen and painful joints do not have rheumatoid arthritis.

Rheumatoid arthritis causes joint deformities and disability as a result of a long-term destructive process affecting typically the small joint of the fingers and hands, but progressing to involve the wrists, elbows, shoulders and other joints. The finger joints near the palms of the hands are affected rather than those near the tips, and this causes a characteristic 'spindle-like' appearance. There is constant pain, and spasm of the muscles that contributes to the deformity. The fingers become deviated to the side of the little finger with tight bending of the joints near the tips and extension of those nearest the hand. Clawing of the toes and other foot distortion also occurs.

Rheumatoid arthritis doesn't only affect the joints. There is loss of appetite (anorexia) and weight, lethargy, muscle pain, the development of nodules under the skin, tendon inflammation, bursitis, and often eye inflammation, which may be severe and damaging. The condition may also be complicated by inflammation of the heart coverings (pericarditis), inflammation of blood vessels (vasculitis), anaemia, and cold fingers with sequential colour change (Raynaud's phenomenon). Sjögren's syndrome – with dryness of the mouth, eyes and genitalia – is often associated with rheumatoid arthritis.

As the cause is unknown, treatment is limited to controlling inflammation and complications and relieving pain. This may involve the use of drugs, rest, splinting, physiotherapy and even surgery. Corticosteroids can have a dramatic effect, lasting for weeks or months, but can lead to further joint destruction and other important side-effects. Non-steroidal anti-inflammatory drugs are widely used, as is aspirin in large dosage for those who can tolerate it. The anti-malarial drug chloroquine can be valuable, but, in the dosage needed, may damage the retina unless monitored carefully. Penicillamine and gold are also widely used, but both have side-effects. The immunosuppressive drugs azathioprine, cyclophosphamide and methotrexate are used in severe cases. These are powerful drugs with potential dangers and must be carefully monitored.

The outcome in rheumatoid arthritis is very variable. About one quarter of affected people enjoy full remission within 10 years and 40 per cent suffer only moderate disability. About 10 per cent become severely disabled.

In spite of the name, rheumatic fever does not seriously affect the joints, and, although a passing arthritis does occur, this does not produce any permanent disability. Rheumatic fever is important because it frequently damages the heart. The commonest and most serious effect is scarring of the valves, with narrowing (stenosis) or leakage (incompetence). This may seriously interfere with the heart's action and severely affects health. Heart valve replacement may, eventually, be necessary. The nervous system may also be involved, causing 'St Vitus' dance' (Sydenham's chorea) which features uncontrollable, jerky movements of the limbs and body, usually accompanied by emotional upset. Rheumatic fever always follows a throat infection with a particular strain of streptococcus – the Group A haemolytic strep. It can always be prevented by prompt treatment of the throat infection with antibiotics.

The early acute stage of rheumatic fever is treated with bed rest, aspirin, sodium salicylate and corticosteroids, after antibiotics have been used to destroy any streptococci present. Children who have had rheumatic fever should be protected from further damage by long-term preventive (prophylactic) penicillin, taken until they are about 20 years of age. Sydenham's chorea is helped by tranquillizer drugs and sedatives.

Joint pain can also be caused by gout (see **Pain in the foot**) and by other forms of arthritis that occur in conjunction with various general diseases such as Reiter's syndrome, psoriasis, inflammatory bowel disease, Lyme disease, meningococcal infections, gonorrhoea, syphilis and tuberculosis.

Pain in the joint of the jaw

Many people do not appreciate that the joint around which the lower jaw moves is high up in front of the ear. You can feel the movement if you put a finger on your face immediately in front of the bump of the ear and then open your mouth widely. *Temporomandibular joint syndrome* is the name given to a condition that features pain in this joint and in the surrounding areas on opening the mouth or eating. This condition is thought to be due to spasm of the chewing muscles as a result of emotional tension. It is one of the more obscure causes of headache, facial pain and pain in the ear.

Pain in the knee

Knee pain due to arthritis is not usually localized to one spot but is felt generally in the knee and is made worse by movement and weight-bearing. Arthritis, whether rheumatoid arthritis or osteoarthritis, features long-term swelling. Localized pain suggests a torn cartilage or a torn ligament and there will usually be a history of injury. A torn cartilage usually causes painful locking of the knee and a torn ligament will allow the knee to 'give way' unexpectedly. If the knee is so unstable that you are liable to fall down, you probably have a dislocated kneecap.

Osgood-Schlatter disease is a knee disorder affecting mostly boys, usually around puberty. The bulky group of muscles on the front of the thigh run down together into a heavy tendon which contains the kneecap and which is inserted into a bony lump on the front of the main bone of the lower leg (the tibia). The repetitive strong pulls on this tendon, as the knee is straightened against resistance (an inevitable occurrence in normal boyhood activity), sometimes cause damage at the point of insertion of the tendon. Some authorities believe this to be due to interference with the blood supply of the region. There is swelling of the upper end of the tibia and sometimes acute tenderness on pressure. Fortunately, the problem resolves rapidly with no more treatment than avoiding for a while activities such as climbing, cycling and playing rugby. If these are persisted in, an unsightly protuberance may develop below the knee. In severe cases a plaster cast to prevent bending may be required.

Knee pain may also be caused by secondary bone cancer, occurring as a remote spread (metastasis) from a primary cancer in another organ. Primary bone cancer – cancer arising in the bone – may take several different forms, but the most important is the osteogenic sarcoma. This usually appears at the lower end of the thigh bone (femur) just above the knee and, happily, is rare, affecting only about one person in 1,000,000. It is, however, very serious. It occurs most often in young adults. The first indication is bone pain, especially at night. Such pain, occurring for no obvious reason in a young adult, should never be ignored for there are few other symptoms until a late stage –

at which the chances of cure are remote. ⚠ Often, the next sign is cough, fever and chest pain, suggesting pneumonia, but actually caused by secondary spread of the cancer to the lungs. The tumour forms a swelling in the bone and the X-ray often shows radiating spicules of bone in the ominous 'sun-ray' pattern known to all doctors.

A major advance in treatment has occurred in recent years and this has improved the five-year survival rate from about one person in five to better than one in two. The drugs adriamycin and methotrexate, in conjunction with amputation and radiotherapy, have greatly improved the outlook. In addition, recent immunological studies have shown that the tumour has antigenic properties which can be attacked by specific antibodies. Loss of the limb has been avoided in some cases by a bone graft from a dead donor.

Pain in the muscles

Muscle pain is very common and has many causes. The most common and important of these are:

- muscle cramps;
- muscle spasms;
- pain during exertion (claudication);
- muscle compartment syndrome;
- polymyalgia rheumatica;
- muscle inflammation (myositis).

Muscle pain is medically known as *myalgia*. Most people suffer occasional myalgia after strenuous or unaccustomed exertion or after taking up a new physical activity. Such muscle pain can be expected to settle quickly but you should always be wary of being too enthusiastic when exercising before your body has adapted to the new level of muscular use. This is especially important if you are not in the first bloom of youth.

Many people suffer severely from muscle cramps. In cramp, a single muscle, or a group of muscles, suddenly goes into a state of powerful sustained contraction. This incapacitating state is quickly followed by severe pain which persists until the contraction eases off. Cramp is often caused by excess salt loss from sweating and can be prevented if lost salt is replaced by drinking adequate amounts of fluid containing some extra salt. Salt tablets can be a convenient source, but may irritate the stomach. Avoid overdosage.

Night cramps affect most people from time to time and usually involve the calf muscles. The pain may be severe but the problem does not seem to have excited much medical interest, perhaps because the symptom is usually harmless. The cause of spontaneous night cramps has never been satisfactorily explained, but many people have found that they can be prevented by taking a small dose of quinine.

Swimmer's cramps can affect the abdominal or the limb muscles and sometimes lead to a panic reaction which only make the situation worse. The best response is to tread water gently or float on your back until the spasm has passed, and then you should swim slowly, avoiding strenuous movements.

Writer's cramp is not a physical disorder as it affects only the activity of writing and does not occur when the same muscles are used for other purposes. Soon after starting writing, the muscles involved in holding the pen or pencil go into a state of spasm so that writing cannot continue. The implication is that the sufferer doesn't really want to write and that this psychological effect suggests that he or she may have been unwise in the choice of occupation. Writer's cramp is sometimes included in the group of disorders known as *dystonia*. It seems unlikely that using word processors will abolish the disorder – more likely their use will simply change the name, perhaps to repetitive strain injury (RSI).

Muscle spasm is similar to cramp but may indicate an underlying condition. A spasm is an abnormal state of sustained contraction of a muscle. In health, nerve connections from the brain normally exert a dampening or controlling influence on the natural tendency of voluntary muscles to go into spasm. When these connections are damaged, as in stroke, cerebral palsy or severe head injury, the controlling influence is removed and a *spastic* condition of the muscles results. Spastic paralysis is a common feature of stroke.

Tetany is a characteristic form of muscle spasm most commonly caused by abnormally strong nerve conduction resulting from low levels of blood calcium. It can also result from a reduction in blood acidity, which in turn affects calcium levels, from deliberate or hysterical overbreathing (hyperventilation). Tetany usually affects the hands and the feet, producing a claw-like effect with extension of the nearer joints and bending of the others (carpopedal spasm). If severe, it may, however, extend to involve the facial muscles, the larynx, or even the spinal muscles. The initial minor spasms are painless but, if they persist, they become painful and may even lead to muscle damage.

Tetany is a feature of underaction of the parathyroid glands and was once common following surgical operations on the thyroid gland. Underaction of the gland may occur for other reasons.

A more serious cause of widespread muscle spasms is the similar-sounding, but quite different condition, *tetanus*. This is an infection of the nervous system caused by the germ *Clostridium tetani* which is found in cultivated soil and manure. This germ gets into the body by way of penetrating wounds, which may be small and seemingly trivial, and causes the disease two days to several weeks later. Tetanus is rare in Britain but is still a common cause of death in developing countries where the mortality rate from the disease is around 50 per cent. Babies are commonly infected through the stump of the umbilical cord, and in these the mortality is nearly 100 per cent.

The tetanus organism produces a powerful toxin which triggers off the nerves supplying voluntary muscles, or the nerve endings on the muscles, causing them to go into violent spasms of contraction. The chief early sign is a spasm of the chewing muscles (trismus), causing great difficulty in opening the mouth – hence the name 'lockjaw'. ⚠ This spasm spreads to the muscles of the face and neck, producing a snarling, mirthless smile known as the *risus sardonicus*. The back muscles then become rigid and, in severe cases, the back becomes strongly arched backwards so that the abdominal wall becomes tight, rigid and boardlike. Spasms of contraction occur every few minutes and increase in severity and frequency over the course of a week. There is also fever, difficulty in swallowing, severe stiffness of the limbs, sore throat and headache. Death from exhaustion or from asphyxia in the course of convulsions is common.

Tetanus is treated by giving tetanus antitoxin, preferably human antitetanus globulin (antibodies) and large doses of antibiotics or metronidazole as soon as the diagnosis is suspected. Spasms are controlled by diazepam (Valium), given into a vein, and every effort is made to handle the affected person gently so as to avoid promoting spasms by unexpected stimuli. In severe cases it may be necessary deliberately to paralyse the patient with curare and to maintain respiration artificially. General measures to maintain the airway and the nutrition are also important. Tetanus is a terrifying ordeal and much reassurance is necessary. It is easily prevented by safe immunization with tetanus toxoid and everyone should be protected.

Painful muscle spasm can also result from arthritis in a nearby joint or from local irritation to the spinal nerves supplying them, as may occur in nerve root pressure from a slipped disc (prolapsed intervertebral disc).

Muscle pain occurring during exertion may indicate the condition of *intermittent clau-*

dication. This features a sudden pain in the leg muscles, often in the calf, associated with temporary inability to walk. Intermittent claudication is caused by an inadequate blood supply to the muscles from narrowing disease of the arteries, usually atherosclerosis. It occurs after the affected person walks for a certain, often constant, distance. There is a build-up of waste products in the muscles and these pain-causing substances cannot be dispersed quickly enough. The process is almost identical to that causing angina pectoris (see **Pain in the chest**) and there is the same relationship to the amount of exertion. As the arterial disease process worsens, the symptoms come on earlier.

Intermittent claudication is a clear indication that medical attention is required and that the state of the heart and blood vessels should be investigated. Recent evidence suggests that the performance can be improved by deliberately 'walking through claudication'. This does not mean that one should continue to try to walk in spite of the pain, but that one should resume walking as soon as the pain has gone. People with intermittent claudication are advised to walk for an hour every day, and it has been found that those who do so are usually able to walk a progressively greater distance before the pain comes on. The term is derived from the Latin verb *claudicare*, 'to be lame or limping' and is immortalized in the name of Claudius, Emperor of Rome, who had a limping gait and tendency to stop walking and grimace, as if in pain.

Compartment syndrome is a muscle disorder of increased pressure within a compartment of the body, usually the forearm or the lower leg, which results in compression of the veins followed by the arteries so that the muscles are eventually deprived of their blood supply and become useless, shrunken and replaced by fibrous tissue. The syndrome may follow fractures, crush injuries, gunshot wounds or even drug overdose. There is pain, loss of power, paralysis and absent pulse. ▲ Urgent surgery is needed to open up the tissue planes and relieve the pressure until the swelling subsides.

A similar condition may occur in athletes whose muscles are developed so quickly that they outgrow the space available for them. Surgery may be necessary.

A comparatively rare but important cause of pain in the muscles is *polymyalgia rheumatica*. This features pain and stiffness in the shoulders, neck, back and arms, which is now known to be associated with another, more dangerous condition – *giant cell arteritis* (see **Pain in the temples**). The stiffness is often present on waking or after prolonged sitting, and may be so severe that the affected person can hardly get out of bed. The morning stiffness and disability are severe. Patients describe how they get their husbands (women are affected almost three times as often as men) to pull them out of bed, or, if they are alone,

how they gradually make their way to the edge of the bed by a snake-like wriggling manoeuvre and then get out by a controlled fall.

There is low-grade fever, anaemia, loss of appetite and weight loss. The condition is remarkable for the absence of organic signs. There is no real muscle weakness and wasting is from disuse only. Muscle biopsy is normal as are serum tests for the presence of muscle enzymes which occur in cases of muscle damage. Electrical tests on muscles (electromyograms) are also normal. But when a short segment of an artery is removed, as a biopsy, in people with polymyalgia, about 40 per cent are found to have the obstructive changes in the artery known as giant cell arteritis. The response to the timely administration of steroids is so striking as almost to confirm the diagnosis. On a maintenance dose of steroids there is dramatic relief of stiffness and disability and this is sustained for periods of up to two years.

However, people with giant cell arteritis are at risk of suffering sudden blindness, especially if the arteries on the temples are inflamed and tender. In such cases, urgent high steroid dosage can be sight-saving. Sudden blindness from giant cell arteritis is due to blockage of the end-branches of the main arteries to the eyes (ophthalmic arteries), but this does not usually occur until after some weeks or months of local symptoms such as tender temples with red streaks, transient visual loss (amaurosis fugax), double vision and headache. The headache is increasingly severe, is often worst in the areas of the affected arteries, persists through the day and is worse at night. When a facial artery is involved, there is pain on chewing – 'jaw claudication'. This is a very suggestive symptom which, in any patient over 50, warrants an urgent sedimentation rate test. ⚠

Myositis is inflammation of muscle. This may occur as a result of infection by viruses, as in the aching condition of Bornholm disease, or by other germs, causing actual death of muscle. This latter type of myositis features serious illness and requires urgent surgical and antibiotic treatment. Myositis may also be a response to cancer elsewhere in the body.

Pain in the neck

The commonest disorder of the bones of the neck is *cervical spondylosis*. This is a degenerative condition of the spine, in the neck region, with backward outgrowth of bone causing narrowing of the canal which contains the spinal cord. As a result, there may be compression of the cord or the emerging spinal nerve roots and sometimes serious neurological damage. Affected people may develop neck pain and stiffness. Pain, weakness and atrophy in the arm muscles may occur. In extreme cases there may even be a stiff, scissors-like walking disorder (spastic gait). In some cases, a supportive collar will relieve the symptoms, but it is often necessary to resort to surgery to relieve the pressure on the important nerve tracts in the spinal cord.

Cervical osteoarthritis is a wearing away of the cartilage surfaces of the spinal bones (vertebrae) of the neck. The disorder is commonest in middle age and runs a slow, persistent course with episodes of pain, stiffness of the neck and sometimes tenderness on pressure over the affected area. Although an X-ray may show some bony extensions from the inflamed areas, it is unusual for these to involve the nerve roots or spinal cord and cause neurological effects, as in cervical spondylosis.

Osteoarthritis is commonly a late sequel to bone or joint injury, such as may occur from the whiplash head movement suffered by the occupants of a car struck from behind by another vehicle.

Slipped disc, which is commonest in the lower back (see **Pain in the back**), can also occur in the neck, causing pain, stiffness and pain that may radiate down either or both arms or through to the back. The neck may be tilted forward or sideways and the muscles are tender. Cervical slipped disc usually follows a sudden acute turning, bending or extension of the neck. This, too, may result from a whiplash injury.

Normally there are no ribs in the neck, but about one person in 200 has a short, floating, rudimentary rib attached to the lowest neck vertebra on one or both sides. Most people with cervical ribs are unaware of the fact, but in about 10 per cent the rib gives trouble. The opening into the chest, at the root of the neck, is very narrow and contains many important structures, including the arteries and major nerve trunks running to the arms. Compression of these arteries or nerves can cause pain and tingling in the neck, shoulder or arm and, occasionally, can lead to severe effects, such as partial loss of blood supply to the arm with cold, blue, numb extremities (Raynaud's phenomenon) or even, rarely, gangrene of the fingertips.

The cervical rib syndrome, as this collection of symptoms is called, is commonest in thin, long-necked women in their 40s and may occur after marked loss of weight. It has also been described in men who have developed their muscles to an unusual degree.

Sometimes the condition can be proved by noting that the pulse at the wrist disappears when the arm is raised and the head is turned to the opposite side. Most cases can be controlled by physiotherapy and exercises. Surgical removal of the offending rib, or of other constricting structures in the region, is sometimes needed.

Pain in the shoulder

Shoulder pain is very common and is usually due to muscle or tendon problems or to pain referred from elsewhere. Shoulder and arm pain is commonly caused by the condition of cervical spondylosis (see **Pain in the neck**). This features softening and flattening of the neck vertebrae and pressure on the emer-

ging nerve roots. It is this pressure that causes the shoulder pain and there may be nothing wrong with the shoulder itself.

Another source of referred pain to the shoulder is coronary artery disease of the heart. Angina pectoris or the pain of a heart attack (see **Pain in the chest**) is commonly referred to the shoulder, especially the left shoulder. Similarly, pain may be referred from disease processes occurring in the chest. A lung cancer, for instance, might lead to referred pain in the shoulder. Pain can be referred to the right shoulder from a liver abscess that irritates the underside of the diaphragm, the muscular sheet that separates the abdomen from the chest.

Pain caused by actual shoulder problems may arise from the many tendons in and around the shoulder joint. Inflammation of these tendons is called *tendinitis* and it may be due to the deposition of calcium hydroxyapatite around certain of the tendons. Fortunately, this condi-

231

tion usually settles within a few weeks.

Frozen shoulder or *adhesive capsulitis* is a painful condition in which the capsule of the joint stiffens. This, too, is a form of tendinitis but, in addition to the pain, it causes fairly severe restriction of shoulder movement. The condition usually settles after a few months but stiffness may persist. Manipulation under anaesthesia may be needed.

The rotator cuff is the tendinous structure around the shoulder joint comprising the tendons of four nearby muscles. These tendons blend with the fibrous capsule of the joint and provide additional support during movement of the shoulder. Injury to the rotator cuff may result from a fall. It is more common in the elderly when these tendons have worn a little. A partial tear may cause pain when the arm is moved away from the body at a particular angle. A complete tear may prevent this movement altogether, although other shoulder muscles usually compensate by tilting the shoulder blade

and allowing some outward movement. If a complete tear causes severe disability, surgical repair by stitching may be required.

Pain in the temples

Ordinary headache often involves the temples. However, there is a particular condition in which the pain is associated with exquisite tenderness on pressure and with visible red streaks. These features indicate a disease of small arteries causing inflammation, with swelling tenderness and possible blockage. This is called *temporal arteritis* or *giant cell arteritis* and it involves arteries in the scalp and brain. The immediate concern is that the condition, once established, may affect the main artery to the eye, causing blindness. There is no time to be wasted. Urgent treatment with corticosteroids is required if sight is to be saved. ▲ See also **Pain in the muscles**.

Pain in the testicle

Probably the commonest cause of pain in the testicle

is frustrated adolescent sexual interest. This causes a prolonged ache well known to young boys. The symptom is harmless and will usually pass with growing experience. The testicles are very sensitive to injury and even a minor blow to the area can cause great pain. In most cases, however, this soon settles.

Mumps most commonly affects children and in these cases the testicles are rarely affected. In adult males, however, mumps is often associated with a painful inflammation of the testicles called *orchitis*. This complication occurs in about a quarter of the adolescent or adult males who contract mumps and it may cause much distress. As a rule, only one testicle is affected, but this may become considerably swollen, exquisitely tender and painful and may remain so for several days, before returning to its normal state. Padding with much loose cotton wool may be needed. Occasionally mumps orchitis leads to sterility of the affected testicle, but

this seldom affects fertility. Total sterility from this cause is rare.

Torsion of the testis is the acutely painful condition in which the spermatic cord, from which the testicle hangs, becomes twisted within, or just above, the scrotum. The veins in the spermatic cord are soon blocked so the return of blood is obstructed. There is great swelling, tenderness and bruising. Early surgical correction is necessary if fertility, in the affected testicle, is to be preserved.

Three quarters of cancers of the testicle are painless and are detected only by noticing a swelling or lump. The remainder do cause pain and this may be associated with inflammation and tenderness. Cancer of the testicle affects young and middle-aged men and appears as a hard swelling on one side. Unless routine self-examination is being performed regularly, a testicular cancer is likely to be missed until well advanced. The outlook, in early cases, is excellent, but worsens with delay in diagnosis. Any new lumps should be reported at once. ⚠

Pain in the throat

Sore throat, or pharyngitis, is a common condition, usually caused by viruses or bacteria. Most cases respond well to simple treatment. There is discomfort on swallowing, occasional earache, redness and swelling of the throat, enlarged and tender lymph nodes in the neck, and slight fever. Pharyngitis is often the starting sign in glandular fever, influenza and scarlet fever but may also be caused by scalding from hot fluids or contact with corrosives or abrasive foreign material in the food.

Although commonly of minor importance, pharyngitis is sometimes serious, with high fever, general upset, swelling (oedema) of the soft palate or larynx – a potentially life-threatening emergency which may require tracheostomy – and the formation of an adherent, dirty-white membrane over the throat. It may also lead to a hard swelling of the soft tissues in the floor of the mouth (Ludwig's angina).

Tonsillitis – inflammation of the tonsils – is often caused by streptococcal bacteria but may be caused by many other kinds of germs. The tonsils become swollen and red and the surfaces may show spots of pus exuding from the clefts (tonsillar crypts). Sometimes material from the crypts forms a whitish membrane over the surface. The lymph nodes in the neck, just behind or under the angle of the jaw, are swollen and tender to the touch. There is sore throat, pain on swallowing, headache, fever (which may be very high in young children) and a feeling of unwellness. Constipation and earache are common. The tongue is often furred and the breath unpleasant. There may be slight difficulty in opening the mouth and thickened speech.

Tonsillitis responds well to antibiotic treatment and this should always be given if the infection is streptococcal. Recurrent, severe or complicated tonsillitis may justify surgical removal of the tonsils.

Complications of tonsillitis are uncommon, but may include abscess in the back of the throat, otitis media, rheumatic fever, glomerulonephritis, septicaemia and quinsy. A *quinsy* is an abscess between the capsule of the tonsil and the adjacent wall of the throat. Quinsy usually follows a severe attack of tonsillitis. The abscess is almost always on one side only, and the swelling appears above the tonsil, near the soft palate, so that the small floppy part of the soft palate (the uvula) is pushed across to the unaffected side. The throat is extremely painful and there is high fever, headache, and other signs of general upset. The speech is impaired and there is much salivation and dribbling. The neck lymph nodes are enlarged and tender. Antibiotics, given at an early stage before the abscess has fully developed, may bring the infection under control, but once the quinsy is established they are of little value and surgical drainage is necessary. This is followed by rapid relief. When the condition has fully settled it is advisable to have the tonsils removed, to avoid recurrence.

The most serious cause of pain in the throat is *diphtheria*. This is a highly infectious disease now, happily, rare in developed countries, thanks to immunization. Diphtheria can progress to serious illness within a day of the appearance of the first symptoms. There is sore throat, fever, headache, difficulty in swallowing and enlarged lymph nodes in the neck. The organism produces a powerful poison (toxin) which is released into the surrounding tissues, causing severe damage and the formation of a greyish-white membrane which can obstruct the upper air passages causing asphyxiation. This may necessitate an emergency artificial opening into the windpipe (a tracheostomy).

The toxin gets into the bloodstream and is carried throughout the body, where it may cause serious damage to the heart, the nervous system – causing permanent muscle weakness – or the kidneys. Many children have died from severe heart damage within a few days of onset. Even today, the death rate from diphtheria is about 10 per cent. In underdeveloped parts of the world it is much higher.

Because of the success of the immunization programme, a generation of parents has grown up with no knowledge of the horrors of the disease. There is a risk that immunization may be neglected.

Pain in the wrist

Surprisingly, wrist pain is often caused by a condition that has nothing to do with the wrist. This is a degenerative disorder of the spine in the neck region, called *cervical spondylosis* (see **Pain in the neck**), in which the bones (vertebrae) flatten a little and develop bony spurs that can press on the emerging nerve roots. Because these nerves go to all parts of the arm, pressure on them can cause referred pain to any part especially the elbow and the wrist.

Wrist pain may also be caused by osteoarthritis, rheumatoid arthritis, tuberculosis or by inflammation in the sheaths of some of the many narrow tendons that pass across both the front and the back of the wrist. This inflammation is called *tenosynovitis* and is usually made worse by forming a fist or stretching the fingers widely.

The scaphoid or navicular bone, so called because of its resemblance to a boat, is one of the eight wrist bones – the outermost, on the thumb side, in the row nearest the body. It is a curved bone, narrower in proportion to its length than the other wrist bones and is readily fractured across its waist by a fall on the outstretched hand. This causes persistent pain and tenderness on the back of the wrist between the two tendons which extend the thumb. Early scaphoid fractures often show up poorly on X-ray, and delay in treatment may result, sometimes with serious consequences, such as

236

osteoarthritis, with worsening of the pain and limitation of movement. Repeat X-rays are ordered by wary doctors, especially if wrist tenderness persists.

De Quervain's disease is an inflammation and thickening of the sheath of a tendon that extends the thumb. It is commonest in women aged 30 to 50 and is usually due to excessive local trauma as from wringing out washing or overenthusiastic use of secateurs in pruning roses. There is a painful point over the prominent thumb tendon and the pain is increased if the thumb is extended against resistance.

Pain on bowel movement

This may be caused by *anal fissure* – a tear in the inner lining of the canal of the anus often caused by hard faeces. The pain on defaecation may be severe and there is sometimes bleeding. Anal fissures usually heal in a few days but will tend to recur unless the cause is removed. You should keep your stools soft by ensuring that there is plenty of fibre in your diet and that your fluid intake is adequate.

Another cause of pain is anal fistula. This is an abnormal connection or passage between the inside of the anal canal and the outer skin near the anus. This usually results from infection and abscess formation in the tissues around the anal canal, but may be caused by cancer or bowel inflammation. Anal fistulas discharge pus onto the skin and there may also be visible pus in the stools. If you see anything of this sort you should report it to your doctor.

Piles, or haemorrhoids, are another possible cause of pain (see **Itching anus**).

Pain on deep breathing

If the pain comes with a sudden catch, this is probably pleurisy (see **Pain in the chest**).

Pain on menstruation

Dysmenorrhoea – painful menstruation – is experienced, from time to time, by almost all women who have not had babies. The symptoms occur just before or at the beginning of the period, and consist of cramping, rhythmical pain in the lower abdomen and back, lasting usually for a few hours, but sometimes for a whole day. In severe cases the pains may last throughout the whole menstrual period.

The pain is caused by strong contractions of the womb and with the opening of the neck of the womb (the cervix). In effect, dysmenorrhoea is a kind of mini-labour. There may also be nausea, vomiting and diarrhoea, and cramping, colicky pain in the bowels. Some women have faintness and dizziness. About 10 per cent of women are so severely affected that they are temporarily unable to work or carry on with their normal daily routine.

Dysmenorrhoea is almost always cured by having a baby, but less drastic remedies can also be effective. Drugs of the antiprostaglandin type (ibuprofen, paracetamol and aspirin) are useful, and in severe cases, menstrua-

tion can be stopped altogether by means of oral contraceptives taken continuously. You should do this only under medical supervision.

The condition may also result as a secondary effect of pelvic infection and other local disease, such as womb fibroids or endometriosis and, in these cases, antibiotics for infection and surgery may be necessary to bring about a cure.

Pain on sexual intercourse

The medical term for this is *dyspareunia*. When a woman feels pain on intercourse it is usually the result of one of a range of gynaecological disorders that include:

- a thick, persistent (imperforate) hymen;
- any inflammation of external genital area (vulvitis);
- inflammation of the mucus-secreting glands in the labia (bartholinitis);
- inflammation in the urine tube (urethritis);

- inflammation of the vagina (vaginitis);
- old episiotomy scars;
- dryness of the vagina, often from oestrogen deficiency after the menopause;
- senile or post-radiational atrophy of the vagina;
- a congenital central vaginal partition (septate, or double, vagina).

This list does not cover all the possibilities but includes the majority of organic causes of the problem. Dyspareunia is often caused by a powerful vaginal spasm (vaginismus) of psychological origin. This may be so severe that even a finger can barely be admitted. Vaginismus is usually caused by disinclination for sexual intercourse with a particular partner or by a very real fear of sex. The spasms are reflex and uncontrollable, and may involve not only all the muscles of the pelvis, but also the muscles which press the thighs together.

Obviously, the treatment of dyspareunia from any of these factors is the treatment of the cause. Ironically, the treatment of vaginismus is often more difficult than that of the physical causes. In some cases, depending on the people involved, treatment of vaginismus may not be a good idea. It involves full investigation, skilled psychotherapy and counselling, a careful explanation of the origin of the problem, training in relaxation, strong encouragement in self-familiarization with the genitals, and when appropriate, the use, by the affected woman herself, of progressively larger smooth, rounded metal or plastic vaginal dilators. The last thing a woman with vaginismus needs is to be forced to have sexual intercourse by an assertive male. This simply causes pain, and makes the whole situation worse.

Pain on urination

By far the commonest cause of pain on urination is cystitis. This is an inflammation of the urinary bladder caused by infection. The symptoms are

239

well known, especially to women, who are more prone to the disorder than men, mainly because of the shortness of the tube from the bladder to the exterior (the urethra). There is burning or scalding pain on passing urine (frequently in small quantities), an unduly frequent desire to visit the toilet, and sometimes involuntarily letting out a small squirt of urine when coughing or laughing. This is called *stress incontinence*.

Sometimes a little blood is passed in the urine and affected people often have to get up during the night. Occasionally there may be fever, shivering, pain in the lower back (the loins) and general upset with nausea and a sense of illness (malaise). Cystitis in men is often associated with infection and inflammation of the prostate gland (prostatitis).

Examination of the urine often shows that germs are present. These are commonly *coliform* organisms (*Escherichia coli*) which normally, and harmlessly, inhabit the bowel. However, cystitis is often due to other organisms, including those acquired during sexual intercourse such as *Chlamydia trachomatis*, *Trichomonas vaginalis*, *Haemophilus vaginalis* or *Candida albicans*.

Treatment with antibiotics should be rapidly effective. If not, further investigation is called for in case the infection should be of wider extent or should be connected with some other bladder or kidney disorder.

You can often avoid cystitis by drinking lots of fluid so as to 'flush out' the urinary system. Another tip is to make deliberate attempts to empty the bladder after urination seems complete ('double urination'). This may involve some patient waiting. It is also a good idea to pee after sexual intercourse, and avoid nylon underwear and vaginal deodorants. In menopausal women, cystitis may respond better to vaginal oestrogen creams than to antibiotics.

Pale stools

Pale stools or faeces, resembling clay in colour, indicate

the absence of bile, usually because of a liver disorder or obstruction to the flow of bile into the intestine. The stools are likely to be greasy and difficult to flush away because of poor absorption from the intestine of dietary fat. The urine may also be very dark because of excretion of bilirubin accumulating in the blood. For the same reason, the skin and whites of the eyes may be yellow.

This state of affairs implies either hepatitis or some mechanical obstruction to the bile duct that carries bile from the liver to the duodenum. This could be a gallstone or it might possibly indicate a cancer of the head of the pancreas pressing on and obstructing the bile duct. Do not delay – see your doctor at once. ▲

Palpitations

This simply means consciousness of your heart beat, either because it is faster than normal or more commonly because it is irregular. A rapid heart rate is, of course, normal during exercise or emotion. Brief periods of irregularity are common and are usually due to premature beats followed by unusually prolonged pauses. These are called *extrasystoles*. They are felt as a fluttering or thumping in the chest, sometimes with a brief but alarming sense that the heart has stopped beating. Extrasystoles do not normally indicate heart disease. Remember that heart muscle, by its nature, will go on beating so long as it is supplied with oxygen and nutrients. Hearts do not stop for no reason. It is one of the inherent properties of heart muscle to continue to contract rhythmically. It will even do so after it is removed from the body.

Another cause of palpitations is *atrial tachycardia*, a condition in which, for periods of seconds to days, the heart beats very rapidly – sometimes over 200 beats per minute. The onset is sudden and causes faintness and breathlessness and the affected person becomes very anxious. The rate can be controlled by medical treatment.

Atrial fibrillation is a condition in which the upper chambers of the heart (the atria) beat in a wholly disorganized manner and only the strongest impulses are passed down to the main lower pumping chambers (the ventricles). The result is a grossly irregular heart beat. In the early stages, affected people have palpitation with an unpleasant awareness of the irregularity of the heart's action but, with time, they usually become accustomed to the symptom and fail to notice it. See also **Irregular pulse**.

Panic attacks

Panic disorder is a condition featuring spontaneous, intense episodes of anxiety, usually lasting for less than an hour and occurring about twice a week or more often. About two thirds of people with agoraphobia have panic attacks. The attacks consist of an acute sense of fear, with a conviction of impending death, and mental confusion. The heart beats rapidly, breathing is fast and deep, and there is sweating and great distress. Overbreathing (hyperventilation) often makes the attack worse.

The condition has a genetic basis and brain imaging has shown that there is an increased blood flow in a particular part of the brain, on the non-dominant side, during a panic attack. An injection of sodium lactate brings on a panic attack in 70 per cent of those who are subject to the disorder but in only 5 per cent of others. This substance is thought to lead to a marked increase in adrenaline production in the susceptible individuals. About half of those who suffer from panic attacks have a minor abnormality of the mitral valve of the heart (mitral valve prolapse) which occurs in only five per cent of the general population, usually harmlessly. Overactivity of the thyroid gland is also associated with panic attacks.

Panic attacks are treated with antidepressant drugs, especially tricyclics and monoamine oxidase inhibitors (MOAIs). Properly used, these are effective and may completely remove the attacks.

Anxiety from anticipation of further attacks can be controlled by behaviour therapy.

Penis problems: ballooning

When a tight foreskin with a very narrow opening (phimosis) is drawn back to the neck of the glans of the penis, an awkward and distressing thing may happen. The narrowed outlet of the foreskin causes tight constriction of the neck of the glans of the penis. In this situation, while the blood in the arteries of the penis, which is under pressure, is able to get into the glans, the veins, which are softer and contain blood under lower pressure, are firmly compressed and the blood cannot escape. As a result, the glans swells progressively causing the constriction to get tighter and the situation to get rapidly worse. This unfortunate state of affairs is called *paraphimosis*. It can be extremely painful and there is some danger of gangrene of the glans unless the paraphimosis is rapidly reduced. ⚠

The treatment is to return the foreskin to its normal position by squeezing fluid back out of the swollen glans until it is small enough to allow the narrowed opening of the foreskin to pass forward over it. Usually, squeezing with the fingers will succeed. This might need to be supplemented by injecting an enzyme that aids the dispersion of fluid – it breaks down the cement substance in tissues (hyalase). In some instances, surgery under general anaesthesia may be necessary. After the paraphimosis is reduced, it is wise to agree to circumcision because this will prevent any possibility of the ordeal happening again.

Penis problems: bending

In *Peyronie's disease* the penis bends at an angle when it is erect. This is caused by a nodular contraction in part of the fibrous sheath surrounding the erectile tissue. The penis is unable to enlarge uniformly as it fills with blood, and so it bends upwards or to one side. Sexual intercourse may be impeded or painful. The local fibrous thickening may extend into the columns of erectile tissue so that the normal passage of blood is obstructed and the erection compromised. The cause is unknown.

Some cases settle without treatment after several months. Surgical removal of the scar tissue has been tried, but the results have not been uniformly good. Local injections of corticosteroids are sometimes successful.

Angulation of the penis, usually from a patch of scar tissue that impedes erection at one point, as in Peyronie's disease, or from the congenital deformity of hypospadias (see **Penile outlet displacement**) is known as *chordee*.

Penis problems: discharge

Inexperienced men sometimes worry that the clear mucin discharge noted at the tip of the penis indicates a venereal infection of some kind. Analysis of the situation will, however, show that this occurs only after or during episodes of sexual arousal, however slight. The effect is physiological and is provided by nature in anticipation of the need for lubrication.

The main causes of genuine penile discharge are chlamydial infection and gonorrhoea. Chlamydial infections are caused by *Chlamydia trachomatis* and gonorrhoea by *Neisseria gonorrhoea*. The urethral discharge, accompanied by severe irritation, occurs two to five days after intercourse in the case of gonorrhoea, and seven to twenty-one days in the case of chlamydia. It may be yellow (pus) or clear. The discharge, which at first may be profuse with severe discomfort when urinating, will gradually become less, and complications are not very common. A proportion of men, however, do suffer spread of infection to the testicles or prostate gland and these infections may last for months or years. Some men, after repeated attacks of gonorrhoea, develop a local narrowing (stricture) of the urine tube (urethra). This can obstruct the flow of urine and may have serious long-term consequences. In addition, about one man in a hundred with chlamydial infection develops a severe form of arthritis affecting mainly the ankles, knees and feet and possibly involving also the eyes and even the heart. This condition is called *Reiter's syndrome*.

If caught early, both gonorrhoea and chlamydial infections will respond well to treatment with suitable antibiotics, and a cure is to be expected. But once the secondary complications have developed, treatment is difficult. Surgery may be required and even this may be unsuccessful.

Penis problems: early orgasm

Most ejaculation problems, such as failure to achieve ejaculation, or to achieve it at the right time, are psycho-sexual in origin and have nothing to do with organic disease or defect. In most cases the problem lies in the nature of the relationship between the partners and it is a commonplace observation that a man may have major problems, even complete sexual failure, with one woman and yet be highly effective with another. Mutual understanding, sympathy, the use of sex as an expression of love and affection – rather than as a form of entertainment or a display of macho virility – are basic to sexual success and satisfaction.

Premature ejaculation is very common. This is when the man has an orgasm at the time of penetration, or very soon after, or even, in extreme cases, before any physical contact has occurred. This is a feature of early sexual experience and is a normal occurrence when the level of mental sexual excitement is high enough to trigger the orgasm. It can often be helped by the trick of squeezing the penis tightly, just behind the bulb (glans), between the finger and thumb. According to sex manuals, this should be the woman's task, performed at the man's urgent request, after the matter has been frankly and freely discussed.

In more experienced men, premature ejaculation is often induced by anxiety, especially over the ability to maintain the erection. Any form of fear brings the sympathetic side of the autonomic nervous system into operation. This is the 'fright and flight' mechanism and is neurologically antagonistic to the parasympathetic system, which is trying to get on with the sexual process. There is a blocking of the arousal state, a failure to build up to orgasmic excitement, the beginnings of erectile failure, and a premature triggering of ejaculation.

Since the fear of failure sets up this vicious cycle the removal of fear should prevent it. Much experience has shown that this is so. When this fear is removed, the problem corrects itself. It is interesting to note that a major industry – the Masters and Johnson-based sex therapy business – has been founded on the simple observation that if you tell people that they may engage in prolonged physical intimacy *but are on no account to have sexual intercourse*, male sexual problems rapidly clear up.

Absence of ejaculation is rare. It may be due to overindulgence, in which case the problem is temporary, or to inadequate penile stimulation from a very lax vagina, which may require manual assistance from the woman or even a vagina-tightening gynaecological operation. Another possible cause is age-related loss of penile sensitivity or poor erection, in which case more manual assistance is needed. Very uncommonly, structural (anatomical) abnormality is the cause – if ejaculation can be achieved by masturbation, this is ruled out.

Penis problems: inflammation

The medical term for inflammation of the glans of the penis and the inside of the foreskin is *balanitis*. This uncomfortable condition causes tremendous itching and, in severe cases, pain from rawness of the affected area. Probably the commonest cause of balanitis is neglect of simple personal hygiene in uncircumcised men which leads to the accumulation, under the foreskin, of a white, cheesy, smelly material called *smegma* that soon gets infected and becomes very irritating. Other causes include:

- thrush, which is usually contracted during sexual intercourse;
- various other infections – gonorrhoea, boils, chlamydial infections and so on;
- an unduly tight foreskin;
- irritation by contraceptive creams.

It is essential to wash the area under the foreskin thoroughly every day – this is a cure in many cases. An antibiotic or an anti-fungal cream may be required. If the condition is sufficiently troublesome and intractable, circumcision is the complete answer.

Penis problems: itching

See **Penis problems: inflammation.**

Penis problems: outlet displacement

Normally, the opening of the urine passage – the urethra – is at the tip of the glans. In rare cases, the urethra may open on the underside of the penis, sometimes as far back as the root. Later, this can, of course, cause both urinary and sexual problems. Fortunately *hypospadias*, as it is called, can be corrected by a plastic procedure and the results are usually good. A similar condition, in which the urine tube opens on the upper surface of the penis, is called *epispadias*. Surgeons have discovered that the essential lining for the new tube can be grown from the man's own cells by artificial tissue culture.

Occasionally, the opening of the urethra at the tip of the penis is so narrow that the urine is hardly able to get out. This uncommon condition, known as *urethral stenosis*, is very easily remedied by a simple operation. It should not be confused with tightness in the opening of the foreskin.

Penis problems: persistent erection

This is called *priapism* and it is no joke. The medical term, which comes from the Greek *Priapus*, the God of male sex, is singularly inappropriate as priapism is a painful and dangerous condition. It means that a prolonged and painful penile erection occurs in the absence of sexual interest. Priapism results from the failure of the normal return of blood from the *corpora cavernosa* of the penis to the circulation at the end of a period of sexual excitement.

This may happen for a variety of reasons. In some cases there is a disturbance of the nervous control of blood flow to and from the penis due to disease of the spinal cord or brain. In others, blood disorders, such as leukaemia or sickle cell disease may be causing partial clotting (coagulation) of the stagnant blood in the penis. Alternatively, there may be other disease processes, such as inflammation of the prostate gland (prostatitis), stone (calculus) in the bladder, or urethritis, which interfere with the normal outflow of blood from the penis.

Long-sustained erection is dangerous because of the risk of clotting in the corpora cavernosa of the penis. Such thrombosis produces serious and permanent loss of erectile function, so treatment must be prompt and effective. Feeling embarrassed about the problem must not prevent you from consulting your doctor. ⚠ Unfortunately, treatment is not always easy, often because the cause of the problem remains obscure, or cannot be quickly established. The first priority is to help the penis to return to its normal state after an erection. The longer this is delayed the more difficult it becomes, for the blood soon acquires the consistency of thick oil. Spinal anaesthesia may help but surgical decompression, by letting out blood through a wide-bore needle, may be necessary. The bulb (glans) of the penis is never affected and it is sometimes possible to drain the corpora (erective tissue) internally into the glans.

Penis problems: shrinkage

The normal penis will commonly shrink, especially in the cold, to surprisingly small dimensions. There is, in fact, no genuine organic disorder in which the penis shrinks to nothing. Millions of people, however, believe that there is.

Koro is the name for a delusional disorder prevalent in South-east Asia, affecting males and sometimes occurring in epidemics. The sufferer becomes obsessed with the belief that his penis is shrinking and that it will disappear into his body, so causing his death. To prevent this, he will tie his penis to a heavy stone or persuade friends to keep hold of it, in relays. Sometimes he will even pass a safety-pin through the foreskin. The delusion is widespread in the areas where koro occurs and is related to the belief that ghosts have no genitals. Koro is a purely cultural and conceptual disorder with no foundation in fact.

Penis problems: ulcer

A *chancre* is the painless, hard-based primary sore of *syphilis*, which appears on the genitals within four weeks of exposure. The chancre is a shallow ulcer with a base resembling wet chamois leather, which oozes a clear serum that is teeming with the spirochaetes that cause the disease. You must never ignore a chancre. ⚠ By the time it has healed on its own, the organisms have spread into the body where they will later cause all kinds of serious problems. Syphilis can be proved by taking a fluid sample from a chancre. Even after the chancre has completely healed, a blood test for syphilis (VDRL test) will always show, retrospectively, whether or not a suspicious genital sore was a chancre.

Penis problems: unresponsiveness

Impotence is the inability to achieve a penile erection of sufficient firmness to allow normal vaginal sexual intercourse. A very small proportion of cases of impotence are actually caused by organic disorders; most are of psychological origin. Even those cases with an organic cause often have a psychological element. At the same time, some cases in which there are obvious psychological or social causal factors also have a physical element. Almost all men experience erectile failure from time to time. There are many causes.

Male potency is a delicate flower which wilts easily and much apparent erectile inadequacy is actually due to fear of failure, lack of desire or unsatisfactory macho attitudes to sex. It is notorious that a man may be useless with one woman and a stallion with an-

other. Lack of desire may simply be due to anything from boredom with the partner to active dislike of her, but may also be due to repeated past failure – a circumstance which many men find deeply humiliating and which they may become determined to avoid, even at the cost of damaging a relationship.

Psychological erectile failure usually comes on fairly suddenly and tends to be intermittent and related to one particular partner. A good erection is achieved during masturbation and during the periods of rapid eye movement (REM) sleep. An erection is commonly present on waking. The problem is likely to affect anxious, tense men with poor skills in communication, little idea of sexual technique or of how to express affection and with strong sexual taboos. Other factors may contribute to non-organic failure. Alcohol may add to sexual desire, but it can detract from the performance – so can several drugs, both respectable and otherwise.

Premature ejaculation affects the man's attitude and may lead to erectile failure, but should not, in itself, be classed as a form of impotence. Although followed, like all ejaculations, by a rapid loss of erection, this is not the basic problem.

Organic impotence may be due to:

- loss of male sex hormones, usually in the elderly;
- anti-hormonal medical treatment;
- diabetic nerve damage;
- various neurological conditions;
- heart output insufficiency;
- local arterial disorders;
- multiple sclerosis;
- spinal cord disorders.

In organic impotence there is often total loss of interest in sex, no fantasies or erotic dreams, and sometimes loss of the male secondary sexual characteristics. Organic impotence usually begins gradually and erection does not occur during attempts at masturbation or during sleep. The penis tends to be small and cold.

Full medical investigation is required in all such cases, unless the underlying disorder is already known. The treatment of psychological impotence depends on education, the use of methods such as the temporary prohibition of sexual intercourse, the encouragement of touching and sensual massage (sensate focus technique) and sexual counselling. Physical treatments include injections of papaverine, using vacuum condoms to suck the penis into a state of erection, wearing a 'penile ring' to exert a mild compression at the base and help to sustain erections, and various implantable inflatable prosthetic devices. In some cases, due to thrombosis of a major artery, blood vessel surgery can effect a cure.

Penis problems: warts

Venereal warts, known medically as *condylomata acuminata*, are pink cauliflower-like growths on the penis. Although often profuse, they are essentially the same as other warts and are caused by the same human papilloma viruses. They are, however, acquired during sexual intercourse and are readily transmitted to women in whom they can contribute to the risk of cervical cancer – so men with penile warts should remember this.

Penile warts should not be confused with *condyloma lata*. These are flat, moist, highly infectious venereal warts occurring on the glans of the penis or on the vulva in secondary syphilis.

Period pains

See **Pain on menstruation.**

Pins and needles

This is the sensation felt when something has affected the passage of nerve impulses in a sensory nerve. If the nerve is totally blocked there will be no feeling at all, but if it is capable of partial conduction, abnormal impulses are passed to the brain and the abnormal sensation – 'pins and needles' – is felt in the area of skin from which the nerve comes. Disturbance of normal nerve conduction is usually temporary and commonly results from pressure on the nerve or on the blood vessels supplying it. This might happen, for instance if you were to fall asleep with your arm over the back of a chair. Pressure on the nerves in the armpit could cause 'pins and needles' when you wake. The effect is well demonstrated by the sensations experienced before and after having a local anaesthetic.

Potato nose

See **Nasal deformity.**

Pounding headache, disturbance of vision and weakness

Everyone has blood pressure – without it we would die in a few minutes. Normal blood pressure is caused when the heart muscle squeezes and blood out into the arteries. These are elastic and stretch under the pressure, so the blood pressure constantly varies. Considerable increases occur during exercise and stress, and blood pressure falls during sleep. The peak pressure occurring at the time of the heart beat is

Progressive muscle weakness

called the *systolic* pressure. The minimum running pressure between beats is called the *diastolic* pressure. Both are measured when blood pressure is checked.

Unfortunately, abnormally raised blood pressure hardly ever causes symptoms until it reaches a dangerous level at which it is causing small arteries to burst. Prior to that stage it is silent and must be detected by routine checking. Raised blood pressure is dangerous because it damages arteries, leading to serious arterial disease that may interfere with vital blood supply to parts such as the heart and the brain. The effect on the larger arteries is also to make them less elastic so that they cannot give under pressure. This leads to a worsening of the blood pressure and a vicious cycle. *Malignant hypertension* is the critically dangerous condition in which runaway blood pressures occur and small blood vessels rupture. This causes pounding headaches, usually disturbances of vision and sometimes weakness or temporary speech

defects. Untreated malignant hypertension is rapidly fatal, usually from a massive stroke. ⚠

Abnormally raised blood pressure is called *hypertension* and is a major risk factor for stroke. This is one of the commonest causes of death and of severe disablement. So everyone should have their blood pressure properly checked at regular intervals, especially after middle age. If the pressure, especially the diastolic pressure, is found to be consistently high, treatment can be given to bring it down to normal levels and to relieve the danger.

Premature ejaculation

See **Penis problems: early orgasm.**

'Prickly heat'

See **Itching after heavy sweating.**

Progressive muscle weakness

Muscular dystrophy is a disorder in which slow, progressive degeneration occurs, leading to increasing weakness and disability. There are three main types. *Duchenne dystrophy* is almost confined to males. The first signs usually appear before the age of three and in most cases the muscles appear bulkier than normal (pseudohypertrophy). The bulk of actual muscle tissue is not, however, increased and there is progressive weakening. This initially affects the buttocks and leg muscles, causing a characteristic waddle in walking. The weakness causes the child to get up from lying in a typical way – by rolling on his or her face and using the arms to push himself or herself up by 'hand-walking' up the legs. Unfortunately, nothing can arrest the progress of the disease, which is usually fatal by the mid-teens.

There are two other main forms of muscular dystrophy – the *limb girdle* type, affecting the shoulders, pelvic and uppermost limb muscles, which usually causes severe disablement within 20 years; and the *facio-scapulo-humeral* type, affecting the muscles of the face, upper back and upper arm, which progresses very slowly and does not necessarily shorten life.

Protruding teeth
See **Buck teeth.**

R

Rash

Reading difficulty in children

Red eye

Red spots on trunk (with fever)

Restless legs

Rumbling tummy

Running ears

R

Rash

If with fever, see entries under **Fever**; alternatively see entries under **Skin**.

Reading difficulty in children

See **Word blindness**.

Red eye

See **Eye inflammation**.

Red spots on trunk (with fever)

See **Fever and neck stiffness**.

Restless legs

This is a condition, associated with insomnia, in which the legs ache and are constantly moved about in the attempt to achieve comfort. The cause is obscure but the condition is not dangerous and relief can be obtained by the use of the alpha blocker drug tolazoline.

Rumbling tummy

There is an impressive name for this common and unimpressive phenomenon – *borborygmi*. Borborygmi are the sounds caused by air and fluid passing through the intestines as a normal part of the digestive process. Everybody has them but sometimes they are more conspicuous than usual, especially if the victim is of an anxious disposition and unduly sensitive about the workings of the bowels. They are a feature of irritable bowel syndrome (see **Diarrhoea**). Severe borborygmi may also occur in association with abdominal pain, vomiting and distress as features of an obstruction to the intestine. This is, however, rare compared with the millions of cases occurring for completely innocent reasons.

Running ears

You should never neglect discharge from the ears. There are two main causes – *otitis externa* and *chronic suppurative otitis media* (CSOM) which involves a perforation in the ear drum.

Otitis externa is an inflammation of the skin of the ear canal. The skin of the external ear (pinna) may or may not be involved. Otitis externa may be a local disorder or part of any general inflammatory disorder of the skin. These include a wide variety of infections. Staphylococci may cause a painful boil in the canal; herpes viruses, both simplex and zoster, may cause the characteristic blisters (vesicles) and crusting;

and fungi of various kinds, including thrush (*Candida albicans*), may cause persistent and sometimes intractable inflammation. This is called *otomycosis*. Eczema and seborrhoeic dermatitis are common causes of otitis externa. Most forms of the disorder cause pain, sometimes severe, and there is usually a discharge from the ear (otorrhoea). Unless the canal becomes blocked, hearing is not usually affected.

Otitis externa may be persistent (chronic) and difficult to treat, and the management varies with the cause. Thorough cleaning of the canal and specific antibiotic or anti-fungal treatment are often necessary, and solutions of such drugs may be applied locally on gauze 'wicks'.

Otitis media is an inflammation in the middle ear cavity, usually as a result of infection spread from the nose or throat by way of the eustachian tube. Although this is the route of access, outward drainage through the eustachian tube is also important in maintaining the health of the middle ear, and blockage commonly leads to infection. Eustachian tube obstruction may be caused by adenoids or by inflammation in the tube itself as a result of repeated infection.

Acute suppurative otitis media is a form in which the onset is sudden with a rapid production of pus in the middle ear so that the pressure rises and the eardrum bulges outwards. There is severe pain and fever with general upset and a risk of perforation of the drum. Urgent treatment with antibiotics is necessary. ▲ In chronic suppurative otitis media, there is a perforation in the drum, usually with a persistent discharge. Deafness and otitis externa are common complications.

S

Sadness	Sense of being a stranger
Salty skin	Separation anxiety
Scaly eyelids	Shivering
Scaly patches on hairline	Short sight
Scaly red patches on body	Shortness of breath
	Sight problems
Scissors gait	Skin blisters
Seasickness	
	Skin blisters around mouth or nose
Secret binge eating	
Seizures	Skin blisters that crust over

Skin bruising without injury

Skin inflamed under nappy

Skin inflammation

Skin marks present at birth

Skin oiliness

Skin reactions to insect bites

Skin rings that expand

Skin spots in adolescence

Skin spots in elderly people

Skin swelling, hard and doughnut-shaped

Skin swelling, inflamed and tender

Skin tingling and with painful blisters around the flank

Skin with large, black boils

Skin with multiple, reddish-brown or bluish nodules

Skin with raised, purplish swellings

Skin with scales

Sleeping difficulties

Slow pulse

Slurred speech

Sore throat

Spastic walking

Speech difficulties

Spider-like fingers

Spinal stiffness and fixation

Spontaneous fractures

Squinting

Squits

Stammering

Stealing without wanting

Stiff neck (with fever)

Stoppage of menses

Stoppage of urine output

Stuttering

Sunken eyes

Swallowing difficulty

Swelling and tenderness near the vaginal opening

Swelling behind the knee

Swelling of the abdomen

Swollen ankles

Swollen testicle

Sadness

A mood of sustained sadness or unhappiness is called *depression*. The distinction between normal reactive unhappiness, which is experienced at times by all, and genuine depressive illness, known as *clinical depression*, is important. Clinical depression involves a degree of hopeless despondency, dejection, fear and irritability out of all proportion to any external situation. Often there is no apparent cause. It is associated with a general slowing down of body and mind, slow speech, poor concentration, confusion, self-reproach, self-accusation and loss of self-esteem. There may be restlessness and agitation. Insomnia, with early morning waking, is common. Sexual interest may be lost and suicide is an ever-present threat.

Depression is especially common in elderly people, and the highest incidence of first attacks occurs between 55 and 65 in men and between 50 and 60 in women. It is usually precipitated by a distressing major life event, such as a bereavement, retirement or loss of status. Postmenopausal depression is a reason for the higher incidence in women than in men. This is often attributed to hormonal changes but there is no positive proof of this.

The causes of depression remain speculative and this has been a fruitful field for the psychoanalytic theorists. To date, their ideas have not been especially enlightening or useful as a basis for treatment. Cognitive psychologists regard depression as the result of a negative view of oneself as being unwanted, unloved, undesirable and worthless. The depressed person, they believe, views the world as a hostile place in which failure and punishment are to be expected and suffering and deprivation inevitable. Women are particularly vulnerable, especially as their sexual attraction and energy declines, and the loss of reproductive capacity, after the menopause, adds to this sense of uselessness.

The recognition of medically abnormal (pathological) depression is very important so that treatment can be given. ▲ The condition of the depressed is pitiable and, since it can in most cases now be relieved, no time should be lost. Many depressives who could have been restored to a normal emotional and social life have committed suicide. Effective antidepressant drugs, such as lithium, the tricyclic antidepressants, the monoamine oxidase inhibitors (MOAIs) and the serotonin re-uptake inhibitors, are available. Note particularly that these drugs do not show their effect until about two weeks after the treatment is started.

Salty skin

This is an uncommon sign that should always give rise to the suspicion of cystic fibrosis. Cystic fibrosis is a genetic disease that affects the millions of tiny mucus and watery secreting glands of the lining surfaces of the body. The salivary glands, the glands of the intestine, the pancreas, the gall bladder, the lungs and the skin either produce excessive quantities of secretion, or a thick, sticky mucinous discharge which clogs them or obstructs the passages into which they normally open.

Babies with cystic fibrosis often get early bowel blockage from sticky contents. Others have swollen tummies and pass frequent oily stools. Appetite is very good but growth is slow. About half have lung complications because the air tubes are blocked with excessive mucus secretions and plugs of thick muco-pus. There is troublesome cough, wheezing and difficulty in breathing and the chest becomes barrel-shaped from the effort of breathing. Sinusitis and nasal problems are common. The sweat contains excessive salt and the skin may be powdered with dried sweat. This is a common early sign of cystic fibrosis.

Children with cystic fibrosis suffer growth retardation and delayed puberty and cannot participate normally in games and sport. The possible complications of the condition include:

- collapse of a lung;
- heart failure;
- cirrhosis of the liver;
- pancreatitis;
- diabetes.

The medical management of cystic fibrosis involves skilled and comprehensive care and much-needed psychological support, both for the child and the parents. The gene for the condition is now easily detected. It is a recessive condition, so both parents must have the gene to produce the disease in a child.

Scaly eyelids

See **Itching scalp.**

Scaly patches on hairline

See **Skin with scales.**

Scaly red patches on body

See **Itching elbows and knees.**

Scissors gait

Spastic paralysis, or *cerebral palsy*, is a non-progressive disorder of the brain control of movement. It affects about one child in five hundred, appears early in life and varies in degree, from only slight to almost total disability.

There is stiff 'spasticity' of the muscles, lack of coordination and sometimes involuntary jerks and movements. There is almost always some difficulty in walking. Commonly the legs press tightly together, causing a characteristic 'scissors gait'. Often speech is affected and about half of the affected children have some degree of mental retardation. About a quarter also have fits.

Cerebral palsy may be caused by brain injury at birth, especially lack of oxygen during delivery; physical malformations; rhesus incompatibility with severe jaundice causing brain damage; infections such as encephalitis and meningitis; and head injury early in life. Many babies who develop cerebral palsy are small at birth – less than 200 kilograms.

Severe spastic paralysis can impose a terrible burden on parents but attitudes should always be as positive as possible. Much can be done to help children to control muscular action and to prevent deformity from muscle contractures.

Seasickness

See **Travel sickness.**

Secret binge eating

Bulimia is a disorder, mainly affecting young women, that features uncontrollable overeating usually followed by induced vomiting and purging. The condition is often kept secret, and is usually unsuspected, but damage to the teeth from stomach acid and to the backs of the fingers (from abrasion by sharp teeth during self-induced vomiting) may give a clue to what is going on.

Bulimia is often a form of anorexia nervosa in which the morbid fear of becoming fat is repeatedly overtaken by a craving for food. It commonly occurs after the years of near starvation typical of anorexia nervosa, but sometimes occurs without such a history. Most people suffering from bulimia are of normal weight or may be very thin. They are often greatly distressed by their compulsive behaviour and are sometimes suicidal.

It is very important to seek treatment for bulimia. ⚠ There is always a real problem and it can be managed, but cooperation is necessary. Sufferers may have to be strongly persuaded to agree to medical management. Control of the depression, alone, can greatly relieve the distress of the condition, but dietary control is also necessary.

Seizures

See **Convulsions**.

Sense of being a stranger

People who have a strong sense of being a stranger, even in familiar surroundings and among familiar people, are said to suffer from *alienation*. If you have this problem you feel you have no sense of identity with those around you and cannot share their interests or concerns. Often alienation is a normal consequence of an actual difference in interests and values and is common in adolescence. It may arise from cultural, educational, racial or financial differences. It is usually easy to recognise alienation of this kind. But a strong, persistent sense of alienation that is not based on obvious differences may be an early symptom of schizophrenia or may be a feature of a personality disorder.

Separation anxiety

This is a childhood disorder in which excessive and inappropriate anxiety is shown whenever there is separation, or the threat of separation, from one or both parents. The child suffers unrealistic fears of abandonment, and of danger to the parent. In addition to demonstrating concern dramatically at the time of separation, by a show of terror or panic, the child may complain of headache, tummy pain and nausea, and may often vomit. Such children make abnormal demands to be held and cuddled and can readily obtrude too much into adult affairs. They will persistently refuse to go to school or to sleep away from home and may refuse even to go to bed unless accompanied by a parent.

Separation anxiety is managed by constant reassurance of love and support, fair treatment, explanation, firmness and natural responses. Occasionally, a doctor may prescribe tranquillizer drugs and night sedatives.

Shivering

Shivering is a rapid succession of contractions and relaxations of muscles and is one of the main ways extra heat is produced in the body. Shivering occurs automatically when extra heat is required to maintain body temperature and is thus a normal feature of exposure to cold. The power of the contraction depends on the rate of heat production needed and may be considerable, leading to a rigor (violent shivering). The correct response to shivering from cold is to improve the body's insulation with suitable clothing and so reduce heat loss.

The body contains a thermostat, in the form of certain temperature-sensitive nerve cells in the hypothalamus of the brain. When these nerves sense a drop in blood temperature, the shivering reflex is initiated. In fever from infection, the germs and their toxins release from some of the white cells of the blood a substance called *interleukin-1*, and this resets the thermostat at a higher point. The nervous system then responds as if the blood were too cold and shivering results. In this case, the extra heat production may or may not be beneficial, depending on the cause but, in general, you should encourage heat loss from the body. Fever can, however, discourage bacterial reproduction so it is not always a good idea to try to bring down moderately high temperatures.

Short sight

See **Vision worse for near.**

Shortness of breath

See **Breathing difficulty.**

Sight problems

See entries under **Vision.**

Skin blisters

A blister is a collection of fluid (serum) between the outer layer of the skin (the epidermis) and the main layer underneath. Blisters are due to injury from persistent rubbing that causes a shearing force between the skin layers or from strong irritation by radiation – such as sunlight – or a penetrating chemical substance. The serum in a blister is usually sterile. Blisters also form spontaneously in a number of skin and general disorders. Impetigo is a common skin infection causing small blisters to form. Other common blistering conditions include chickenpox and shingles. Rarer conditions, such as pemphigus, erythema multiforme, epidermolysis bullosa and dermatitis herpetiformis, also feature blistering.

In most cases the cause of blistering is obvious and in many case it can be avoided. Don't deliberately prick or cut blisters. To do so is to incite infection. Unexplained blistering should always be reported to your doctor.

Skin blisters around mouth or nose

Most people will have no difficulty in identifying 'cold sores' or herpes simplex infection. There are two strains of herpes simplex viruses – type 1 (HSV-1), which causes 'cold sores' around the mouth and nose and type 2 (HSV-2), which causes venereal herpes. Regrettably, these two types have now become rather mixed up. Herpes viruses are highly contagious and few people are free from them. Most of us carry herpes simplex viruses lying dormant in the nerves at the junction of skin and mucous membranes. These viruses may have been present for long periods, often for years. Every now and then, dormant viruses become active, reproducing rapidly, moving to the skin and causing the well-known itching, tingling discomfort and spreading clusters of painful little crusting blisters.

It is not known, for certain, why the dormant viruses flare up, but they often do so during a feverish illness, or at times of stress or emotional upset or after exposure to bright sunlight. Some people get an attack after taking certain foodstuffs or drugs. It is probable that the fighting strength of the viruses is kept under control most of the time by the immune system and that herpes only flares when the immune system is coping with demands elsewhere. People whose immune systems are deficient, as in AIDS, have a very bad time with herpes, which often spreads to parts of the body not normally affected.

One problem in trying to treat herpes simplex infections is that, because the available drugs act to stop the viruses reproducing, it is hard to know when is the right time to start. Unfortunately, before each flare-up, viral reproduction has gone on quietly for quite a while, so there are always plenty of viruses around before there seems to be any reason to start treatment. Short of treating all the time, the ideal is to start treatment at the earliest possible moment – at the

first suggestion of a tingle. The most effective drug is acyclovir (Zovirax). Acyclovir is a remarkable drug which remains virtually inert until it contacts herpes viruses. These contain an enzyme which converts acyclovir to its active form, acyclovir triphosphate, and it is this which stops the virus from reproducing by interfering with its DNA.

Acyclovir can safely be taken by mouth and it is widely distributed throughout the body. It is excreted in the urine and about half the dose has gone in three hours. It is also available as a cream for the treatment of herpes on the lips and eyes. Genital herpes is best treated by the tablets, because the cream may encourage resistant strains of the virus to emerge. The dose will be prescribed by the doctor and one should on no account try to economize. Large doses are used for primary attacks, but, unfortunately, do not eradicate the infection. Those who suffer severe recurrent herpes can reduce the frequency and severity of the attacks by taking a tablet three times a day, but this should not be done without medical advice.

Skin blisters that crust over

Blisters that ooze and form sticky golden crusts could be impetigo. This common, infective skin disease is characterized by small blisters, often ring-like, which soon crust and form scabs. If neglected, the condition may quickly become widespread, suggesting poor standards of baby or child skin care. Both staphylococci and streptococci can cause impetigo. Antibiotics, such as erythromycin, in ointment form, are usually effective, but recurrence is likely unless the child is carefully washed all over every day.

Impetigo is much commoner in Europeans living in tropical areas than it is when they are at home.

Skin bruising without injury

Most bruises are caused by an obvious injury and are seldom of more than temporary importance. They result from the release of blood into the tissues from small blood vessels (capillaries). Over the course of a week or two, the blood is gradually absorbed and the bruise turns from black to yellow and then disappears. Bruising can be minimized by applying a cold compress as soon as possible after the injury. See also **Eyelids bruised after injury.**

A bruise that appears *without* injury is a different matter and suggests a disorder of small blood vessels or of blood clotting. This should always be reported for investigation.

Purpura is a group of bleeding disorders which cause haemorrhages into the tissues from small blood vessels. These may often be seen under or in the skin either as the tiny pinhead *petechiae* or as larger 'black and blue' bruises (ecchymoses). Purpura arises in two ways – from damage to small blood vessels or from a shortage of blood platelets (thrombocytes), which are necessary for normal clotting.

'Simple' or 'senile' purpura is the commonest of all bleeding disorders and is seen most often in post-menopausal women. Unsightly, and sometimes extensive, bruising is readily seen through the thinned skin, often on the thighs or arms. Bleeding may also occur under the mucous membrane lining of the mouth. This form of purpura is due to increased fragility of small blood vessels and is sometimes related to oestrogen deficiency.

Allergic purpura, or Henoch-Schönlein purpura, often follows a streptococcal infection in children. It arises when the lining of small blood vessels is damaged by the resulting immune complexes (the antibodies linked to the material causing the allergic reaction). In addition to the signs of bleeding, the skin may show redness and urticaria. This form of purpura causes local inflammation and itching and may affect a wide range of organs, especially the kidneys, the joints and the bowels. Kidney disease occurs in about 10 per cent of cases. There may be swollen and painful joints, abdominal pain and sometimes blackening of the stools from altered blood (melaena). Sometimes there is bleeding into the brain, causing headaches, dizziness and confusion.

Platelet deficiency (thrombocytopenia) is a common cause of purpura and can occur in many ways. These include:

- inadequate production by the bone marrow;
- bone marrow tumour;
- infection;
- drug reaction;
- radiation;
- increased platelet destruction by drugs;
- alcohol excess;
- increased platelet usage from burns, septicaemia or severe injuries.

Thrombocytopenia from increased platelet destruction often occurs for no determinable reason, but the condition commonly follows a virus infection, especially in children and young adults, and is probably due to an antibody-antigen reaction. This is called *acute idiopathic thrombo-cytopenia.*

Platelet deficiency interferes with normal clotting and the result is an abnormal tendency to bleed anywhere in the body. The skin shows petechiae and bruising, there may be nose bleeding, bleeding into the bowel, urinary system, vagina, brain, spinal cord and joints. Such haemorrhages cause varying effects depending on the site but, in addition, the persistent blood loss tends to lead to anaemia with fatigue, weakness and even heart failure. The condition is very variable in severity, showing, at the one extreme, only a few petechiae, and at the other, severe and barely controllable bleeding.

Spontaneous bruising has other causes. It may result from:

- vitamin C deficiency, when it is called scurvy;
- hereditary blood vessel weakness;
- excessive antibodies in the blood (hypergammaglobulinaemia);

- autoimmune reaction to the person's own red blood cells.

The treatment of spontaneous bruising depends on the type. Common purpura in menopausal women may be helped by hormone replacement therapy (HRT) or by corticosteroids. Immunosuppressive therapy has been found helpful in severe cases, as has a plasma exchange (plasmapheresis). Thrombocytopenic purpura is treated according to the cause. In many cases it is necessary to transfuse platelet concentrates. Scurvy is cured by vitamin C.

Skin inflamed under nappy

Babies with nappy rash show obvious discomfort and cry a lot. An extensive rash is usually caused by prolonged skin contact with a wet nappy in which the urine has been acted on by bacteria so that some of the urea in it has been converted to ammonia. You can smell the ammonia in these cases and, not surprisingly, this strong alkali is highly irritating to the baby's skin. The remedy is to change nappies frequently and to try to keep the nappy area of the skin as clean and free from contamination as possible. Disposable nappies are better than towelling ones. Disposable liners are available from most chemists. As the problem is primarily due to bacteria, a mild antiseptic cream like cetavlon is helpful.

If the rash is confined to the area immediately around the baby's anus, it is probably due to irritants in the faeces. These irritants also irritate the bowel, so there is likely to be diarrhoea. Never neglect diarrhoea in a baby. When the diarrhoea settles, the rash should settle also. The affected skin should be kept as clean as possible. A bland protective barrier cream, such as Dimethicone cream, applied after washing and thorough drying, can be helpful. Waterproof pants should be used only when strictly necessary.

Skin inflammation

Inflammation of the skin from any cause is called *dermatitis*.

Note that dermatitis is not a specific disease. Different kinds of dermatitis may have a similar appearance, but the causes can be diverse. They include:

- infection by viruses, bacteria or fungi;
- injury by insects, such as the scabies mite, or lice;
- chemical injury by irritants, solvents or defatting agents;
- poisons;
- allergy to particular substances such as metals, plants, cosmetics, drugs, foodstuffs or a wide range of chemicals.

Eczema (atopic dermatitis), runs in families and is commonly associated with hay fever and asthma. The appearance of many of these forms of dermatitis is similar, with redness, blister formation, swelling, weeping and crusting. There is itching and burning and a strong impulse to scratch, which often makes the condition worse and may, in itself, keep it going. Dermatitis calls for skilled medical attention. See **Itching elbows and knees.**

Skin marks present at birth

These affect about one third of all babies at birth or soon after. They are harmless tumours of skin blood vessels and are of cosmetic importance only. They take various forms. The strawberry naevus is a small, bright red, raised tumour which grows to its full size during the first six months of life and then subsides. In most cases it disappears altogether by the age of five. No treatment is needed.

The port-wine stain, or capillary haemangioma, is a flat tumour of the smallest blood vessels. It is present at birth and is permanent. It usually occurs on one side of the face and is often a conspicuous blemish. Even worse is the cavernous haemangioma which is raised, lumpy and highly coloured and consists of a mass of medium blood vessels and blood spaces. It is also permanent. However, if small enough, haemangiomas may be removed and the skin edges brought together with stitches. Larger haemangiomas may require a skin graft. Lasers and freezing have been tried, with limited success.

One in three newborn babies have small pinkish-red skin blemishes around the eyes and at the nape of the neck. These are called 'storkbites' or 'salmon patches', and those on the face nearly always disappear in the first year of life. They are actually benign tumours of tiny blood vessels (haemangiomas) and are entirely harmless. Salmon patches on the neck may, however, persist.

Skin oiliness

A great many of the hair follicles in your skin – and there are millions – have their own particular oil supply in the form of tiny sebaceous glands that secrete sebum into the follicle around the shaft of each hair. There are large numbers of sebaceous glands on the face, upper part of the back and on the chest and they are very much under the influence of the sex hormones. This is why they become more active at puberty and why adolescents are so plagued by acne.

To say that sebum is an oil is a bit of a simplification. It is produced by the breakdown of the sebaceous glands, and is actually a highly complex substance consisting of triacyl glycerols, wax esters and squalene. Sebum leaves a thin oily or fatty film over the skin that has a useful antibacterial effect and that also helps to make the skin more waterproof so as to retain moisture. Without sebum, the skin becomes very dry and powdery.

For some people, especially those with black skin, plenty of sebum is a good thing as, in these, the powdery effect is more conspicuous. People with white skins, however, often consider the oily appearance unattractive. It's all a matter of your point of view. Excess sebum is easily removed with soap and water but do remember that it has a

purpose and that too much washing can be damaging to the skin. As in many other things, moderation is everything.

Skin reactions to insect bites

Most bites from midges, mosquitos and fleas cause little trouble apart from the annoying irritation and an occasional allergic reaction. Dog and cat fleas populate domestic areas where the animal commonly lies, and may jump onto humans to suck blood. They usually cause bites in clusters, often in areas of skin in close contact with clothing. These can cause persistent itching. More severe reactions can arise from harvest mites and grain mites. Sandflies can cause severe and persistent skin spots.

The common skin mite of scabies burrows into the skin to lay her eggs and these hatch into larvae in a few days, causing such intense itching that the burrows are often obscured by scratching (see **Itching wrists**). Severe itching is also a feature of infestation with lice.

All these reactions are allergic in nature. Scratching should be avoided, if possible, and the itching relieved by applying a soothing lotion.

Skin rings that expand

The two principal conditions that can cause this odd effect are *tinea* and *Lyme disease*. Tinea, commonly known as 'ringworm', is not a worm but a fungus infection of the skin, often called *epidermophytosis*. The fungus starts as a progressively enlarging reddish, slightly raised spot. Soon the skin first affected acquires resistance so the centre of the spot heals and returns to normal. The result is a gradually enlarging ring of fungus infection.

Tinea occurs most often in the moist areas of the body – the groin, armpits and feet, but can also affect the scalp and the nails. It is commoner in the tropics than in temperate climates. Antifungal treatment, either ointments or tablets, is effective, but may have to be continued for long periods.

The other condition causing expanding skin rings is much more important. Lyme disease was first recognized in Old Lyme, Connecticut, USA, in 1975. It is caused by a spirochaete transmitted by the bite of a tick. It occurs throughout the temperate regions of the world. The natural hosts are deer and dogs and it is now occurring increasingly in Britain.

The first sign is a slightly itchy red spot at the site of the mite bite. This expands steadily and forms a slowly growing ring. In about half the cases other similar rings appear and there may be as many as 100, scattered all over the skin. These are not due to multiple bites. There is fatigue, a feeling of illness, headaches, fever, stiff neck, aches in the muscles and joints and enlarged lymph nodes. In some cases there is sore throat, cough, conjunctivitis, other more severe eye complications and tummy pain with enlargement and tenderness of the liver. ▲

Weeks or months later, one in six of affected people develop meningitis, encephalitis, paralysis of various nerves, muscle weakness or shingles-like pain in the skin. Mental illness or deep fatigue and weakness, lasting for months or years, may occur. Half of those who contract Lyme disease suffer joint problems, usually mild, but sometimes severe, with damage similar to rheumatoid arthritis. Heart damage may occur. Lyme disease can be passed from a mother to her unborn baby, and the spirochaetes have been found in children with severe congenital defects.

It is a pity that the disease is not better known to the public, for if the early skin pattern is recognized for what it is, all these unpleasant complications can be entirely prevented by a course of antibiotics.

Skin spots in adolescence

Acne is a persistent skin disorder, mainly troubling adolescents, in which the tube-like hair-forming pores (the follicles) and the oil-producing sebaceous glands, become affected by sex hormones. The oily secretion of the sebaceous glands increases and thickens to form plugs that block the hair follicles. The altered material irritates the surrounding skin which becomes inflamed. The tip of the plug, exposed to the air, changes chemically and turns dark brown, producing a blackhead. This is not caused by dirt. Contact with any oily material, including cosmetics, can make acne worse.

Acne most severely affects skin areas with the largest numbers of sebaceous glands, such as the face, the shoulders, the upper back and the centre of the chest. There are blackheads, whiteheads, pimples, purplish nodules under the skin and small abscesses.

Be careful about squeezing out blackheads. It is only too easy to rupture the walls of the hair follicle and release the irritating material into the surrounding tissue, causing worsening inflammation and leading to permanent scarring. Blackheads do not leave permanently widened pores. Your skin is growing all the time. There are effective treatments to unblock the pores and remove sebum, and drugs that can counter the basic defect. But the treatment of severe acne is a job for a skin specialist (dermatologist). If necessary, acne scars can be reduced by sandpapering (dermabrasion), performed by an expert.

Skin spots in elderly people

Elderly skin almost always features large freckles and a variety of other blemishes such as slightly raised, scaly, brownish or yellow patches, red pinpoints on the trunk, or enlarged skin blood vessels. Most age spots are harmless and require no treatment but skin cancers are common in the elderly so you should report anything in the least unusual or suspicious. Cancers are commonest in skin areas exposed to the sun. Small brownish spots on exposed skin areas with scaly tops that become white when you pick at them (don't!) are called *solar keratoses*. It is best to report these, as a small proportion of them turn to local cancers. Any spot that changes shape or colour or that bleeds readily should be reported to your doctor. See also **Itching mole.**

Skin swelling, hard and doughnut-shaped

This could be a basal cell carcinoma, a form of skin cancer also known as a *rodent ulcer*. It is the commonest skin cancer and affects about 30,000 people each year in Britain. It occurs mostly on the face, often around the eyes or on or near the nose. Although locally destructive if neglected, it does not spread remotely to other parts of the body. Basal cell carcinomas (BCC) are definitely related to overexposure to bright sunlight. You are most likely to suffer a BCC if you are fair-skinned and over 50.

Basal cell carcinomas are usually hard, flat and round-edged with a dimple in the centre. They may have a few fine, red lines – blood vessels – running across the surface. Sometimes they have a pearly appearance. They grow slowly and can spread down into the depth of the facial structures, even involving bone or the eye socket. For this reason, you should always report any suspicious nodule on the face or elsewhere to your doctor without undue delay. ⚠ Rodent ulcers are easy to remove in the early stages and this is a complete cure.

Skin swelling, inflamed and tender

You are not likely to be in much doubt as to whether or not you have a boil. These angry, inflamed, pus-filled swellings, usually on the back of the neck or in an armpit or groin are unlikely to be mistaken for anything else. Boils start as infections of hair follicles and develop into abscesses usually with a yellow head where the pus is trying to get out. Occasionally, a 'blind boil' develops

without a head and this may cease to be inflamed and persist for months as a simple swelling.

Boils discharge millions of bacteria and these may set up secondary boils nearby or on a remote part of the skin. So if you have a boil, you should be particularly careful about your daily overall washing. Don't deliberately burst boils. It is better to let nature – in the shape of your immune system – kill off as many of the bacteria as possible. You can help this by applying hot, moist pads of cotton wool or other clean material every two or three hours. If you get a sequence of boils, see your doctor.

Skin tingling and with painful blisters around the flank

Shingles is a painful and sometimes debilitating disease caused by the same virus that causes chickenpox (the varicella-zoster virus). Shingles is not an infection in the ordinary sense. The virus is acquired, as a general rule, during childhood when it causes an attack of chickenpox – usually a very mild and transient illness and one which may even go unnoticed. In the course of the chickenpox attack, varicella-zoster virus is believed to enter the sensory nerve endings in the skin and travel up the nerves to the collections of nerve bodies (ganglia) near the spinal cord. The virus has been isolated from these ganglia at postmortem examination of patients who died while suffering from shingles. Later, often many years later, the viruses become reactivated and produce an acute inflammation in the ganglion (ganglionitis). This is the cause of the pain experienced in the area supplied by the nerve, prior to the onset of the rash. Reactivation occurs because of a drop in the efficiency of the immune system which had been keeping the virus in check. Replication of the viruses now produces a large number of new individuals and these travel down the nerve to the skin where further reproduction occurs and the characteristic rash, from cell damage, appears.

The first indication of shingles is usually a tingling sensation (hypersensitivity) in the area to be affected and this is followed by pain, often severe, in the same area. The area involved is the skin distribution of one or more sensory nerve roots supplying a strip of the skin of the chest or abdominal wall on one side, or on the face, above the eyebrow, also on one side. There is often fever and sickness and on the fourth or fifth day after the onset, the skin becomes red, and typical crops of small blisters (vesicles) appear in the area affected.

These vesicles are initially full of clear fluid, which is teeming with herpes viruses, but about three days after appearing, they turn yellowish and within a few days flatten, dry out and crust over. In the following two weeks or so, the crusts gradually dry up and drop off, leaving small, pitted scars. Occasionally, the rash is more widespread and the vesicles may join up to form large areas of damaged skin. In these cases healing may take many weeks and residual scarring may be severe. Widespread rash should arouse the suspicion of an underlying malignancy or a compromised immune system. Herpes zoster of the face, which occurs in 10–15 per cent of cases, is especially distressing, because the eye may be involved and vision affected.

Unfortunately, shingles is often followed by persistent pain in the site of the rash. This misfortune, which is known as *post-herpetic pain*, is the real reason why shingles is so important. The pain affects about 30 per cent of shingles patients over the age of 40, and the older the person, and the more severe the pre-rash pain, the more likely this is to happen. Persistent pain of this kind can have a devastating effect on the life of the unfortunate sufferer. Many are old, frail and ill-equipped to tolerate the resulting debility and the

deeply depressing effects of unremitting pain. For many, the will to live may, all too easily, be lost.

Shingles can hardly be avoided, but an important recent advance has made it possible to ensure that the effects are mild and the post-herpetic pain minor. This is the development of the anti-herpes drug acyclovir (Zovirax) which should be given in large dosage as soon as the diagnosis becomes clear. The earlier the drug is given, the more effective it is.

Skin with large, black boils

Happily, this eventuality is rare in developed countries. It suggests the severe bacterial infection of *anthrax*, a disease of animals that sometimes affects people handling affected livestock or animal products. Anthrax is occasionally imported on hides or wool and has been caused by infected shaving brushes.

The disease starts in the skin, causing large boils with

black central scabs and swelling and inflammation of the surrounding tissues. In non-immune people who receive no treatment, infection may spread from these boils to other parts of the body causing blood poisoning and severe and sometimes fatal illness. Antibiotics are effective. Anthrax of the lungs is acquired by inhaling anthrax spores from infected animal fibres, and is usually fatal.

Skin with multiple, reddish-brown or bluish nodules

Multiple, firm, plaques or nodules of this colour, some of which may be ulcerated, suggest *Kaposi's sarcoma*. In this condition, these nodules appear simultaneously anywhere on the skin or on the mucous membranes, such as the lining of the mouth. They are commonest on the legs. Kaposi's sarcoma is a multiple tumour, thought to be of small blood vessels, that affects mainly men.

Although the condition has long been known to affect elderly men, especially of Eastern European origin, it was a rare disease in the West, until the advent of the AIDS epidemic in 1981. It is now estimated to be 20,000 times more common in people with AIDS than in the general population. If you think you have this condition, you need urgent medical attention ⚠. Non-AIDS Kaposi's sarcoma is rarely fatal but untreated Kaposi's sarcoma in a person with AIDS is an aggressive and dangerous disorder. Treatment is with anti-cancer drugs such as etoposide, doxorubicin, bleomycin and vinblastine.

Skin with raised, purplish swellings

If this occurs only in cold weather and affects your fingers and toes, you are likely to have *chilblains*. The condition, together with other related disorders, is dignified by the title of *perniosis*. The disorder is essentially due to the severe narrowing that cold can cause in the small arteries supplying the part with blood. Lack of circulation through the part leads to tissue damage from shortage of oxygen and glucose fuel. At the same time, damaging bodies such as immune complexes and bacteria accumulate at the sites. Things are made worse if garters or other constricting clothing interfere with the blood supply. Chilblains can be avoided by keeping the extremities warm.

Alternatively, these swellings may be the condition of *angioedema*. This is a form of allergic reaction that features large, slightly raised purplish swellings of the skin and sometimes of the internal structures of the body. The swellings may last for days. Angioedema is usually a response to food, but sometimes occurs after contact with drugs, certain plants or other substances. The main danger is from obstruction to the airway when the lining of the voice box swells. In this case there will also usually be swelling of the face and neck. Severe angioedema that obstructs air entry can cause potentially fatal suffocation and may require an emergency cutting into the windpipe (a tracheostomy). Angioedema of the intestine causes nausea and vomiting. Don't be casual about angioedema. Most cases are fairly mild but a dangerous attack is always possible. Ask your doctor whether you need any special precautionary measures. ⚠

Skin with scales

All skin is a bit scaly because it is normal for the dead surface layer of the skin to be shed. The average adult loses 5–10 grams of skin scales each day. There are, however, a number of conditions in which the rate of skin shedding is increased. These include:

- dry skin in the elderly;
- any itching disorder;
- eczema;
- psoriasis;
- Hodgkin's disease;
- icthyosis.

There are several articles on itching disorders in this book. For information on eczema, see **Itching elbows and knees.**

Psoriasis is a common, non-infectious skin disease featuring non- itching, bright red or pink, sharply outlined, dry plaques with silvery scaling surfaces. These affect mainly the elbows, knees, shins, scalp and lower back. The nails can also be affected, causing severe distortion. The plaques are caused by increased thickness, from rapid growth, of the skin outer layers (the epidermis and the keratin surface). This is associated with the abnormal presence of nucleated cells in the skin above the basal cell layer. There are also widened (dilated) blood vessels and sometimes migration into the plaques of white blood cells (polymorphs) to produce sterile pus. The patches vary in size from a few millimetres to many centimetres.

The cause of psoriasis is unknown. It may start at any age, but usually shows itself in early adult life, often after a period of severe stress, including illness or childbirth. There is sometimes a family history. Plaques often appear at the site of a minor injury and usually clear on exposure to sun. Psoriasis is sometimes associated with arthritis of the fingers and toes, or of a single large joint.

Psoriasis is usually very persistent. Severe attacks require management by a dermatologist. Coal tar is a long-established remedy for simple psoriasis and the tar may be supplemented by salicylic acid which helps to reduce scaling. Dithranol is widely used and is highly effective, but is damaging to normal skin and must be applied with great care. Some doctors advise a 'short-contact' application for no more than half an hour, followed by a bath. Other treatments include ultraviolet light in association with psoralens (PUVA), derivatives of vitamin A called *retinoids*, hydrocortisone and, in very stubborn cases, the powerful cytotoxic drug methotrexate. Recurrence is common.

Ichthyosis is a scaly, fish-like disorder of the skin, sometimes called 'fish skin disease' – *ichthyos* is Greek for 'a fish'.

The condition is usually genetically determined and present from birth. The skin is unable to form the normal waterproof horny outer layer so that it cannot retain water and tends to dry out.

The treatment consists in soaking the skin, cleaning with aqueous cream or emulsifying ointment instead of soap, removing excessive scales by scrubbing or fine sandpapering, and using a protective, waterproof cream. Ichthyosis is always worse in cold weather when the low atmospheric humidity encourages water loss. Sufferers fare better in warm moist climates. The condition often improves with age.

Sleeping difficulties

See **Insomnia; Nightmares; Night terrors; Night waking**.

Slow pulse

Doctors talk of a *bradycardia* when they really mean an unusually, but not necessarily abnormally, slow heart rate – below about 60 beats per minute instead of the usual 70 to 80. Very fit people often have a naturally slow pulse and athletes who engage in sustained exertion, such as long-distance running, almost always have a bradycardia when they are not exerting themselves. This allows them to increase the heart rate, and the volume of blood pumped per minute, to a much greater degree than other people can during strenuous activity.

If you are not athletic, a persistent bradycardia might indicate a heart disorder, such as an interruption of the conducting fibres in the heart muscle (heart block), or possibly underaction of the thyroid gland, so that your whole body is slowed down. Short periods of bradycardia may result from a temporary overaction of the nerves that control the heart rate. This can cause fainting because the supply of blood to the brain is diminished. Beta-blocker drugs are often used to slow the heart and improve its performance, but overdosage can lead to undesirable bradycardia.

Slurred speech

There are several things that can go wrong with the production of speech in a person who has previously spoken normally. These are classified under the term *dysphasia* This is an impairment of speech or of the production or comprehension of spoken or written language, due to damage to certain parts of the brain. Dysphasia is most commonly caused by local interference with the blood supply and is a common feature of stroke. Dysphasia may be:

- *motor*, in which the comprehension is normal but the execution defective;
- *sensory*, in which there is a receptive defect;
- *global*, in which both are affected.

It may also be of widely varying degrees of severity. Any such change should be reported immediately. ▲ See also **Speech difficulties.**

Sore throat

See **Pain in the throat.**

Spastic walking

See **Scissors gait.**

Speech difficulties

There are many causes of this. They may result from:

- hearing loss;
- emotional upset;
- developmental delay;
- lack of stimulation;
- psychological or physical difficulty in articulating speech.

Articulation problems may be due to cerebral palsy or to abnormalities of the mouth, such as a cleft palate or poor alignment of the teeth.

Stammering (which is the same thing as stuttering) usually starts in childhood, almost always before the age of eight and persists in about one per cent of the adult population. Temporary stammering is common in children of two to four. About half those whose stammer continues after five will have a permanent stammer. Stammering is commonest in males, twins, and left-handed people. The cause is disputed, but it is generally believed to be a psychological problem and it can usually be improved or cured by speech therapy.

Spider-like fingers

Doctors call this *arachnodactyly* and it is the most obvious feature of an inherited condition called *Marfan's syndrome*. This is a rare genetic disease in which all the collagen connective tissue of the body is abnormally weak. Affected people grow tall and thin and characteristically have extraordinarily long spidery fingers. The joints dislocate easily, the suspensory ligaments of the lenses of the eyes break easily so that the lenses become displaced, and the main artery of the body, the aorta, is unusually elastic and floppy. There is a strong tendency to develop heart disease.

Spinal stiffness and fixation

Ankylosing spondylitis is a long-term disease of the spine in which the joints between the bones (vertebrae) become inflamed and eventually fuse together so that the spine be-comes very stiff and inflexible. Initially there is pain and stiffness in the lower back, which is worse after lying in bed and is reduced by exercise. Sometimes other joints are also involved. Gradually the stiffness becomes worse and the range of possible movement less. There may also be general symptoms such as tiredness and loss of appetite and weight. The condition is often associated with a form of internal eye inflammation which may be severe. Eventually, in severe cases, the spine may become almost solid with curvature of the back and severe restriction in chest expansion from involvement of the rib joints. In many cases the outcome is less serious. Constant attention to movement and regular exercise are important in limiting the effects. Don't ignore persistent pain and stiffness in the lower back. Report them to your doctor so that the matter can be investigated.

Spontaneous fractures

See **Brittle bones.**

Squinting

See **Eyes crossed.**

Squits

See **Diarrhoea.**

Stammering

See **Speech difficulties.**

Stealing without wanting

Most people who steal do so because they think they want what they steal. There is one kind of stealing, however, in which that is not the motive. Kleptomania is a rare condition characterized by a recurrent compulsion to steal things, usually from a shop, that are neither wanted nor needed. The object is not acquisition and the things stolen are often given or thrown away or are carefully hidden. Most kleptomaniacs could easily pay for the things they steal. The disorder, although rare, occurs in all levels of society.

The act is not usually preplanned and the object is the theft itself. The stealing is not usually reckless, and reason-able precautions are taken to avoid discovery, but sometimes kleptomaniacs seem to give no thought to the probable consequences of their actions and some of them appear outraged when arrested. In the course of the act there is a rising sense of tension focused on the theft. Afterwards, if the act is successfully accomplished there is relief of tension and a sense of elation. This may, however, be followed by strong guilt feelings and intense fear of discovery.

Kleptomania is often put forward as a defence against an indictment for theft, but it is in fact very uncommon. Less than five per cent of people arrested for shoplifting are found, on questioning, to respond in a manner consistent with the diagnosis. The condition is associated with stress, such as bereavement or separation, and kleptomaniacs also tend to suffer from persistent depression (see **Sadness**) and anorexia nervosa (see **Loss of appetite**). It has also been associated with starting fires (pyromania). The cause remains obscure, but many kleptomaniacs feel that they have been wronged, and are unwanted or neglected and are thus entitled to steal.

Kleptomania tends to be persistent and may, indeed, be a life-long disorder. In many cases it is compatible with an otherwise apparently normal life and few affected people receive treatment unless this has been ordered by judicial authorities after arrest. Treatment involves a course of psychotherapy designed to provide the affected person with a clear insight into the nature of the condition. Behaviour therapy has also been successful.

Stiff neck (with fever)

See **Fever and neck stiffness.**

Stoppage of menses

See **Absence of menstrual periods.**

Stoppage of urine output

Total stoppage is called *anuria* and is always a serious matter as it indicates either that the kidneys have stopped functioning or that there is an obstruction to the outflow. In either case, urgent attention is needed. ⚠ You should have little difficulty in deciding which of the two causes is operating. Obstruction to outflow – usually from an enlarged prostate gland in men – causes acute pain, distention of the lower abdomen and great distress. Failure of the kidneys to produce urine only occurs after serious injury or prolonged kidney disease such as glomerulonephritis. An apparent cessation of urine production in a healthy person is probably the result of temporary dehydration or inadequate fluid intake and is very unlikely to be a genuine anuria.

Stuttering

See **Speech difficulties.**

Sunken eyes

See **Eyes sunken.**

Swallowing difficulty

Doctors call this *dysphagia*. One of the commonest types

of swallowing difficulty is due to a condition known as *achalasia*. This is a failure of the muscle ring at the bottom of the gullet to relax. As a result swallowed food cannot pass normally down into the stomach. The gullet above the obstruction becomes wider and tends to become blocked with food. The cause is unknown. There is pain after swallowing, felt in the lower part of the chest, bad breath and bringing up of food that has been swallowed some time before. The condition tends to worsen until even liquids cannot pass down.

Similar effects are caused by cancer at the lower end of the gullet. Any swallowing difficulty should be reported to your doctor without delay. ⚠ Achalasia is treated by surgical widening or by cutting the muscle ring.

Another cause of dysphagia is pharyngeal pouch. In this disorder there is a blind-ended sac of mucous membrane, at the junction of the pharynx and the oesophagus, which bulges backwards and downwards from the back of the throat to lie between the oesophagus and the spine. The pouch seldom occurs before middle age and when fully formed pushes the oesophagus forward and causes difficulty in swallowing. A person with a pharyngeal pouch has a constant sense of something stuck in the throat and on swallowing the neck swells and a gurgling sound may be heard. Food accumulates in the pouch and becomes offensive so that there is often severe bad breath. Because of the proximity of the larynx, the pouch may also cause interference with breathing, and inhalation of the contents of the sac may lead to pneumonia.

The treatment is surgical and aims to remove the pouch and to close the opening completely. This must be done with great care, as subsequent leakage into the central partition of the chest (the mediastinum) is dangerous.

See also **Lump in the throat.**

Swelling and tenderness near the vaginal opening

The Bartholin glands lie on either side of a woman's vaginal opening and secrete clear lubricating mucus during sexual excitement. Infection of the glands causes bulging, red, acutely tender swellings and may progress to abscess. Often this can be prevented by timely use of antibiotics – assuming you report the matter quickly enough – but, if not, a minor operation involving a small incision will be needed to drain the pus from the infected gland. This is usually done under general anaesthesia. Sometimes the affected gland has to be removed. This doesn't usually cause too much of a problem as there are two Bartholin glands and vaginal secretions can make up the deficit in lubrication.

Swelling behind the knee

A Baker's cyst is a firm, fluid-filled, slightly squashy lump at the back of the knee caused by ballooning backwards of the lining of the joint. Baker's cysts are commonest in joint disorders such as rheumatoid arthritis. Most of them are painless and it is fairly common for them to disappear after some months. A Baker's cyst may rupture, causing pain and swelling in the calf as the fluid contents pass downwards. If you get a Baker's cyst you should report it to your doctor.

Swelling of the abdomen

This is common and most of the causes are not especially alarming. Some of them, such as obesity and pregnancy, are, or should be obvious, but sometimes unexpected pregnancies occur. In the case of pregnancy, you will not usually notice any swelling until about 10 to 12 weeks after the last period. Gas in the stomach or in the intestine – usually swallowed air – can cause distension of the abdomen, as can premenstrual fluid retention.

If you are certain that none of these causes apply, then the swelling may indicate something more serious. Obvious and progressive swelling in women may be due to an ovarian cyst. This may be mistaken for a pregnancy and can grow to a considerable size. An accumulation of fluid in the abdomen – fluid that shifts from one side to the other as you change position – is called *ascites* and needs urgent investigation. ⚠ This may be a symptom of heart disease, kidney disease, liver disease or cancer. In the cases of the first three there may be fluid swelling elsewhere in the body, such as swollen ankles or oedema of the lower back

Swelling of the abdomen can also be caused by a blockage in the intestine but this will also cause severe pain and probably vomiting.

Swollen ankles

An acute swelling on one side that follows an injury such as 'twisting' the ankle is obviously related to that injury. Spontaneous swelling of both sides, causing tightness of the shoes, is another matter. This is *oedema* – an abnormal accumulation of fluid in the tissues. It may be part of a general problem, in which case the oedema may be due to heart failure (see **Breathlessness**) or to kidney problems (see glomerulonephritis in the article on **Facial puffiness**).

A much more common cause of swollen ankles is a partial interference with the return of blood to the heart via the veins of the leg. This may be due to:

- pressure on the veins from pregnancy;
- tight clothing around the thighs and hips;
- clotting of blood in the veins;
- defective vein valves;
- surgery on the veins;
- varicose veins.

Varicose veins in the legs affect millions of people and are especially troublesome to women, to whom much distress is caused by their unsightly appearance and the associated symptoms. Varicosity does not simply mean the cosmetic problem of ugly, purplish, bulging veins. For many, varicosity means persistent swelling of the ankles, aching and tiredness, brownish-blue discoloration of the skin, a strong tendency to ulceration after minor knocks or abrasions and sometimes, although happily rarely, profuse and even dangerous bleeding from a ruptured vein.

Varicosity implies stagnation of blood flow; a poor supply of oxygen, glucose and other nutritional requirements to the surrounding tissues; and the accumulation of toxic products of metabolism which, normally, are diluted and washed away by a brisk blood flow. It is this combination of inadequate nutrition and local damage that causes both the symptoms and the liability of the skin to break down to form persistent ulcers. The small blood vessels become abnormally leaky and fluid passes out into the tissues where it accumulates.

Varicose veins tend to run in families and it is probable that there is a genetic tendency to weakness and incompetent vein valves. Obesity certainly contributes,

as does any factor that impedes the free flow of blood up the veins, such as pregnancy, prolonged standing and local constriction from underwear elastic or garters. Insufficient exercise, with resulting stagnation of blood in the veins, is another known factor.

Adequate external support of the surface veins – as by well-designed and properly selected compression hosiery – can be a great help in the treatment of varicose veins. This will prevent blood stagnation, relieve local oxygen lack and help to prevent accumulation of pain-causing metabolites. (These form following chemical reactions in the body and are normally washed away and diluted by the bloodstream.) Supporting the veins will divert blood from the surface into the deep veins where the pressure of the moving muscles on the veins effects an upward pumping action. Symptoms are relieved and even established varicose ulcers will often heal. The most effective support hosiery applies the greatest compression at the ankle with a progressively graded reduction in pressure up the leg to the thigh.

The definitive treatment for varicose veins is to remove them by an operation known as *stripping*. So long as tests show that the deep veins are working properly, these can be relied on to carry all the blood back to the heart. The results of this operation are usually excellent.

Swollen testicle

See **Pain in the testicle.**

T

Teeth grinding

Teething

Tender arteries

Thirst

Threatened abortion

Throbbing swelling in the abdomen

Thumbsucking

Tics

Tight shoes

Tightness in the throat

Tingling hand

Tinnitus

Tiredness and weakness

Toes turning black

Tongue-tie

Tooth abscess

Toothache

Travel sickness

Trembling	Tunnel vision
Tripping out	Twitching

Teeth grinding

Habitual, rhythmic grinding or clenching of the teeth is called *bruxism*. This is common and usually occurs during sleep. Bruxism while awake generally implies some emotional problem. The contraction of the muscles that clench the jaw can be observed in front of the ear. Sometimes bruxism is performed unconsciously. It may also result from an unsatisfactory arrangement between the upper and lower teeth (faulty occlusion)

In most cases bruxism does little harm but in severe cases it can lead to the teeth being worn away or loosened and pain and stiffness in the jaw joint. Occasionally it is necessary to protect the teeth during sleep with a dental bite plate.

Teething

The time of appearance (eruption) of the milk (primary) teeth is very variable. Some babies are actually born with one or more teeth, much to the alarm of the breast-feeding mother. Others still have no teeth by one year. Both extremes are normal and need cause no concern. In most cases, the first teeth – the central incisors (biting teeth) – appear around 6 to 9 months, followed, in a month or two, by the other incisors. Around 10 to 16 months, the first molars (grinding teeth) appear and at 16 to 20 months, the canine (tearing teeth) appear. The second molars usually erupt sometime between the second and third years of life.

Teething causes gum tenderness, some pain, and dribbling – and your baby will spend much time investigating his or her mouth. Teething can certainly lead to fractiousness and crying, but this is seldom a serious problem. Other conditions may cause these symptoms which may be wrongly attributed to teething. Evidence of undue distress should lead to investigation.

Teething powders and chewing rings should be avoided. Aspirin should not be given because of Reye's syndrome, but a suitable dose of a paracetamol preparation can be a great comfort to all concerned. A mild local anaesthetic preparation with an astringent to reduce salivation may be helpful.

Tender arteries

Inflammation of arteries usually results in narrowing or blockage with serious consequences from loss of a blood supply to tissues. If the arteries supplying the eyes are blocked, for instance it commonly causes permanent blindness. Blockage of the main leg arteries – a condition that sometimes affects heavy smokers – causes gangrene of the legs. *Polyarteritis nodosa* is a form of arteritis that can affect arteries in any part of the body, causing serious heart and kidney damage and abdominal pain.

Elderly people should be aware of the dangers of red, tender arteries under the skin of the temples (temporal arteritis). This should always be reported as a matter of urgency as sight can readily be saved by injections of steroid drugs. ⚠

Thirst

See **Excessive thirst**.

Threatened abortion

See **Bleeding during pregnancy**.

Throbbing swelling in the abdomen

Ballooning of an artery from weakening of the wall is called an *aneurysm*. Aneurysms may affect any artery but are commonest in the largest artery of the body – the aorta. Aneurysms of the aorta are mainly caused by weakening from the important artery disease *atherosclerosis*. An enlarging aneurysm of the aorta may cause abdominal or chest pain, backache or a throbbing swelling in the abdomen. It may also press on a nerve running up to the voice box and cause hoarseness.

Don't confuse this condition with the normal strong pulsation of the aorta that can be felt, especially in thin people. But if you are in any doubt that you have a pulsative swelling in your abdomen, see your doctor without delay. ⚠

Thumbsucking

This harmless habit is common and normal in young children. It may safely be ignored unless persisted in after the age of six or seven, when it may lead to some displacement of the central teeth (incisors). In this case, the child may require orthodontic treatment and possibly the use of a dental appliance at night.

Tics

Tics are repetitive, twitching movements occurring at irregular intervals and always at the same site. Simple tics occur in about a quarter of all children and usually disappear within a year. They are three times as common in boys as in girls and are absent during sleep and when the child is deeply absorbed. They are made worse by stress and by the child's awareness that he or she is being observed. A small proportion of tics persist into adult life and most of these are minor.

However, some tics become so severe and widespread as to call for medical assistance. Such major tics occasionally affect the diaphragm causing a grunting sound. In the worst cases, tics may progress to the extraordinary condition of *Gilles de la Tourette's syndrome*. This begins in childhood with simple tics such as shrugs, twitches, jerks or blinks. Instead of disappearing spontaneously as childhood tics usually do, these progress to a repertoire of ever more extensive and grotesque manifestations. Initially, they are complex bodily movements only, but eventually the sufferer begins to emit noises, at first minor barks, grunts or coughs, but later in the form of compulsive utterances, usually of an obscene nature. *Coprolalia* – involuntary scatological remarks – occur in about half the cases and so the condition becomes a severe social disability.

The condition requires skilled treatment with antipsychotic drugs (neuroleptics) which cause emotional quieting, promote indifference and slow down bodily and mental overactivity. Serenace (haloperidol) is often used.

Tics do not indicate any organic disorder, but reflect a psychological disturbance. They can be controlled by an effort of will, but since they appear to release emotional tension, such control is unpleasant.

Tight shoes

See **Swollen ankles.**

Tightness in the throat

See **Lump in the throat.**

Tingling hand

See **Pain in the hand.**

Tinnitus

See **Noises in the ears.**

Tiredness and weakness

One of the commonest causes of people feeling tired and weak is *anaemia*. This is a reduction in the amount of haemoglobin, the iron-containing, oxygen-carrying constituent of the red cells in the blood. Because a good supply of oxygen is so vital, anaemia has widespread effects, causing weakness, fatigue, tiredness and breathlessness on minor effort. The skin may appear pale and there is lowered resistance to infection. There are several different kinds of anaemia including:

- simple iron deficiency anaemia;
- haemolytic disease, due to an abnormal rate of red-cell breakdown;
- pernicious anaemia, due to the absence of an essential blood-forming factor;

- sickle-cell anaemia which features a genetic defect in the haemoglobin of the red blood cells;
- aplastic anaemia in which the bone marrow simply fails to manufacture red blood cells.

Aplastic anaemia is the most serious type of all. Anaemia is uncommon in children but all kinds can occur. It most often affects young women, especially those with heavy periods and a poor diet.

Another less common cause of tiredness and weakness is *Addison's disease*. This condition results from a shortage of the steroid hormones normally produced by the adrenal glands, situated on top of the kidneys. This occurs when any disease process, such as an immune disorder or an infection, destroys the outer layers of the glands. The effects of inadequate steroids include tiredness, weakness, loss of weight and a striking darkening of parts of the skin, such as the creases of the palms, the pressure areas and inside the mouth. If an infection or injury occurs, or if a surgical operation is needed, the deficiency of natural steroids causes severe problems – muscle weakness, low blood pressure, faintness, confusion, and sometimes loss of consciousness and death. It is therefore essential to make a diagnosis as early as possible so that maintenance steroid treatment can be given and precautions taken against increased demand. You should always report undue weakness and tiredness, especially if associated with unusual pigmentation of the skin or mouth. ▲

The term 'fatigue' has more than one meaning. It may mean the feeling of exhaustion that follows sustained physical exertion or lack of sleep; or it may mean a feeling of extreme tiredness that is unrelated to work of any kind. Physical fatigue is due to the accumulation in the muscles of the breakdown products of fuel consumption and energy production (metabolism). Resting for a short period will allow time for the normal blood flow through the muscles to 'wash out' these *metabolites*. To the extent that the affected person is aware of the symptoms caused by the metabolites, physical fatigue may be said to have a mental component.

In many cases, however, purely mental fatigue, that masquerades in most of its features as physical fatigue, can occur. While it is true that sustained, intense intellectual work can produce a sense of fatigue that urges a period of relief from the work, most cases of non-physical fatigue have nothing to do with over-use of the mental faculties. Usually, they are the result of boredom, over-long concentration on a single task, anxiety, frustration, fear or just general disinclination to perform a particular job of work. Even during periods of fatigue, the contemplation of work that is rewarding and absorbing is pleasurable, and resumption is anticipated with satisfaction.

Perhaps the most distressing cause of tiredness is the so-called *myalgic encephalitis*, which is commonly abbreviated to ME. This term is not medically approved. *Encephalitis* means 'inflammation of the brain' and *myalgic* means 'relating to muscle pain'. Sufferers from this condition may have muscle pain but they do not have brain inflammation. The concept of ME has deeply divided the medical profession for years and has provoked sometimes acrimonious and dismissive argument between those who believe the condition entirely imaginary and those who think it has an organic basis. The often derogatory remarks made about people with this problem and the implication that most of them are malingerers or manipulators betrays a common but somewhat outdated dualistic concept of the mind-body problem – the idea that the two are entirely separable.

There is no questioning the existence of a common entity, affecting predominantly women (but also both male and female members of the medical profession), featuring severe fatigue and emotional disturbance and made worse by exercise, a single act of which may cause fatigue for weeks. Unfortunately, these effects have been variously associated with a great number of other symptoms and signs, and a range of names has been applied to what may or may not be the same condition. These names include:

- Royal Free disease;
- epidemic neuromyasthenia;
- Otago mystery disease;
- Icelandic disease;
- institutional mass hysteria;
- benign myalgic encephalomyelitis;
- post-viral fatigue syndrome.

The basic difficulty, so far as medical attitudes are concerned, stems from two points. The first is medical awareness that complaint of persistent fatigue is often a feature of 'non-organic', 'neurotic' illness in which the sufferer is seeking a resolution of some major personal or social problem. The second is the failure of medical investigation to find a cause.

Virus infection has been widely proposed as a cause of the syndrome and a wide range of viruses including cox-sackie, herpes, polio, varicella-zoster (chickenpox and shingles) and Epstein-Barr (glandular fever) have been cited. Unfortunately, finding antibodies to these or other viruses in people with ME proves nothing – the world is full of people with such antibodies who do not have ME. Moreover, it is well known that psychological stress increases susceptibility to infection, so even a higher than normal prevalence of these antibodies in ME sufferers would not prove that this was the cause. Extensive immunological studies into people with ME have been inconclusive.

Although the condition is called an encephalitis, none of the normal neurological tests, such as electroencephalography, show that this is present. Some tests on muscle fibres have shown abnormalities in some cases but these have not been universally accepted.

It is clear that the fatigue experienced by ME sufferers is not a matter of the muscles alone and is quite different from the weakness experienced in muscular disorders such as myasthenia gravis (see below). The fatigue of ME has a strong cognitive element and is commonly associated with mild to severe depression. A comparison of the bodily (somatic) effects of depression – fatigue, headache, breathlessness, chest pain, dizziness and often bowel upset – with those of ME shows a striking similarity. The prevalences of ME and of depression are also very similar. In some cases the syndrome has responded well to treatment with antidepressant drugs.

Critical attitudes on the part of doctors and others have not been helpful and have caused great distress to sufferers who have often been forced to turn to alternative therapists. Whether the condition is of external organic origin or otherwise is, currently, the central point at issue. But it is surely equally important to acknowledge that people whose lives are as severely affected as those of ME sufferers deserve as much help as any similarly affected people, whatever

the cause. Such a gross and persistent disruption of normal living indicates a major disorder of the whole person and can, in no sense, be considered to be 'all in the mind'.

By contrast, *myasthenia gravis* is very much an organic disorder. It is a disease in which muscles weaken abnormally rapidly on use. The symptom becomes worse towards the end of the day and after exercise. Myasthenia gravis is an autoimmune disease caused by an abnormal antibody which blocks or damages the sites at which nerves act on muscle fibres to make them contract. These are called receptor sites and they are stimulated by the neurotransmitter acetylcholine released by the nerve endings. In some cases, the abnormal antibody production is known to be due to an abnormality in the thymus gland, which processes T-lymphocytes. In about 15 per cent of cases there is a benign tumour of the thymus gland.

Myasthenia usually appears after the age of 15 and may start at any age up to about 50. Women are affected about three times as often as men. In the early years, the disorder tends to be intermittent. Often the first sign is drooping of the eyelids or double vision. Other early signs are difficulty in swallowing, rapid fatigue of the chewing muscles, difficulty in speaking and general weakness of the limbs. If weakness of the muscles of respiration occurs, life may be threatened. The ability to cough may be so reduced that there is a risk of asphyxia from accumulated secretions.

The diagnosis of myasthenia is often confirmed by observing the effect of a small injection of the drug Tensilon (edrophonium hydrochloride) which has a brief but specific effect at the nerve endings, causing a striking improvement in muscle power within half a minute.

Acetylcholine is broken down by an enzyme, cholinesterase, and this can be antagonized by drugs such as neostigmine and pyridostigmine. These are called *anticholinesterase* drugs and are useful in the treatment of myasthenia. Removal of the thymus gland can be helpful and in some cases a procedure to remove the antibodies from the blood (plasmapheresis) may be justified.

Toes turning black

See **Blackening and loss of the extremities**.

Tongue-tie

Tongue tie is a rare defect in which the soft partition under the tongue (the frenulum) extends too far forward and is too tight, thereby limiting tongue movement. This may affect speech, but is easily corrected by surgery in which the frenulum is snipped.

Tooth abscess

This is a collection of pus around the root of a tooth. It results from infection and destruction of the pulp that fills the central cavity of the tooth. Infection usually follows tooth decay (dental caries), which destroys a small area of the hard outer enamel and the inner dentine, allowing bacteria to reach the pulp. This can happen very rapidly in young children and is especially common in those given sweetened comforters or neat syrups in feeding bottles.

A dental abscess causes great pain and the gum around the tooth is tender, red and swollen. There may also be severe swelling of the face. Untreated, an abscess will work its way through the bone of the jaw to the gum surface, where it forms a gumboil. This may burst, discharging the pus into the mouth and relieving the pain. A child with a dental abscess should always be seen, without delay, by a dentist. ▲ Antibiotics may be needed. Permanent teeth may often be saved by skilled dental care.

Toothache

Pain in a tooth is usually caused by tooth decay (dental caries) in which the outer layer, the enamel, has been breached so that germs have been able to reach the central pulp and cause inflammation. The pulp contains sensory nerves and it is the stimulation of these that causes the pain.

Caries reduces the thickness of the hard material between the exterior and the tooth nerve and leads to undue sensitivity to cold, heat, acid materials or even to sweet substances. In the presence of caries all of these can cause toothache. Toothache can also be caused by a broken tooth or by inflammation of the supporting tissue around a tooth (periodontitis). The roots of the upper teeth project into the sinuses (maxillary antrums) in the cheeks and inflammation in these sinuses can cause toothache. An unusual cause of toothache is the condition of *aerodontalgia*. This is pain in a tooth from a reduction in surrounding air pressure, as during flying or sucking at the tooth. The symptom results from the expansion of air within the pulp cavity of the tooth and usually indicates infection or a badly filled tooth.

Toothache is a symptom that always indicates that something is wrong, probably with one or more teeth. Neglect will usually lead to a worsening of the situation and possibly to the loss of an otherwise reclaimable tooth. See your dentist without delay.

Travel sickness

This is the effect on certain people when they are exposed to sustained movement, whether in a car, aircraft, boat or train. After a variable period there is a feeling of uneasiness increasing rapidly to distress. There is yawning, overbreathing, salivation, nausea, tummy discomfort, pallor, sweating of the face and hands, headache and vomiting. Air-swallowing, dizziness and an intense sense of fatigue may also occur. If the motion continues, these symptoms persist for several days and there is apathy, depression and total loss of appetite.

The probability of sickness is greater in a stuffy or smelly enclosure than in the fresh air, and a full stomach doesn't help. Sickness is relieved if you can fix your eyes on some unmoving point or line, such as the horizon. A steady draught of fresh air is often helpful, as is sitting with your head tilted backwards, and taking frequent small meals.

Travel sickness is most effectively treated with small doses of whichever drug has been found, by experience, to be most effective. Useful drugs include belladonna (atropine) and hyoscine, and antihistamine drugs such as Phenergan, Avomine, or Dramamine. Any drugs must be taken at least an hour before the motion starts, for once the vomiting has started, tablets or capsules may be rejected. Also, these drugs take a little time to act.

Trembling

Doctors tend to describe trembling using the alternative word 'tremor'. This is a rhythmical oscillation of any part of the body, lasting for at least a few seconds, and affecting especially the hands, the head, the jaw or the tongue. Tremor is very common, especially in elderly people, and does not necessarily imply disease. A minor degree of tremor, known as *physiological tremor*, is normal and from time to time everyone experiences exaggeration of this into an obvious, coarse shake, especially when the muscles concerned are being tensed. Tremor during excitement or anxiety, due to raised adrenaline levels, is an exaggerated physiological tremor.

Essential-familial tremor is an embarrassing condition which runs in families and produces an effect of nervousness. It does not progress to more serious disease and is usually temporarily relieved by alcohol. It may be suppressed by beta-blocking drugs.

Persistent tremor at rest, with a frequency of four or five cycles per second, may indicate *Parkinson's disease*, even if the tremor disappears on complete relaxation. Such tremor may be extreme but has less effect on voluntary movement than would be expected, and a person who normally has a violent tremor may be able to drink from a glass without mishap. Severe tremor is also a feature of:

- multiple sclerosis;
- accumulation of copper in the body (Wilson's disease);
- cerebellar ataxia;
- encephalitis;
- mercury poisoning;
- thyroid gland overactivity.

Tremor caused by brain disorder (encephalopathy) from liver failure or other metabolic disorders is called *asterixis*.

A variety of drugs can cause tremor. These include:

- amphetamines;
- antidepressant drugs;
- caffeine;
- corticosteroids;
- lithium.

A marked tremor is a common feature of patients under drug treatment for certain psychiatric disorders.

Tripping out

See **Drug abuse effects.**

Tunnel vision

See **Vision lost to the sides.**

Twitching

See **Tics.**

Undescended testicle

Unreasonable fears

Urinary frequency

Urination stopped

U

Undescended testicle

You should be able to feel two, but if you can only feel one testicle n your little boy's scrotum the other one is either in the abdomen – where they both originate – or part way down the canal. Often, an undescended testicle will come down of its own accord within the first few months of life, but don't count on it. A permanently undescended testicle doesn't produce any sperm and is significantly more likely to develop cancer, later in life, than a testicle in the right place. If both are undescended, and nothing is done, your boy will be sterile. See your doctor and take his advice sometime before your child is one. The operation to bring down and retain the testicle – orchidopexy – is usually successful. Don't confuse this condition with *retractile testicles* – testicles that pop up in the cold or if touched. These are common in little boys and the undue mobility ceases by puberty.

Unreasonable fears

These are called *phobias*. They are intense, irrational fears which cannot be ignored or overcome even when the sufferer is fully aware, as is usually the case, that there is no reason for the fear. Phobias take many forms and include fear of:

- humiliation or embarrassment (social phobias);
- high places (acrophobia – See **Fear of public places**);
- open places (agoraphobia);
- spiders (arachnophobia);
- enclosed places (claustrophobia);
- cats (ailurophobia);
- water (hydrophobia);
- dead bodies (necrophobia);
- night (nyctophobia);
- crowds (ochlophobia or demophobia);
- animals (zoophobia).

Phobias may relate to almost any situation, idea or object and most people have at least one mild phobia. Severe phobias, however, are very disabling and can seriously disrupt normal living.

Freud interpreted phobias by suggesting that they are the effect of a hidden and forbidden unconscious drive striving for expression, but being strenuously repressed. They are, he thought, the result of conflict arising from an infant oedipal situation with castration anxiety. It seems more likely that a phobia is a simple, forgotten conditioned reflex which is kept active (reinforced) by the repeated drive to avoid the unpleasant experience. This view is supported by the success of behaviour therapy in removing phobias. The physiological responses to phobias – fast pulse, sweating, high blood pressure and so on – can be controlled by the use of beta-blocking drugs.

Urinary frequency

The most obvious feature of this is having to get up at night to pee, and the commonest cause is the urinary infection *cystitis* (see **Pain on urination**). Urgency or frequency does not necessarily imply infection. It may be caused by local irritation from shampoos, bubble baths, biological washing powder residues on underclothes, fabric softeners, tight garments, emotional stress or threadworms.

In men, by far the commonest cause of urinary frequency is prostate gland enlargement. The prostate is very liable to enlarge, especially after the age of about 60, probably because of a falling off in the secretion of male sex hormone. About a quarter of men over 65 have moderate to severe symptoms from this cause. Enlargement is liable to interfere with the outflow of urine from the bladder by narrowing the urethra, or even by expanding upwards into the bladder so as to form a kind of ball valve. This makes it much harder to empty the bladder – there is a reduction in the force of the urine stream and seriously incomplete emptying of the bladder. It is this that leads to increased frequency of urination, with the repeated necessity to get up at night. This is simply because once a small amount of urine is passed, the desire to pee ceases, only to return soon afterwards as the bladder fills up again.

Sudden acute stoppage may occur, requiring an emergency passage of a tube (catheter) or, if this is impossible, drainage of the bladder through a wide needle passed through the abdominal wall. Back pressure can damage bladder function and the kidneys. Enlargement of the prostate often has to be treated by removal of part or all of the gland. This is most commonly done through the urethra, using a special viewing and cutting instrument called a resectoscope. If the enlargement is considerable, a direct surgical approach through the lower part of the wall of the abdomen and the wall of the bladder may be necessary. The results are usually excellent.

Urination stopped

See **Stoppage of urine output.**

V

Vagina itching

Vaginal bleeding between periods

Vaginal discharge

Vaginal discharge in children

Verrucas

Vertigo

Vision affected by floating specks

Vision blurred

Vision defective after injury

Vision defective from birth

Vision doubled

Vision lost in a painful red eye

Vision lost or dimmed for short periods

Vision lost to the sides

Vision missing in the middle

Vision partly obscured by black curtain

Vision persisting on looking away

Vision severely defective in dim conditions

Vision unequal in the two eyes

Vision unequal for objects of different orientation

Vision worse for distance

Vision worse for near

Visual loss with changing perception of colour

Vomiting

Vagina itching

See **Itching genitals.**

Vaginal bleeding between periods

This is called *breakthrough bleeding* and it usually occurs in women taking contraceptive pills. Breakthrough bleeding is commonest with low dose preparations, especially in the first few months after starting the pill. Don't worry about it.

If you are not on the pill, however, bleeding between periods or bleeding during pregnancy should always be considered potentially serious, so see your doctor. ▲

Vaginal discharge

This is one of the commonest of women's complaints. You should clearly distinguish between normal secretion from the womb and vagina and a discharge due to a local disorder. Sometimes the normal secretions may seem profuse enough to persuade you that something is wrong, but remember that normal secretions are not offensive and do not cause irritation.

The wall of the vagina is kept moist, not by producing its own fluids but by water that passes through from the tissue fluid in the pelvis. This is called a *transudate* and, as it passes, it carries away cast-off cells from the vaginal lining and these make it look white or creamy. This transudate becomes mixed with mucus secreted by glands in the lining of the cervix and by glands in the lining of the womb. Cervical mucus is usually fairly sticky and viscous but becomes more watery around the time of ovulation.

The normal vaginal secretion varies in amount at different times in the menstrual cycle, being most profuse in the few days before the onset of bleeding. During sexual excitement the area around the entrance to the vagina is lubricated by further clear mucus from the two Bartholin glands lying in the labia. This source may add to the amount of the discharge. Vaginal secretions are also inclined to be more profuse during pregnancy. The term *leukorrhoea*, which does not imply any disease process but which was once synonymous with abnormal vaginal discharge, is now often applied to the normal condition. Vaginal discharge is sometimes caused by a tampon which has been pushed up into the cul de sac (fornix) behind the cervix and forgotten.

Before the menopause, discharge resulting from bacterial infection of the vagina is uncommon. This is because the vagina is kept at a significantly acid pH by lactic acid formed by normal commensal germs which break down sugars in the lining. The loss of these 'healthy' bacteria is undesirable and is one of the reasons for vaginal problems, especially after the menopause. The commonest causes of abnormal vaginal discharge are thrush (candidiasis), and infection with the single-celled organism *Trichomonas vaginalis* (known as trichomoniasis). You can read about the Trichomonas vaginalis and what it does in the article on **Itching genitals.**

Vaginal discharge in children

Inflammation of the vagina (vaginitis) is common and causes discharge and itching. Most cases are caused by infection, especially with the *Candida* fungi which cause thrush. *Trichomonas vaginalis* infection is uncommon in children but may affect adolescents, especially the sexually active. Gonorrhoea may affect little girls who are susceptible because of the thinness of the vaginal lining. The usual source of infection in infantile gonococcal vaginitis is the mother, and infection may be acquired during birth.

Vaginal discharge is sometimes caused by a foreign body which has been pushed into the vagina, but more common causes are those which also cause frequency and urgency of urination (see **Urinary frequency**).

Verrucas

See **Warts**.

Vertigo

This is a feeling, actually an illusion, that the world is spinning around you. Occasionally, the illusion is that you are spinning around. The effect may be slight and only just noticeable, or may be so severe that you fall instantly to the ground as if you had been thrown down. Mild vertigo is very common and such cases are seldom due to underlying disease, or require any treatment. Vertigo can be caused by:

- fear of heights;
- travel sicknes;
- overbreathing (hyperventilation);
- alcohol;
- various drugs.

More severe vertigo may indicate disorder of the balancing mechanisms in the inner ears, such as Ménière's disease or labyrinthitis, or a disorder of the neurological mechanism for balance in the brain, usually from an inadequate blood supply (vertebrobasilar insufficiency) or from a tumour or multiple sclerosis.

Many elderly people suffer from vertigo and so long as there are no other obvious symptoms the problem is likely to be benign. Even so, if vertigo comes on for no obvious reason, you should certainly see your doctor.

Vision affected by floating specks

Floaters are semi-transparent, cobweb-like floating shadows seen in the field of vision. Floaters move rapidly with eye movement, but drift slowly when the eyes are still. The rapid movement, often seen 'out of the corner of the eye' has given rise to the name *muscae volitantes*, which is Latin for 'flitting flies'. Floaters do not affect vision and, in most cases, are important only to those who are unable to treat them with the healthy disregard they deserve.

Most floaters are shadows of developmental remnants in the jelly-like vitreous body of the eye. Some are shadows of condensed vitreous and these are especially common in people in their 60s and 70s when the vitreous body tends to shrink away from the retina. Such floaters are of no significance, and will usually disappear in time.

Should a sudden cloud of dark floaters appear, especially if associated with bright flashes of light, the implication is that a small tear has occurred in the retina and that there is an incipient risk that the retina will become detached. Such a symptom warrants immediate referral to an eye specialist. A large red floater, partly or wholly obscuring vision, suggests bleeding into the vitreous (vitreous haemorrhage). This is commonest in long-term diabetics, and this, too, calls for an urgent specialist opinion. ⚠

Vision blurred

Temporary blurring of vision can be caused by discharge from *conjunctivitis* (see **Eye inflammation**) or from watering of the eyes. Permanent blurring may be due to a cataract or to an opaque patch on the cornea following a *corneal ulcer*. But the great majority of cases of blurred vision are due to an eye focusing problem. If you are middle aged and have had no previous difficulty, but are now finding that close objects are unclear, the problem is probably *presbyopia*. This is the effect of a gradual loss of elasticity of the internal lenses of the eyes. You will need reading glasses. See also the following articles on defective vision.

Vision defective after injury

Injury to the eye is an important cause of cataract – an opacification of the internal lens of the eye situated behind the pupil. A concussive force such as that caused by a flying stone or high-speed squash ball, a sharp poke from a finger or a severe blow to the face, may cause cataract even without any external injury to the eye. Penetrating wounds of the eye are even more likely to cause cataract, especially if the lens capsule is torn. In such cases, water immediately enters the lens and, within a matter of hours or days, a dense cataract will develop.

Vision defective from birth

Cataract present at birth (congenital cataract) is often caused by the mother had German measles (rubella) early in pregnancy or, less often, is due to the effects of drugs taken by the mother during the early weeks when the eyes of the fetus were developing. Down's syndrome is commonly associated with cataract as are various rare hereditary conditions. *Galactosaemia* is a condition in which the infant is unable to break down galactose into simpler sugars so that it accumulates in the body. Unless a galactose-free diet is given, cataract is inevitable.

Vision doubled

Double vision is the perception of a single object as two images. It is medically known as *diplopia*. Although we see with both eyes simultaneously, single vision is normally experienced because the brain makes the eye-moving muscles align the eyes accurately enough to superimpose and fuse the two images into one. This fusional capacity of the brain is what is meant by binocular vision and is the highest level of visual development. Binocularity develops in infancy and early childhood only if all is well with the focusing and alignment capability of both eyes. Early interference with the development of binocularity, as from squint (strabismus), may eliminate binocularity altogether and many people grow up without it. Such people are incapable of experiencing double vision although they may have excellent single vision in each eye. They must, of course, use only one eye at a time.

Diplopia may be a normal (physiological) effect, as when a finger held in front of the eyes is seen double when we look past it into the distance. It is also common, and usually harmless, to experience double vision when turning the eyes to the extreme right or left. Some people who have had injudicious or unsuccessful orthoptic or surgical treatment for squint may have persistent diplopia, dating from the time of the treatment. This may be distressing but is not dangerous and should, if possible, be ignored.

However, diplopia that appears spontaneously and that cannot be controlled, or recently acquired diplopia, occurring on looking a little to one side, is likely to be a sign of disease, either of the eye muscles or of the part of the nervous system concerned with the control of eye movement. Possible conditions causing this include:

- thyroid eye disease affecting the external eye muscles;
- disease of the arteries supplying the brain;
- diabetes;
- stroke;
- brain tumour;
- aneurysm on the brain arteries.

Diplopia that has recently occurred must never be ignored and requires full ophthalmic or neurological investigation. ⚠

Diplopia perceived with *one* eye is rare but possible. It should be distinguished from the slight doubling of simple blurred vision, and is usually due to an internal eye problem, such as a partially dislocated crystalline lens, an unusual type of cataract or a glass foreign body within the eye.

Vision lost in a painful red eye

The symptoms of acute glaucoma are so severe that you are unlikely to be in any doubt that a serious condition has arisen. The affected eye is acutely painful, intensely red and congested, and very hard and tender to the touch. The pupil is enlarged and oval and the cornea steamy and partly opaque. The vision is grossly diminished. There is shock and sometimes pain in the abdomen. Urgent treatment to reduce the pressure is needed, so no time must be wasted. ▲

Vision lost or dimmed for short periods

This usually affects one eye, and is known as *amaurosis fugax*. The symptom results from temporary blockage of the blood supply to the eye. The blockage is caused by tiny particles of blood clot or other material carried along in the blood stream from patches of disease on larger arteries or sometimes from the lining of the heart. Amaurosis fugax is an important warning sign that the affected person is in danger of having a stroke. It should never be ignored. ▲ It indicates a distinct and serious possibility that any of the vital arteries supplying the brain could be blocked – medical action is needed to counter this risk. The effects of stroke are so devastating that such an outcome must be prevented at all costs. Amaurosis fugax is also a risk factor for heart attack because artery disease is seldom confined to one group of arteries and it is likely that the coronary arteries of the heart are also involved. Amaurosis fugax is the commonest form of *transient ischaemic attack* (TIA) – the principal warning sign of impending stroke.

Vision lost to the sides

This is called visual field loss and it is always important. There are several possible causes. Loss of half of the field of vision of each eye may occur and may be temporary or permanent. Most commonly, the line dividing the seeing from the non-seeing areas runs vertically through the point at which the affected person is looking. Both outer halves may be lost (bitemporal hemianopia) or there may be loss of both right or both left halves (homonymous hemianopia).

Bitemporal hemianopia almost always indicates a tumour of the pituitary gland pressing on the central crossing of the optic nerves behind the eyes. At this point fibres from the inner half of each retina cross and their destruction causes blindness in the outer halves of the field of vision. Loss of the same half of the field in each eye (homonymous hemianopia) in elderly people is usually caused by a stroke, when the blood supply to the back

of one side of the brain is cut off. If the field loss has a sparkly edge and clears up in 20 minutes it is almost certainly caused by migraine and is usually of no great significance. Homonymous hemianopia may also be due to damage to the back of the brain from other causes such as gun-shot wound or other injury, brain tumour, brain abscess or inflammation of the brain (encephalitis). Hemianopia of this kind cannot be caused by any disorder of the eyes themselves.

Another important cause of loss of vision to the sides is chronic simple glaucoma. This is one of a group of eye diseases in which the pressure of the fluid within the eyeball is too high. A certain minimum pressure is required to maintain the shape and size of the globe so that it can function efficiently as an optical instrument and not be easily indented by minor external force. But if the pressure is too high it will exceed the pressure of the blood in the small arteries inside the eye and these will be flattened and occluded. Certain arteries supplying the beginning of the optic nerve are especially susceptible to such excess pressures, and it is this region which suffers most in glaucoma.

Long-term, minor deprivation of blood to the optic nerve head gradually kills off the nerve fibres from the retina, which bundle together to form the optic nerve, and the visual capacity is gradually eroded. The disorder is insidious because the fibres first affected are those coming from the periphery of the retina which subserve the outer parts of the fields of vision. It is a feature of visual function that one is largely unaware of the quality, or even the presence, of vision in those areas to which attention is not directed. Since we can, in general, direct attention only by looking straight at something, thus using the central retina, defects in the peripheral visual fields pass unnoticed. Unless looked for, therefore, glaucomatous damage to the fields of vision is often extensive

before it is detected. Chronic simple glaucoma, the commonest form, is a major cause of blindness, and visual field loss is irremediable. If detected early, the pressures can be controlled and the damage stopped. ▲

Chronic simple glaucoma runs in families and is more likely to occur in relatives of people with the disease. Only in the late stages will there be obvious signs and, by that time, so much peripheral visual field will have been lost that the affected person will probably be constantly bumping into others on busy pavements. Central vision is usually the last to go and one eye may be completely blinded before it is appreciated that anything is amiss.

About one person in 100 has glaucoma at the age of 40, but the incidence rises steeply with increasing age so that, by 70, about one in 10 have significantly raised eye pressures. If glaucoma is to be detected before severe damage is done, it must be looked for. One of the signs is a hollowing out (cupping)

323

of the optic nerve head, and this can be detected during a routine eye examination. But the real test is to measure the internal pressure by a technique known as tonometry. If the pressure is found to be above the upper limit of normal, the visual fields are checked and arrangements made for follow-up investigation. If glaucoma is diagnosed, eye drops are given to keep the pressures within normal limits. Occasionally, medical treatment fails and an operation may be needed. In other, less common, forms of glaucoma, the outlet obstruction can be caused by mechanical or disease processes and the effects may be much more sudden and severe, with great pain and sudden loss of all vision. This is the case in acute congestive glaucoma or in glaucomas caused by inflammatory eye disease with adhesions.

Vision missing in the middle

Macular degeneration is a disorder of the retina usually affecting elderly people and causing progressive loss of the central part of the field of vision. It is caused by defects in the insulating layer between the retina and the underlying choroid so that fluid leaks into the retina with progressive destruction of the rods, cones and connecting nerves. Destruction of this part of the retina has very damaging consequences. The eye never becomes completely blind, but whatever you are looking at is blanked out. This means that you cannot read, tell the time or recognize faces. Vision to the sides remains normal.

Macular degeneration can affect both eyes simultaneously, but usually one eye is affected weeks or months before the other. In some cases the process can be arrested by laser treatment. If you notice a central gap in the field of vision in one eye you should report this at once. ⚠ You should check by covering one eye at a time.

Another possible cause of a hole in the centre of your field is vision is *multiple sclerosis*

(MS). This long-term disease of the central nervous system affects about one person in 2,000 in Britain. In spite of intensive research and many advances in understanding, the cause remains unknown. MS may occur at any age, but it is rare before puberty and after 60. In most cases it starts between the ages of 20 and 40.

Multiple small scattered plaques – areas of degeneration and loss of the insulating myelin sheath of nerve fibres – occur in a random manner anywhere in the brain or spinal cord. These can be seen on MRI scanning. Where these plaques occur the conduction of the nerve fibres is blocked and the function served by them is lost. As a result, affected people develop any of the wide range of disabilities resulting from loss of nervous system function – weakness, paralysis, loss of sensation, visual loss, incoordination and mental disturbances. Attacks do not destroy the whole of the function concerned, because only a proportion of the nerves are affected, but if repeated attacks occur, the disability is usually progressive.

The loss of central vision caused by involvement of an optic nerve (retrobulbar neuritis) is a common initial feature, as is limb weakness. There may be patches of skin without sensation, double vision, vertigo, staggering, disorders of speech, facial paralysis or epilepsy. The visual damage and the other effects nearly always clear up in about six weeks and sight is restored, but sensitive tests will show that some permanent damage has occurred to the nerves concerned. Recurrent attacks can make this damage progressively worse.

The disease is characterized by long periods of freedom (remission) followed, in many cases, by recurrences. The course is very variable. Some people have an attack and then are free from trouble for up to 10 years or longer. The condition can even be found on post-mortem examination in a person who had never suspected that anything was wrong. Relapses may occur at any time and in some cases each of these seems to be followed by complete recovery. In other cases relapses lead to increasing disability. Eventually, about half of all those with MS become permanently and increasingly affected. The disease is often associated with unexpectedly high morale, even euphoria, but appropriate depression is also common. Late in the disease there may be intellectual impairment.

Research into the cause takes account of a number of known facts. The incidence of MS varies widely in different parts of the world, being very low in the tropics. People who, before adolescence, move from places of high incidence to places of low incidence enjoy a reduced risk; and young people who move from areas of low incidence to those of high incidence acquire the greater risk. After the age of 15, a move of location does not affect your chances of developing MS. There is a higher incidence of the disease in people of certain tissue type groups (HLA groups) than in the general population, and there is also a higher incidence in relatives of MS sufferers. It seems probable, from this and other evidence, that the disease may occur in people with a genetic susceptibility who become infected, early in life, with an unknown slow virus.

Unfortunately, there is no effective treatment for MS but much may be done to support and encourage those affected and to relieve or ameliorate many of the symptoms and effects. Undue bed rest should be avoided and mobility maximized. Walking frames, wheelchairs and adapted motor vehicles should be used, as necessary, together with all required physical aids. Association with other sufferers and the promotion of the highest attainable degree of intellectual activity are important in the attempt to promote the best possible quality of life.

Vision partly obscured by black curtain

If the black curtain is totally obscuring part of the field of vision of one eye, this is an emergency ⚠. You have developed a major retinal detachment in the affected eye. *If the curtain came down from above*, your retina is detached below and *you can safely sit up*. Remember that there is fluid under the detachment and this will tend, by its weight, to strip the retina further off. This must be avoided. So *if the curtain came up from below*, you have an upper detachment and should *lie down flat*. If from the right, lie on your left side and vice versa. The important thing is to avoid losing central vision. This makes the probable outcome for vision worse.

Retinal detachment is a job for an ophthalmic specialist in hospital, so get someone to telephone a hospital and tell them what has happened. Don't wait until the next day. If central vision is retained, the outlook is excellent, but even if it is not, vision can often be restored by surgery.

In case you are wondering why the victim sees the black area in a manner that is the reverse of what is actually happening, the explanation is that the images formed on our retinas by the lens system of the eyes are actually inverted and reversed right to left.

Vision persisting on looking away

Perseveration is the name given to a strange phenomenon in which, on shifting your gaze away from a particular scene, you continue for a short time to see what you were seeing before. This is a rare symptom but it is one you should never ignore. Unfortunately, perseveration usually indicates a disorder of brain function, affecting the frontal lobes. The same condition can make it difficult for someone to move on from one task to another. This is a case for a neurologist. ⚠

327

Vision severely defective in dim conditions

The most striking cause of severely defective vision in dark conditions is *retinitis pigmentosa*. This is a slow degeneration of the rods and cones of the retinas of both eyes. It starts at any time from adolescence to late middle age and progressesg to a variable degree. In some cases there is little disability, but in many the eventual loss of vision is profound. The condition usually has a genetic basis but spontaneous cases occur.

The first sign of the disease is defective night vision due to loss of function of the rods, which are necessary for vision in dim light. This observation usually leads to ophthalmic examination and the visual field test shows a ring-shaped area of loss well out from, but surrounding, the point at which the affected person is looking. At first this ring is fairly narrow but, over the years, it gradually extends, both outwards and inwards, to destroy an increasing area of the field of vision. This ring *scotoma* corresponds to an area on each retina in which the retinal pigment, normally evenly and smoothly distributed, has become clumped into scattered masses. Fortunately, central vision is retained, often for many years. There is, as yet, no treatment for retinitis pigmentosa.

Another cause of night blindness, rare in developed countries, is vitamin A deficiency. In this case, there is also severe dryness of the eyes and often a foamy white appearance, on the whites of the eyes, at the corners.

Vision unequal for objects of different orientation

When a small spot of light (*stigma* is Greek for 'a spot') is focused by an astigmatic lens, the image formed is a smeared line instead of a sharp point. A minor degree of astigmatism is normal – nearly every eye has some – and glasses are unnecessary for this. But more severe astigmatism causes objects in a particular direction to be blurred. A person with astigmatism might, for instance, see horizontal lines clearly while vertical lines are blurred; or the meridian of greatest blurring may be at an oblique angle.

The cornea is the main focusing lens of the eye and should, ideally, be curved like the surface of a perfect sphere. In astigmatism, although the eye is perfectly healthy, the cornea is curved like the surface of an egg, so the lens is more powerful in one meridian than in the others. Ordinary spherical eyeglass lenses cannot correct astigmatism and lenses are needed which have more optical power in the appropriate meridian than in that at right angles. For pure astigmatism, a lens is required which has no optical power in the normal meridian but appropriate curvature in the others. These are called cylindrical lenses and must, of course, be set in the frame at exactly the correct orientation.

Hard contact lenses bridge over the anomalous corneal curve and present a perfect spherical surface for focusing. They thus give excellent vision in astigmatism. Ordinary soft lenses, however, tend to mould to the astigmatic curve. Special toric soft lenses, which have an uneven curve, are available for astigmatism. Unfortunately, they are more expensive and are difficult to fit satisfactorily.

Young children with undetected high astigmatism frequently develop a form of visual loss, known as *amblyopia*, which is confined to the out-of-focus meridia. This is called *meridional amblyopia* and, unless detected early in life and treated with accurately prescribed glasses, will be permanent and uncorrectable. High astigmatism, in one eye only, very commonly causes severe amblyopia in that eye.

Vision unequal in the two eyes

This is called *anisometropiacan*, and can be very troublesome and is an inequality in the focusing power of the two eyes. One eye may be normal and the other shortsighted or longsighted, or one may be markedly more shortsighted or longsighted than the other. Sometimes one eye is short-sighted and the other long-sighted. When longsighted, a young person can usually learn to use one eye for close work and the other for distance viewing, so that glasses are unnecessary. Glasses do not correct anisometropia very efficiently and there is often discomfort from a noticeable difference in the apparent size of objects. Contact lenses reduce this difference and often give more comfortable vision

Vision worse for distance

Short sight, medically known as *myopia*, is the condition in which the focusing power of the eye is too strong so that the images of distant objects come to a focus in front of the proper focal plane (the retina). Rays from near objects, however, are diverging more when they enter the eye, and these focus further back, often on the retina. So a myopic person cannot see distant objects clearly, but sees near objects well. The condition is the result of a failure of the proper relationship between the curvature of the cornea, the length of the eye, and the power and position of the internal crystalline lens. To compensate for myopia, *weakening* (minus or concave) lenses are needed.

Myopia usually appears around puberty, but may arise at any age up to about 25. It is rare for myopia to appear after body growth is complete. The earlier it starts, the higher the final degree is likely to be. Those whose myopia appears late in adolescence never develop high myopia. Since the condition is of dimensional origin, it is not surprising to find that it runs in families. Myopia is, in most cases, no more than a nuisance, calling for contact lenses or glasses. But in the higher degrees there is a raised probability of eye trouble such as retinal detachment, retinal degeneration and bleeding (retinal haemorrhages).

Vision worse for near

Long sight, or *hypermetropia*, is the condition in which the eyes, when in a state of relaxed focus, are unable to see distant or near objects clearly. The greatest difficulty is experienced in viewing near objects. The term 'farsightedness' or 'long-sightedness' has been a cause of confusion because, even on distant viewing, people with hypermetropia must exert a focusing effort (accommodation) to see clearly. This is easy for young people, whose focusing power is considerable and whose hypermetropia is thus usually concealed by an automatic and unconscious effort of accommodation.

Since the power of accommodation declines steadily with age, sooner or later hypermetropia becomes manifest and glasses are needed. The more severe the hypermetropia, the lower the age at which the difficulty appears. Initially there are problems with close work but, later, the distance vision becomes blurred also. In hypermetropia the eye is too short for the focal length of the combined cornea and internal lens. Or, considered in another way, the lens system is insufficiently strong to focus on the retina. Hypermetropic defects are corrected by ordinary convex lenses.

Presbyopia is the effect, usually noticed around the age of 45, of the progressive loss of the ability to focus the eyes for near vision (accommodation). The power of accommodation is greatest in childhood and gradually weakens with age until, around the age of 65, very little focusing power remains. The effect of this steady weakening is that the nearest point at which clear vision is possible gradually moves further away. A person will still be able to read print which is large enough, but the diminishing effect of perspective may make it impossible to read small print.

Simple lenses with low magnification, prescribed as reading glasses, are used to compensate for presbyopia.

Assuming the distance vision is normal, the first prescription, at about 45, will be lenses of the power of one dioptre (a lens with a focal length of 1 metre). These will need to be progressively increased in strength, at intervals of a few years, over the course of about 20 years, until, eventually, all the focusing is done by the glasses.

It should seldom be necessary to change reading glasses more often than about once every four or five years, the power rising by about half a dioptre, each time. The usual reading correction, at 60, for a person with normal distance vision, is about two and a half dioptres. Lenses of this power focus at 40 cm – a convenient reading distance – with no accommodation. The power needed in the reading glasses is affected by the basic refraction at distance. A long-sighted person will need stronger lenses and a short-sighted person (see **Vision worse for distance**) weaker lenses. A person with two or three dioptres of myopia will never need reading glasses.

Visual loss with changing perception of colour

Cataract is an opacification of the internal focusing lens of the eye (the crystalline lens) due to irreversible structural changes in the orderly arrangement of the fibres from which the lens is made. Cataract never causes complete blindness in the sense of total absence of perception of light. People with dense cataracts can still usually distinguish an open from a closed door and will always see windows in daytime. But as the transparency of the lenses is gradually lost, image clarity slowly declines and perception of detail becomes less and less until eventually it is lost. Contrary to popular belief, cataract is not readily visible to the external observer. The fears, commonly expressed, that cataract is going to progress to a disfiguring blemish are quite without foundation. People over 75 will usually have some visual loss from lens opacity. Few people in their 80s are free from appreciable visual loss from this cause. So cataract in the elderly should be considered almost normal.

Progressive hardening of the centre of the lens (nuclear sclerosis) is common in cataract and this often leads to a special form of short sight (index myopia) in which the bending power of the lenses increases. Index myopia can progress steadily to high degrees which is why glasses need to be changed over the years. However, it should be appreciated that this is a transient stage in the development of cataract and that the vision is likely to get worse. People with index myopia who can read without glasses will, of course, need spectacles for vision in the distance.

One of the most constant effects of cataract is a change in the perception of colours. Red, yellow and orange are accentuated at the expense of blue. But, because of the very gradual nature of the change, this effect may remain unnoticed. After cataract operations, however, patients are regularly surprised at, and often comment on, the brilliance of blues. The irregular opacification of the lenses, which is a common feature of cataract, causes some rays of light entering the eye to be scattered while some are not. This may occur even at an early stage, and may be very annoying. The effect is particular noticeable when the headlights of approaching cars shine in the eyes while driving at night. Many people, otherwise barely affected, find they have to avoid night driving because of this.

There is no possible way to restore transparency to a cataractous lens and it is unrealistic to imagine that cataract can be cured by any form of medication or by any means other than cataract surgery. Happily, this is one of the most successful of all operations and the expectation of an excellent result, the eye being otherwise healthy, is well over 95 per cent.

Aphakia is the state of an eye without an internal lens. The crystalline lens may have been surgically removed in the treatment of cataract or punctured in the course of a penetrating injury and subsequently have absorbed. The result is a severely defocused eye requiring strong glasses. Spectacle correction, however, results in a much enlarged image on the affected side and this is seldom tolerable. A better alternative is a contact lens or a lens implant. Aphakia on one side causes a distressing difference in the focus of the two eyes.

Vomiting

Vomiting is a sign of some particular disorder. There is always a cause and this should, if possible, be found and removed. It is usually preceded by severe nausea, sweating, excessive salivation, pallor and slowing of the heart rate.

Vomiting may result from many causes. These include:

- allergic sensitivity to various foods;
- undue distention of the stomach from overeating;
- severe indigestion;
- early pregnancy;
- appendicitis;
- peritonitis;
- infection of the intestine, as in food poisoning;
- heavy roundworm infestation.

Bowel obstruction, from causes such as congenital pyloric stenosis or telescoping of the bowel (intussusception) will, unless relieved, inevitably lead to vomiting.

Vomiting is also an important sign of a rise in the pressure within the skull from any cause such as brain tumour, encephalitis, or hydrocephalus. These may cause unexpected, forcible, 'projectile' vomiting, often without nausea. Cyclical vomiting is a condition, tending to run in families, which causes recurrent attacks of vomiting and headache. It often starts in childhood and is associated with migraine.

Waddling gait in children

Walking problems

Warts

Watery eye

Weakness on one side of the body

Weight excess

Whiteness of hair and skin

Whites of the eyes blue

Womb contractions during pregnancy

Word blindness

Worms in stool

Wry-neck

W

Waddling gait in children

Congenital hip dislocation is a condition, present at birth, in which the sphere-like head of the thigh bone does not fit normally into its socket in the side of the pelvis. One or both joints may be affected. In most cases the condition recovers without treatment, but if not, or if not detected, treatment is necessary to prevent a severe walking defect. This features a characteristic waddling gait. The untreated condition will also tend later to cause arthritis. The earlier the condition is spotted the easier it is to treat and there is a routine test which all babies should have in a baby clinic.

In infancy, light splints for two or three months are an effective cure. If left till later, traction with weights or even an operation and several months in a plaster cast may be needed.

Walking problems

Nine out of 10 children are walking by 15 months. Infants still making no attempt to walk by this age may possibly be suffering from developmental delay (see **Delay in development**) and should be seen by a doctor.

Abnormal walking may also be due to one of a number of causes including:

● cerebral palsy;

- congenital hip dislocation or other hip disorders such as Perthe's disease;
- muscular dystrophy;
- severe spinal problems;
- foot deformities, such as club foot.

Some of these conditions are remediable and every child with walking problems deserves full paediatric investigation.

Warts

Warts are very interesting to children, annoying to parents and badly understood. They occur when a small patch of cells at the base of the outer layer of the skin is forced to overgrow by the presence of a virus, called a human *papillomavirus*. They can occur anywhere on the skin. The medical term for a wart is *verruca*, regardless of where it occurs – it does not mean a wart on the sole of the foot, as is widely supposed. Warts are uncommon in babies but very common in older children once they have got around enough to encounter the virus.

Warts are harmless and only matter because of their appearance. They are commonest on the hands and often last for years. Half of all new warts go away in a month or two without treatment. If they persist, wait until the child is old enough to put up with treatment without too much distress. The exception is a wart on the sole of the foot (plantar wart). These are the same as warts elsewhere but because of their position get pressed in by the weight of the body and are painful and particularly troublesome.

Warts are removed by freezing with liquid nitrogen, burning with an electric cautery under anaesthesia, or by using salicylic acid or other lotions. One should always consider whether treatment is justified. Many children are quite pleased with their warts.

Watery eye

See **Eye watering**.

Weakness on one side of the body

Definite weakness or paralysis

337

affecting one side of the body is caused by brain damage, usually a stroke. This is the result of acute deprivation of blood in a part of the brain, by narrowing or thrombosis in an artery, or of physical damage to part of the brain by internal or external bleeding.

Cerebral haemorrhage – bleeding into or around the brain – is the cause of the most serious kinds of stroke and is often fatal. Bleeding into the brain is usually the result of the rupture of a small artery, damaged and weakened by atherosclerosis, which gives way under the influence of raised blood pressure. High blood pressure contributes to atherosclerosis and is the main risk factor for stroke. The bleeding can occur almost anywhere in the brain and the effect varies with the location.

The pumping action of the burst vessel forces blood into the brain tissue which is disrupted and compressed. The effect is most obvious in those parts in which the nerve tracts concerned with movement, sensation, speech and vision are situated close together and so are involved in common. Haemorrhage into the brain stem, where the centres that control the vital functions of breathing and heart beat are situated, is the most immediately dangerous to life.

The first sign of a cerebral haemorrhage is usually a sudden severe headache. This is quickly followed by obvious functional loss such as paralysis down one side of the body, loss of vision to one side, fixed turning of the eyes to one side and perhaps a major epileptic-type fit. Often consciousness is lost early and if the haemorrhage is large, this may never be regained – more than half of the people affected in this way die within a few hours or days. Those who recover consciousness always have an initial defect of function which is frequently severe. Smaller haemorrhages produce less damage and there may be no loss of consciousness, but simply the signs of functional injury to the nervous system.

This is almost always worst at the beginning and much of

it is caused by recoverable and temporary loss of function in brain tissue surrounding the area of damage. Brain swelling (oedema) occurs and this temporarily interferes with nerve conduction. Recovery also occurs, to some extent, as a result of reabsorption of the released blood. As these recovery processes proceed there is a slow, but usually substantial, improvement and, unless further haemorrhages supervene, the end result may be good. Some degree of permanent disability is, however, usual. Strokes may be caused by bleeding from a ruptured aneurysm on one of the arteries supplying the brain – see subarachnoid haemorrhage under **Pain in the head (headache)**.

Cerebral thrombosis, or a minor embolism, produces effects similar to, but generally less severe than, those of cerebral haemorrhage and recovery is common. Strokes due to thrombosis or repeated embolism may occur in people with atherosclerosis of the carotid arteries or their branches, or in people with diseased heart valves on which small blood clots form and then break loose to be carried up to the brain.

After a stroke, the emphasis should always be on the restoration of maximum function by sustained efforts to achieve as much activity as possible. A person who consistently attempts to walk after a minor stroke is much more likely to recover mobility than one who stays in bed.

Weight excess

See **Obesity**.

Whiteness of hair and skin

An almost total absence of body colouring is known as *albinism*. This is a genetic disorder and people are affected to varying degrees. In most cases the hair and skin are pure white and the irises of the eyes have a pinkish appearance. There is usually some defect of vision and intolerance to bright light. Many albinos have constant, jerky eye movements (nys-tagmus) and squints, and are often short-sighted. Because of the absence of protective colouring in the skin, the effect of sunlight is severe and the skin may wrinkle prematurely. If unprotected it is more prone than normal to cancer. Albino children should always have their eyes checked by a specialist at an early age.

Whites of the eyes blue

See **Brittle bones.**

Wind

Greedy or hungry babies often swallow air along with their feeds and this air becomes compressed by peristalsis and may cause colic, pain and much crying. It often leads to regurgitation of food, much to the annoyance of the mother who has to clean up and may also feel obliged to give another feed. Traditional burping methods help – rubbing or patting the baby's back – but many mothers will ask for something more reliable.

Dill water (or gripe water) may be useful, as may dimethicone which is a silicone polymer oil, useful as a skin barrier cream or ointment base, but used here to reduce surface tension and allow froth to coalesce so that wind may more easily be expelled from either end.

Womb contractions during pregnancy

These are more common than you probably realize. They are called *Braxton Hicks' contractions* and, although they actually involve brief and almost painless tightening of the womb, need not worry you. You are unlikely to appreciate them in the early stages of pregnancy, but an examining doctor may feel them. Later they are more obvious and can even be seen sometimes through the tense wall of the abdomen. Braxton Hicks' contractions don't cause the cervix to widen and are much less uncomfortable than true labour pains. They are a normal part of a normal pregnancy and do not indicate that labour is beginning.

Word blindness

The phrase 'word blindness', as commonly used, is a real exaggeration. Dyslexia – the condition to which it refers – is in no sense a blindness. It may be defined as 'a less than average performance in reading and comprehension that does not result from any social, educational or cultural disadvantage or from lack of intelligence'. Dyslexia is independent of visual or speech defect, and may vary from a very minor disadvantage to an almost total inability to read. It is commoner in males, tends to run in families, and persists into adult life. There are clear indications of cognitive disability, with much greater than normal difficulty in the use, meaning, spelling and pronunciation of words.

In performance, there seems to be difficulty in visual perception and discrimination. Letters and words are perceived as reversed, so that 'd' becomes 'b' and 'was' becomes 'saw'. Complete mirror writing may occur. Children affected in this way seem to show an absence of cerebral dominance and are neither strongly right- nor left-handed.

In spite of major advances in psychology, neurology, brain function studies and linguistics, current views on dyslexia remain controversial. There are even those who deny the existence of dyslexia and claim that the problems are purely of educational or emotional origin. Most authorities, however, recognize the condition and many are convinced that it is a disorder essentially of the language function. Some have suggested that, whereas language came early in the evolution of our species and has its own distinct 'module' in the brain, reading is a later accomplishment, intimately dependent on the structural and functional normality of the language module. Any disorder or abnormality in the language module would inevitably cause reading difficulty.

Some scientists have claimed that dyslexic people

have variations in the normal brain anatomy, and show an abnormal degree of symmetry in the size of the areas in the temporal lobes containing the auditory association areas. These are normally asymmetrical, being larger on the left side. Recent work has shown that certain cells (specifically in what is called the medial geniculate nucleus) of dyslexic people are smaller in the left hemisphere (the language hemisphere) than in the right. This nucleus handles auditory input. Analogous changes have been found in the layers of the lateral geniculate bodies – which handle visual input – in people with lazy vision (amblyopia).

It also seems likely that dyslexic children are anatomically less well equipped than others to recognize sounds presented to them in rapid succession. An interval of about 100 milliseconds is required to separate sounds. This is greater than the interval that separates the component sounds in many common syllables. Phonetic reading is the major problem in dyslexia.

Much can be done to help dyslexic children and it is essential that the condition should be recognized as a specific difficulty and not the result of inattention, laziness or natural perversity. Parents should not add to their children's anxiety by unduly emphasizing the problem, but should be ready and willing to read to the child, or to encourage the use of recorded books long after the age at which the child would normally be able to read fluently. Cooperation with a specialist teacher or educational psychologist can be most helpful. Some educational authorities have been willing to allow dyslexic children extra time during examinations.

Dyslexia should not be confused with alexia (see **Inability to make sense of words**).

Worms in stool

Roundworms are common human intestinal parasites, especially in underdeveloped countries. It is estimated that

98 per cent of people either have a roundworm infestation or have had one at some time. The common roundworm has a life span of about a year and inhabits the small intestine. The females pass microscopic eggs in the faeces and, under suitable conditions, as in moist soil, these can survive for three years or more. Crops or hands are commonly contaminated by eggs and these are passed to other people. Ingested eggs hatch in the small intestine, migrate to the lungs and return to the intestine by way of the air tubes and the gullet.

The commonest symptoms of worms are tummy discomfort and pain, nausea, vomiting, irritability, loss of appetite and disturbed sleep. These symptoms occur only if considerable numbers of worms are present. In heavy infestations, of 500–1,500 worms, pneumonia or obstruction of the bowel may result. Adult worms are 15-30 cm long and will occasionally be seen in the stools. Roundworms are easy to get rid of by using the drug piperazine.

Tapeworms are ribbon-like populations of joined flatworms, which grow from a small common head with hooks or suckers by which it is attached to the lining of the bowel. The body of the worm is composed of segments of increasing size, each of which is a separate individual containing both male and female reproductive organs. Tapeworms extend to about four metres in length and have 800 to 1,000 segments. The younger, smaller segments release sperms which fertilize the eggs in the older segments.

Mature segments with developing embryos break off, usually in groups of five or six, and are passed in the faeces. These are whitish, roughly rectangular and about 12 mm long by 6 mm wide. If these are eaten by an animal (the intermediate host), the larvae develop, travel to the animal's muscles and form cysts. Pork containing tapeworm cysts is called 'measly pork' and if this is eaten, undercooked, the worm is released in the intestine, attaches itself, and the life cycle is continued. Tapeworms can be eliminated fairly easily with suitable drugs.

Threadworms are the commonest worm parasite of children in temperate areas. At least 20 per cent of all children are affected at any one time. The mature female worm is about 1 cm long, white, and with a blunt head and a fine, hair-like, pointed tail. The male is shorter and is rarely seen, as he remains in the intestine. The pregnant female worm may contain 10,000 eggs, which almost fill her body. Her movement on the skin around the anus to deposit her eggs cause a strong tickling sensation. The child scratches and the eggs adhere to the fingers and nails. These are then transferred, either directly to the mouth to cause re-infestation, or, by way of toys, blankets and so on to other children. The eggs can survive for three weeks. Diagnosis is easy, because the worms are easy to see and may appear on the faeces. In cases of doubt, Sellotape can be applied to the skin around the anus to pick up eggs, which can then be identified microscopically.

It is unlikely that threadworms ever do any real harm except to disturb the sleep of children and the sensibilities of fastidious parents. If re-infestation is avoided, the problem will disappear within a month. Ointments will allay the anal itching and there are various effective de-worming drugs, such as mebendazole, piperazine or pyrantel. You must treat all the members of the family.

Wry-neck

See **Head permanently on one side.**

Yellow baby

see

Yellowing of the skin and eyes

Yellow baby

It is quite common for a new-born baby to have a slight yellow tinge to the skin and this is usually harmless. Even so, every jaundiced baby should be fully investigated because raised levels of bile pigment (bilirubin) in the blood can be very damaging to the brain. The most important cause of yellowness in babies is rhesus factor incompatibility.

After the A, B, AB and O blood groups, the rhesus factor is the most important. The gene that makes a person rhesus positive is called D. This is present in 85 per cent of the population. Rhesus positive

fathers may carry two D genes (homozygous) or one D gene and one non-D gene (heterozygous). All the offspring of homozygous fathers are rhesus positive. With a heterozygous father, each pregnancy will have a 50 per cent chance of producing a rhesus positive baby.

When a rhesus positive father produces a rhesus positive baby in a rhesus negative mother, the baby's red blood cells will cause the mother to produce antibodies against them. The baby red cells do not normally reach the mother's blood until labour so they are unlikely to cause serious harm in the first pregnancy. But in subsequent pregnancies, the levels of these antibodies in the mother's blood rise rapidly and soon reach a point at which they are able to destroy the red cells of the fetus.

In the most severe cases, the fetus dies in the womb, usually after the 28th week. If born alive, the child is deeply jaundiced with an enlarged liver and spleen and bilestaining of the brain (kernicterus). This leads to paralysis, spasticity, mental retardation and defects of sight and hearing.

A badly affected baby can have an exchange transfusion, via the umbilical cord, as soon as it is born, or even while still in the womb. This corrects the anaemia and gets rid of the bilirubin. Exposure to intense blue light soon after birth assists in converting the bilirubin in the skin to a form which is harmless to the brain.

Rhesus negative women can be prevented from developing antibodies by being given an injection of anti D gamma globulin within 60 hours of the birth of a rhesus positive baby. In order to protect future babies, this is done in all such cases. Gamma globulin is also given when there has been an abortion or if there is any other reason to believe that rhesus positive fetal blood may have gained access to the woman's circulation. The injection is given if an amniocentesis shows blood-stained amniotic fluid.

Yellowing of the skin and eyes

Progressive yellowing of the skin and of the whites of the eyes must never be neglected. This is called *jaundice* and it results from deposition of a natural colouring substance, bilirubin. This pigment is released from the haemoglobin in red blood cells at the end of their working lives. In health, bilirubin is taken up by the liver and passed into the intestine in the bile. But if the liver is diseased, as by hepatitis, so that it cannot secrete the bilirubin, or if the bile ducts are blocked so that the bilirubin cannot get out, it gradually accumulates in the blood and stains the tissues.

Jaundice can also be caused if the red blood cells are broken down more rapidly than normal (haemolytic disease) so that more bilirubin is produced than the liver can cope with.

Some of the increased bilirubin in the blood is excreted in the urine, causing it to become very dark. Because the bile is not getting into the intestine, the stools will be much paler than normal and will look like clay. This combination of yellow skin, dark urine and light-coloured faeces is an unmistakable indication of a serious liver or bile-duct problem. If you have it you need immediate medical attention. ⚠

Index

Index

Index

Index

cystic fibrosis 30, 263
cystitis 189, 239, 311
  and oestrogen creams 240
  and prostatitis 240

D factor 346
dacryocystitis 88
dacryocystorhinostomy 89
Daktarin 140
dandruff 142
dark circles under eyes 89
De Quervain's disease 237
deafness 32, 123, 168, 258
  and acoustic neuroma 125
  and drugs 124
  and ear drum perforation 123
  and ear injury 124
  and ear wax 123
  and noise 124
  and otosclerosis 123
  and speech difficulty 286
death, fear of 8
decongestant nasal sprays 165
decongestants 166
decubitus ulcers 16
deflected nasal septum 166
deformed face 59
dehydration 86
déjà vu 68
dejection 62
delay in development 69
delayed puberty 264
delirium tremens 126
delusion, of bad breath 14
delusions 73, 81
dementia 151
  early signs of 152
  first sign of 4
dendritic ulcer of cornea 205
dental calculus 21
dental caries 305
depression 80, 148, 152, 172, 262
  age incidence of 262
  causes of 263
  and insomnia 133
  and kleptomania 288
  and ME 304
  precipitating factors 262
dermatitis 49, 138, 272
  and insect infestation 272
dermatitis herpetiformis 268

dermatophytes 137
developmental delay 69
  and speech difficulty 286
'Devil's grip' 200
diabetes 85, 264
  and double vision 320
  and gangrene 18
  and genital thrush 139
  and impotence 251
diabetes insipidus 86
Diarrest 73
diarrhoea 71, 181
  frequent 8
  and lactose intolerance 71
  and weaning 71
diastolic pressure 253
diazepam 226
dietary bran 48
dietary fibre 48, 237
difficulty getting out of bed 228
difficulty with reading 341
difficulty in swallowing 289
Diflucan 140
digestion, and breath 14
digitalis 35
dill water 340
dimethicone 340
Dimethicone cream 273
dioptres 331
diphtheria 235
diphtheria immunization 236
diphtheria toxin
  and heart 235
  and muscle weakness 235
diplopia 320
dirt, eating 79
disappearing pulse 231
discharge from urethra 244
discharge from vagina 315
discharging ears 257
disease, fear of 103
disjointed speech 158
dislocation of eye lenses 287
disordered judgement 80
disorientation 4, 153
Distaval 64
dithranol 284
diuretic drugs 35
dizziness 134
dog fleas 275
double urination 240

Index

and faintness 112
heat stroke 112
heel, pain in 211
height, loss of 37
Heimlich manoeuvre 43
Helicobacter pylori 186
hemianopia 322
Henoch-Schönlein purpura 271
hepatitis 241
hereditary haemorrhagic telangiectasia 39
hernia, and hip pain 217
heroin habit 117
herpes
    and AIDS 269
    and immune system 269
herpes meningitis 110
herpes simplex 268
herpes simplex encephalitis 215
    and AIDS 215
    and immune deficiency 215
herpes simplex virus, and eye 205
hiatus hernia 126
hiccups 126
    what to do 127
high blood cholesterol 89
high blood pressure 171, 252
    and headache 213
high spirits 80
high-pitched voice 157
high-roughage diet 73
hip
    congenital dislocation of 336
    pain in 217
hoarseness 154
Hodgkin's lymphoma 83
homonymous hemianopia 322
'honeymoon rhinitis' 165
hormone replacement therapy 38
    and osteoporosis 38
hot flushes 127
house dust mite droppings 165
HRT 38
HSV-1 268
HSV-2 268
human antitetanus globulin 226
human papilloma virus 251, 337
Huntington's chorea 152
Hurler's syndrome 60
hyalase 243
hydrocephalus 65, 152

hyoscine 307
hyperhidrosis 84
hyperlipidaemia 89
hypermetropia 330
hypertension 269
    malignant 253
hyperthermia 113
hypertrophic rhinitis 166
hyperventilation 7, 30, 36, 319
hypnagogic hallucinations 126
hypnopompic hallucinations 126
hypochondriasis 8, 14, 103
hypodermic fibrosis 42
hypospadias 248
hypothermia 113
hypotonia in babies 70
hysteria 152

ibuprofen 216
Icelandic disease 207
ichthyosis 284
ideas, flight of 80
ideas of persecution 74
idiopathic diarrhoea 72
ileostomy 185
ileus 185
illusory sense of touch 125
imidazole drugs 138
immune system 49
Imodium 73
impetigo 270
impotence 250
    and alcohol 250
    and boredom 250
    causes of 250
    and masturbation 250
    nature of 250
    and sexual technique 250
inability to express feelings 158
inability to express thoughts 158
inability to read 230
inability to recognize objects 102
inability to sit still 132
inability to speak 132
inability to write 132
incontinence 153
incoordination 325
index myopia 333
indigestion, and vomiting 334
indomethacin 211
inevitable, abortion 20

362

Index

Index

muscular dystrophy 337
myalgia 223
myalgic encephalitis 302
myasthenia gravis 90, 304
Mycobacterium tuberculosis 199
myopia 331
  age of onset 332
  complications of 332
myositis 229
myxoedema 100, 212

nappies, disposable 273
nappy rash 141, 273
  and ammonia smell 273
  barrier creams 273
  causes of 273
naproxen 211
nasal catarrh 52, 165
nasal congestion, rebound 166
nasal deformity 163
nasal inflammation 165
nasal obstruction 166
nasal partition perforation 74
nasal polyps 166
nausea 8
navel, bulging 40
navicular bone, and wrist pain 236
near sight 331
neck
  compression in 230
  lumps in 81
  pain in 229
  stiffness of 110
  tilted 230
  twisted 67, 122
neck glands 22
neck pain 8
neck stiffness, and headache 213
Neisseria gonorrhoea 244
nervous diarrhoea 72
nervousness, social 24
network pattern on legs 167
neuralgia, trigeminal 207
neurofibromatosis 61
neuroleptic drugs 300
neurological disorders, and impotence 251
night blindness 328
night cramps 224
night driving difficulty 333
night sweats 199
night terrors 167

night waking 168
  what to do 168
night-time bone pain 222
nightmares 167
  and sleeping pills 167
nipple
  discharge from 27
  retracted 27
nipples, milk leaking from 159
nociceptors 178
nocturnal enuresis 17
noises in the ears 168
nominal aphasia 132
non-Hodgkin's lymphoma 83
non-nutritional substances, eating 79
nose
  bleeding 163
  and cocaine sniffing 164
  crusting 163, 166
  deformity of 163
  depressed bridge 160
  inflammation of 165
  obstruction of 166
nose-picking 163
nosebleeds 163
  what to do 163
NSAIDs 191
nylon underwear 140
  avoiding 240
nystagmus 96, 340

obesity 33, 171
  definition of 172
  disadvantages of 171
  and energy expenditure 172
  and exercise 172
obscene utterances 300
obsessive-compulsive disorder 46
obstructed airway 31
obstructed bowel 184
obstruction of gullet 290
obstruction to urination 289
oedema 35
  of ankles 292
  and kidney disorder 100
  of larynx 234
  and nephritis 100
  and raised blood pressure 100
oedema of face 100
oesophagus, ulceration of 186
oestrogen creams, and cystitis 240

Index

pale stools 240, 348
pallor around mouth 112
palms, darkening of 301
palpitations 73, 103, 134, 241
pancreatitis 264
panic attacks 7, 242
papaverine, and impotence 251
paperclips in ear 202
para-aminosalicylic acid (PAS) 199
paracetamol 216
paralysis 110
paralytic ileus 189
paraphimosis 243
  what to do 243
parental affection, lack of 6
Parkinson's disease 132, 152, 308
passing wind 72
pathological fracture 38
patterns of insomnia 133
pelvic floor, weakness of 6
pelvic inflammatory disease 189
pemphigus 268
penicillamine 220
penile itching 139
penile ring aid 251
penile squeeze 247
penile warts 251
  and cervical cancer 252
penis
  ballooning of 243
  bending of 243
  discharge from 244
  hypospadias of 248
  inflammation of 246
  itching of 263
  outlet malplacement 248
  persistent erection of 248
  shrinkage of 249
  small and cold 251
  and smegma 245
  ulcer on 247
  warts on 251
pepsin 186
peptic ulcers 185
  preventing 188
pericarditis, and rheumatoid arthritis 219
periodontitis 306
periods
  absence of 149, 158
  absent 100
  bleeding between 317

  and contraceptive pill 3
  stopped 3
periorbital haematoma 89
peritonitis 184, 187, 188, 334
pernicious anaemia 300
perniosis 282
perseveration of vision 327
persistent cough 199
persistent erection of penis 248
persistent hymen, and painful sex 238
personal hygiene, decline in 152
personality disorder 266
Perthé's disease 217, 337
pertussis 54
  vaccination against 54
pes planus 209
pessimism 81
petechiae 270
Peyronie's disease 243
pharyngeal pouch 13, 290
pharyngitis 234
Phenergan 307
phenylketonuria 23
phimosis 243
phlegm 53
phobias 7, 310
phocomelia 64
phonetic reading 342
physiological tremor 307
pica 79
pigeon chest 58
piles 5, 18, 136, 237
pin-point haemorrhages 270
pink eye 87
pins and needles 252
pinworms 137
piperazine 343, 344
Pityrosporum ovale 143
plantar fasciitis 212
plantar wart 337
plaques of demyelination 325
plasmapheresis 305
platelet deficiency 271
  effects of 272
platelets 270
pleurisy 196
pointed chest 58
polio vaccine 112
poliomyelitis (polio) 111
polyarteritis nodosa 298
polycythaemia 135

Index

reflux oesophagitis 196
Regaine 15
Reiter's syndrome 245
  and joint pain 221
relaxation 8
  and headache 216
REM sleep 167
repetitive strain injury 224
respiratory distress syndrome 29
restless legs 256
restlessness 4, 262
retardation, mental 23
retinal detachment 318, 327
retinitis pigmentosa 328
retinoids 284
retracted nipple 27
retrobulbar neuritis 325
retrograde amnesia 150
Reye's syndrome 113
rhesus factor 346
rhesus incompatibility, and spastic
  paralysis 265
rhesus incompatibility 346
rheumatic fever 112, 220
  and heart valves 220
  and long-term penicillin 221
  and St Vitus' dance 220
  and streptococcus 220
rheumatoid arthritis 203, 218
  age of onset 218
  and carpal tunnel syndrome 212
  in children 219
  frequency in women 219
  and hand pain 212
  and hip pain 217
  outcome 220
  and wrist pain 236
rheumatoid factors 219
rhinitis 165
rhinophyma 164
rib in neck 230
rickets 26, 57
rifampicin 199
rigid big toe 210
rigor 267
ring scotoma 328
ringworm 137
risus sardonicus 226
rodent ulcer 278
Rogaine 15
rosacea 39, 164

rotator cuff 232
  injury to 232
  tear of 232
roundworms 240, 342
Royal Free disease 303
RSI 224
rubella 109
  and blindness 109
  and congenital malformations 109
  dangers of 109
  and defective vision 319
  immunization 110
  and pregnancy 109
rumbling bowels 72
rumbling tummy 256
runny stools 71
rupture of Achilles tendon 211
rye fungus 19

sadness 81, 262
St Vitus' dance 262
salivary gland swelling 108
salivation, excessive 307
salmon patches 274
Salmonella typhimurium 181
salpingitis 189
salt deficiency 224
salt-losing states 87
salty skin 263
sandflies 275
Sarcoptes scabiei 143
scabies 143, 275
  in family 143
scalp itching 142
scalp tension, and headache 213
scaphoid bone fracture, and wrist pain
  236
scarlet fever 108
schizophrenia 158, 266
scissors gait 265
scoliosis 67
scurvy 272
sea sickness 307
sebaceous glands 275
seborrhoeic dermatitis 93, 143, 257
sebum 274
  constitution of 275
  function of 275
secret binge eating 265
seeing things 125
seizures 50, 73

Index

deformity of 64
enlargement of 120
flattening of 57
squaring of 57
skull bossing 66
sleep
nightmares 167
teeth grinding 297
sleep problems 133
sleeping pills 134
slipped disc 191
cervical 230
and hip pain 217
and muscle spasm 226
siow pulse 285
slowing of body and mind 262
slurred speech 285
smegma 246
smell, loss of sense of 76
smoker's cough 52
smoking 35, 197
and gangrene 19
snoring 32
snow blindness 204
social nervousness 24
soggy skin 85, 136
solar keratosis 278
solder 150
solvent abuse 74
something coming down 5
sore throat 22, 234
spasm, of vagina 239
spasm in chewing muscles 221
spasm of muscle 224
spasmodic bending of wrists 31
spasmodic extension of feet 31
spasms
of back muscles 226
of hand and feet 225
violent 226
spastic colon 72
spastic paralysis 264
speaking, defect of 132
speech
difficulties with 286
slurred 285
speech difficulty, and brain tumour
215
speech disturbances 110
spider naevi 39
spider-like fingers 287

spina bifida 67
diagnosis of 68
occulta 67
spinal canal narrowing 229
spinal cord disorders, and impotence
251
spinal curvature 67
spinal nerve roots, compression of 229
spine
angulated 67
curvature of 37, 57
Pott's disease 67
solidification of 287
stiffness of 287
spine deformity of 67
spirochaete 249, 276
spleen – seat of melancholy 104
spontaneous bruising
and autoimmune disease 272
and blood vessel defects 272
and platelet deficiency 272
treatment of 272
and vitamin C deficiency 272
spontaneous pneumothorax 33
spots 277
spotted fever 110
sputum 53
blood-streaked 53, 199
squint 94
staggering 325
stammering 286
and left-handedness 286
and twins 286
staphylococcal toxin 181
Staphylococcus aureus 194
staring appearance 90
stealing 288
steroid hormones 167
steroid ointments 138, 143
stiff neck, and encephalitis 216
stiffness, on waking 228
Still's disease 219
stimulation, lack of 69
stomach cancer 14
stomach ulcers 18, 185
stone tied to penis 249
stools
blackening of 271
blood and mucus in 183
difficulty in passing 48
greasy 117, 241

Index